Two Years
on the
Alabama

Two Years on the Alabama

A Firsthand Account of the Daring
Exploits of the Infamous
Confederate Raider

Arthur Sinclair

TANTALLON PRESS

Text design: Charles Sutherland
Cover and illustration design: Victor Weaver
Text preparation: Kathy Pittman
Proofreading: Deborah Wiseman
Copy editor: Colleen Cook

Cover image: The *Alabama* (*290*) and the *Brilliante*—
drawing by Granville Perkins
LIBRARY OF CONGRESS

Printed in the United States of America
10 9 8 7 6 5 4 3 2 1

CONTENTS

wines and liquors; enemies' ships getting scarce; disposing of prisoners at sea; in the Brazilian high road; washing days for Jack

LIST OF ILLUSTRATIONS

(Following page 164)

PUBLISHER'S PREFACE

This edition of *Two Years on the* Alabama is based on the first edition published in 1895. The text has been copyedited for contemporary punctuation but is otherwise unaltered. A new introduction offers background to the political events that led up to the *Alabama*'s origins, and an epilogue completes her story where the author's narrative leaves off. Sixteen new illustrations have been added as a separate insert.

In drafting the introduction and epilogue, the publisher would like to acknowledge the following sources, which are also recommended for further reading: Cornell University *Making of America* Journal Collection—*Harper's Weekly*; *Memoirs of Service Afloat During the War Between the States*, Raphael Semmes (Kelly, Piet & Co., 1869); *The Naval History of the Civil War*, Bern Anderson (Knopf 1962); Introduction to *Two Years on the Alabama*, William N. Still Jr. (Naval Institute Press, 1989); *The Alabama and the Kearsarge*, William Marvel (University of North Carolina Press, 1996); *Shark of the Confederacy*, Charles M. Robinson III (Naval Institute Press, 1995); *The Alabama: Anatomy of a Confederate Raider*, Andrew Bowcock (Naval Institute Press, 2002); *CSS Alabama*—Builder, Captain, and Plans, Charles M. Grayson Summersell (University of Alabama, 1985); *Raphael Semmes and the Alabama*, Spencer C. Tucker (Ryan Place Publishers, 1996); *The Rebel Raiders*, James Tertius de Kay (Ballantine Books, 2002).

The publisher would also like to thank Norman Cohen and Mike DeWitt for their help in locating picture sources, and Jan Grenci for locating images at the Library of Congress.

PUBLISHER'S INTRODUCTION

Predator and pirate to her enemies, the raider CSS *Alabama* was synonymous with daring and audacity to the Southern cause during the American Civil War, and her commander revered as an icon of the Confederacy. In two short years the *Alabama* inflicted extensive damage on Union commerce from the Caribbean to the China Sea, and her exploits became the substance of a dispute in international law that continued long after the last shot in the war had been fired.

Numerous books have been published about the *Alabama*, many of which are listed in the Publisher's Preface and recommended for further reading, but the majority are secondary works and some very specialized. There are only two other firsthand accounts. *My Service Afloat*, written by Commander Raphael Semmes and published in 1869, is a key source. However, it covers more than just the account of the *Alabama* and runs to some eight hundred pages, much of which explores the underlying legal arguments. The second is *Recollections of a Naval Life* by First Officer McIntosh Kell, published in 1900, again a broad scope beyond *Alabama*'s story. *Two Years on the Alabama*, by Arthur Sinclair, the fourth officer, is the only account specifically about the raider's exploits and is by far the most descriptive and readable account of life on board. Sinclair's narrative has immediacy and color that make the other retellings seem bland by comparison.

If there has been any criticism of his account it has been for, supposedly, romanticizing the character of the crew—in contrast to Semmes's description of them as "a precious set of rascals . . . faithless in the matter of abiding by their contract, liars, thieves and drunkards." Still, a high level of morale must have been sustained for the *Alabama* to have achieved her purpose so effectively and for her crew to have fought her last action with such courage. Semmes's somewhat patrician attitude was almost certainly not typical of his officers.

Sinclair's account did provoke strong reactions from fellow officers Kell and Richard Armstrong upon its publication in 1895, both of whom contributed information to this book. Kell took strong exception to Sinclair's implied questioning of Semmes's judgment in stating that the commander knew that the *Alabama*'s final nemesis, the *Kearsarge*, carried concealed armor on her hull. Sinclair may well have been right. Opinions differ, and there is no way to know for sure today which version is correct. Clearly, Sinclair respected Semmes, and Semmes had brief but good words for Sinclair in his account, so it would not appear that Sinclair had any motive to invent this information.

Armstrong thought too that Sinclair had inflated his role on board in some respects; but there may have been an element of professional jealousy to this. Armstrong also wrote in a letter that he felt Sinclair had plagiarized Semmes's earlier work. While Sinclair obviously used it as a source, this charge is not justified.

Regardless of these comments, *Two Years on the Alabama* is an accurate account in all important respects and is foremost an exciting, well-told story of a fascinating side show to the bloody struggle on land. And not withstanding these animosities in later years, the degree of mutual respect among the officers is evident in the brief biographies Sinclair includes at the end of the book.

Sinclair's story opens with the arming of the *Alabama* in the Azores and her commissioning into the Confederate navy, the author having stated, "The public is already familiar with the events of the *Alabama*'s escape." While true when the book was first published, this does not apply to the general reader today. The building and launching of the *Alabama* was a drama in itself, and a story worth retelling here as background to Sinclair's narrative.

WAR STRATEGY

The Confederate naval strategy evolved, to some degree unwittingly, from the sequence of actions set in motion by the attack on Fort Sumter and the issues of international law that it provoked. President Abraham Lincoln had countered the taking of Fort Sumter by characterizing it as an act of insurrection beyond the power of the law enforcement authorities to contain, and calling for volunteers to help end the rebellion. In retaliation the Confederacy, invoking the threat of invasion, proclaimed the right to defend itself and in turn called for volunteers—including those to take out Letters of Marque to attack Northern shipping.

This stratagem followed a tradition set by the fledgling American republic in the War of Independence and the War of 1812 and to whom the Confederacy compared its role in this new conflict. It also accorded with the underlying Confederate war strategy. In order to win the war the North would have to defeat the South, but for the South to win it believed it had only to wear down the North (where there were many Southern sympathizers at the outset) to the point of acknowledging the Confederacy's right of secession. By disrupting Northern commerce early on, Confederate strategists believed, they would bring the cost of war home to the general population in the North as well as divert the Union navy from any immediate attack on Southern ports. The threat of privateers did alarm Northern merchant ship owners, with many selling their ships to neutral powers to protect them, and drove up marine insurance rates significantly.

After first sounding out the potential reaction from Britain, which was the leading maritime power in the world, Lincoln responded with a blockade of all Southern ports. He wanted to ensure the Confederacy did not gain international support or recognition but needed to take action against the threat presented by privateers. The British minister in Washington, Lord Lyons, made it clear that closing Southern ports and making them inaccessible to all trading commerce could provoke British intervention, but that Britain could not object to a blockade that simply controlled access, something Britain itself had set as a precedent in the Napoleonic War.

However, imposing a blockade implicitly acknowledged the Confederacy as a belligerent power rather than an insurgency, a status confirmed when Britain and other foreign powers declared their neutrality. Nevertheless Lincoln, aided by the Northern press, attempted to characterize the Confederates as rebels throughout the war and, by extension, the Confederate commerce raiders as pirates.

In any event, the Union blockade, combined with international declarations of neutrality, made it impossible for privateers to bring prizes into port and thereby rendered them ineffective. This circumstance obliged the Confederate Secretary of the Navy, Stephen Mallory, to consider other methods.

COVERT CONSTRUCTION

The main objective of Secretary Mallory, who had first-hand knowledge of the latest naval technology from his former post as chairman of the Naval Committee in the U.S. Senate, was to build a fleet of ironclads that could break the blockade. The South had no merchant marine base or ship-yards of any scale, and in 1861 the Confederate navy consisted of a few riverboats and revenue cutters. Ultimately, the South did build some sixty naval vessels, primarily in Nor-folk, New Orleans, and Charleston, but at the outset of the war Mallory knew that it would be some time, perhaps years, before they could be launched. With the effectiveness of the privateers scotched, he sought an alternative means of attacking the Union maritime commerce.

At first he had hoped to find suitable merchant vessels that could be converted to armed cruisers. At the urging of Commander Semmes (subsequently the commander of the *Alabama*) he located a suitable freighter, the *Habana*, which was armed and commissioned into the Confederate navy as the CSS *Sumter*. She ran the blockade out of New Orleans on June 18, 1861, and successfully took some seventeen prizes before being effectively bottled up in Gibraltar by the Union frigate *Tuscarora* and abandoned.

The *Sumter* was not well designed for her purpose, and in any case, there were few other such vessels available. In order to put to sea effective commerce raiders, Mallory realized that he would need to have them built in Europe, and on April 26, 1861, he declared to the Confederate Congress, "I propose to build a class of vessels hitherto unknown to naval services . . . built exclusively for speed, at a low cost, with a battery of one or two accurate guns of long range, with an ability to keep the sea upon a long cruise, and to engage or to avoid the enemy at will."

To carry out this task, an associate recommended that Mallory meet James Dunwoody Bullock, a native of Georgia and former captain in the U.S. Navy. At the moment of secession, Bulloch was master of a merchant ship out of New York and, honorably, had returned his vessel to its owners before resigning his position and offering his services to the Southern cause.

Impressed by their first meeting and by Bulloch's decision to sacrifice a successful career for the cause, Mallory appointed him as purchasing agent for the Confederate navy with the promise that he would command one of the vessels to be built in Liverpool, England. Liverpool was home to some of Britain's finest naval shipyards and a port where the Southern states already had a strong commercial base from the cotton trade.

Bulloch proved effective in his new role. Upon arrival in Liverpool, he first met with the Confederacy's financial agents, Fraser, Trenholm, and Company; then hired F. C. Hull, an attorney qualified to advise him on the intricacies of Britain's neutral status and on the specifics of the British Foreign Enlistment Act. This act, which had been signed into law in 1819, was designed to ensure that Britain's neutrality would not be compromised by acts of private individuals or by that of foreign powers attempting to recruit support from within British territory. It included many provisions, but the one that concerned Bulloch pertained to warship construction.

The act permitted certain trading of armaments and contraband but not the construction of warships for a belligerent power within British Territory. Because it had never been tested in this respect, there was no established legal precedent. After careful perusal, Hull devised the argument that a vessel free of armaments could not be construed a warship and submitted his argument to two eminent jurists, who concurred with his conclusion. Such opinions carried weight in the absence of any court-set precedent. Hull made sure this information was given suitable but surreptitious circulation to serve notice to any future challenger, and to let the authorities and any interested parties sympathetic to the Southern cause—not least the shipbuilders—know that the act provided such latitude.

With this potential obstacle removed, Bulloch contracted for the Confederacy's first raider, careful to do so in his own name. Anxious to get a ship launched at the earliest opportunity, he ordered the first vessel from a firm that had suitable plans already drawn up for a British navy gunboat, which, with some modifications to increase the speed, would fit his needs very closely. Paperwork listed the ship as the *Oreto*, ostensibly for the Italian government.

With construction of the first raider under way, Bulloch approached the firm of John Laird and Sons in Birkenhead to commission a custom-designed vessel, recorded in the order books as vessel *290*, but revealing her true identity in due course as the *Alabama*. As a leading shipbuilder and supplier to the British navy, Laird's main business was, by 1862, in ironclads. Bulloch, however, wanted a wooden-hulled ship that could be readily refitted in any port around the world, built to the highest standards of the day. The contract for vessel 290 was signed in April 1861.

Once satisfied that construction was proceeding satisfactorily to his specifications, Bulloch turned to his other responsibilities. On October 1, 1861, he sailed for the Confederacy with munitions and supplies, planning to return in good time for the completion of the new vessels. He successfully ran the blockade into Savannah and delivered his valuable cargo.

Testing Britain's neutrality

Back home, Bulloch's activities in Liverpool had not gone unnoticed. Unguarded telegraph messages early in the war had revealed his arrival, if not his specific purpose, to Union agents. When the new U.S. consul, Thomas Haines Dudley, arrived in Liverpool shortly after Bulloch's departure, he lost no time in recruiting a detective, former police officer Matthew Maguire, and a network of informers. Maguire soon uncovered the connection to Frazer Trenholm and exposed the fiction that named the Italian government as the future owner of the *Oreto*. Dudley relayed this information to Charles Francis Adams, the Union minister in London, who made strong representations to British Foreign Secretary Lord Russell that the ship be impounded under the Foreign Enlistment Act.

The official position of the British government towards the warring states was one of neutrality, but with the outcome at that stage unclear, they did not wish in any way to damage their relationship with the Confederacy. Lord Russell had not disguised his belief that whatever the outcome, it would not be possible to restore the Union to what had been, and he recognized that the dilution of the United States' world power by permanent division was very much in Britain's interest. But of far more immediate significance was the fact that Britain's textile industry depended on the South for 60 percent of its raw cotton. As long as he did not compromise Britain's neutral status, Lord Russell had every reason not to interfere. But given the nature of the information from Adams, Russell knew he had to be seen to take it seriously and so agreed to have the vessel inspected. Following the letter of the law, the customs agents assigned to inspect the vessel reported back that they could find no grounds for detaining it.

Bulloch, meanwhile, had difficulty returning to England. After many delays trying to run the blockade, he finally returned to Liverpool in March 1862, where he learned of the intense activity by Dudley and Maguire to forestall his plans. He realized the *Oreto* must be put to sea at the earliest opportunity. By now the vessel was nearing completion, so he set out to hire a qualified, trustworthy English ship's master and crew to sail to the Bahamas under the guise of taking the vessel out on a trial run. Bulloch embellished the plan by arranging for a party of invited guests to be entertained on board. Later that day he and his guests disembarked, and the *Oreto* sailed to a rendezvous with her supply ship in the Bahamas. There she was commissioned into the Confederate navy as the *Florida*.

As luck would have it, the crew was almost immediately taken down with yellow fever, and the captain was forced to seek refuge and run the blockade into Mobile by day for lack of a pilot. Although damaged by gunfire, the *Florida* was refitted and ultimately broke out again, taking over twenty prizes before being captured by a U.S. frigate in the port of Bahia—in contravention of Brazilian neutrality.

Chagrined to learn of the *Oreto*'s escape, Dudley and Adams refused to be outwitted again. Within days, Maguire reported on a suspicious vessel number 290 in Laird's shipyard, which from its description could only be a warship. Adams immediately demanded that the British government detain the vessel, but was met with only the now-familiar deflective response.

Work on the *290* progressed, and on May 15 the raider was launched and taken to the graving dock for fitting out. Meanwhile, Bulloch purchased a supply vessel in London, the *Agrippina*, and had it loaded with armaments, supplies, and 350 tons of coal.

By now Maguire's reports were flowing thick and fast, and

Adams made another formal demand to investigate the 290. For appearances' sake, a customs officer again visited the Laird shipyard and reported that although the vessel was clearly designed as a warship, she carried no armaments and had been commissioned by a private individual, not a belligerent power. Therefore, he had no legal grounds to seize her.

ALABAMA MAKES HER ESCAPE

With the *290* (now christened the *Enrica*) within weeks of being fully fitted out for sea, Bulloch readied himself to take command and selected a sailing master, Captain Matthew Butcher, to prepare the vessel and hire a crew. Then in early July, he received a letter from Mallory informing him, to his great disappointment, that command of the new ship would be given to Raphael Semmes, who had been forced to abandon the *Sumter* when it was trapped at Gibraltar. With characteristic dedication and stoicism, Bulloch did not let the news deter him from his current assignment.

Upon learning that the Union frigate *Tuscarora*, which had blockaded the *Sumter*, had sailed for England, Adams saw the opportunity of developing a secondary plan to trap the *Alabama* in the event that the British government continued to forestall him. Upon the *Tuscarora's* arrival in Southampton, Adams summoned her commander, Captain Thomas T. Craven, to London and, exercising his authority as Lincoln's direct representative Adams instructed him to follow the 290 should it leave Birkenhead. The *Tuscarora* would not be able to attack the vessel as long as she was under a British flag, but she would be able to track her and prevent her from carrying out her intended role.

Just when it seemed this would be the only way to contain

the *290*, Maguire's efforts—and wallet—produced the evidence Adams needed to checkmate Russell. The tireless detective finally succeeded in obtaining a deposition from William Passmore, a seaman who claimed he had heard that Lairds was seeking crewmen for a new fighting vessel. Passmore testified that he met with a Captain Butcher, from whom he learned the ship was to go to the Confederate States, that all hired hands had experience on fighting ships, and that James Bulloch was to command her. Adams immediately forwarded this information to Russell and included an independent legal opinion that if the British government did not act on this information, the United States would have strong grounds for retaliation.

Precisely when Russell received this letter is not known, but from this point delays in the British government's response were to be critical to the fate of the *290* and a central issue in the later international dispute. On Friday, July 25, Russell sought a legal opinion from the Queen's counsel, William Lyons. But as if scripted for a melodrama, Lyons suffered a brain seizure that same day. When Russell learned of this the following morning, he referred the matter to the attorney general, the next most senior legal officer, for consideration on the coming Monday.

That same morning, Bulloch, who had been debating whether to wait for Semmes's arrival to take command of the *290*, received a telegram in Liverpool warning it would not be safe to remain in dock another forty-eight hours. He also learned that the *Tuscarora* was leaving Southampton. The source remains a mystery, but twenty years later Bulloch acknowledged that he had a confidant within the British government offices, though he never divulged a name.

Losing no time, Bulloch summoned Captain Butcher, confided in him the rendezvous plans in the Azores, and instructed him to prepare for a sea trial from which the ship would not return. On Monday, replaying the tactic he employed previously with the *Oreto*, Bulloch invited guests to be entertained on board during the trials. He also arranged for a skeleton crew to further dispel suspicions, deciding to acquire additional hands later. That very afternoon, the attorney general in London concluded that the vessel must be seized and determined to advise Russell the next day.

On Tuesday morning, the 29th, Bulloch's guests boarded the festively decorated *290*, and she headed out into the Mersey. In London, the attorney general submitted his recommendation that "without loss of time, the vessel be seized." But it was in the afternoon before a telegram to that effect reached customs officials in Liverpool. The *290* was by then many miles away.

As the day's end approached, Bulloch made the excuse that the ship would have to continue on her trials overnight instead of turning back. He transferred himself and his guests into the accompanying tender for the return voyage to Birkenhead while the ship sailed to a prearranged mooring in a secluded bay some fifty miles out.

Back on the docks and with generous payments to the appropriate go-betweens, Bulloch pulled together the crewmen he needed and, following the standard custom, brought them out to the *290* together with their womenfolk, who wanted both to see their husbands aboard and to collect the first few months' pay. Well aware of his dependence on the goodwill of his new recruits, he served the party a generous meal accompanied with judicious allowances of grog.

Later that evening, the women were put back to shore and the *290* set a course for the Azores, safely eluding both the *Tuscarora* now heading up the coast and the customs agents sent to seize her. It is here that Sinclair takes up his tale.

The vessel

The author gives a good description of the *Alabama* within the narrative, but the ship is so central to this story that many readers may want to know more detail of her design.

The contract that Bulloch signed with shipbuilding firm John Laird and Sons called for "a good staunch and substantial wooden screw steamship" for a price of £50,000, or about $250,000 at the then conversion rate. Most naval ships being constructed at this time were ironclads, but the *Alabama* needed a wooden hull for easy refitting in any port and copper sheathing to resist deterioration in tropical waters, key requirements for extended cruising on the world's oceans. The specifications called for her to be built to the highest standards, mainly from English oak. In fact, it proved difficult to find a suitable single piece of timber for the sternpost—two being rejected after boring out before a suitable one was found. Her sail configuration and long lower mast provided the best combination of speed and maneuverability. She was to be barquentine-rigged—that is to say, with a square foresail and fore- and aft sails on the main- and mizzenmasts to take wind on either side. Several features enhanced her capability, such as a retractable screw to eliminate drag when under sail and winches to retract the funnel in order to obscure her identity, and a condenser supplied constant fresh drinking water.

A report by Matthew Maguire, the detective hired by U.S. Consul Thomas Haines Dudley to track the activities of Bulloch, provides perhaps the best-detailed description of the ship's interior:

Internal description:
State room right aft. The entrance to the cabin from the deck, is abaft the mizzenmast, raised about 2 feet 6 inches.

The stateroom is seated all round, there are two small glass cases in it. At the bottom of the stairs, the communication to the right leads to a small saloon in the center of which, is a small dining table and on each side are state cabins.

Passing from this to a little more forward, is a large saloon, where the chief officers' and chief engineers' cabins are situated on each side, fitted up with book and chart cases. From this you pass through a doorway into the engine room. There is a platform over the engines (which are two in number) and which are most complete and handsome pieces of machinery, only occupying a small space and lying entirely at the bottom; they are on the oscillating principle. From here also you can pass into the stoke holes.

Forward of this, but no communication, are the men's berths, which are quite open and spacious and run entirely forward, in the center is the cooking apparatus. The hooks are slung to the deck, for the men's hammocks. This also is seated all round. Under these seats are places for the men's bags with iron grating, which forms the front of the seats. The entrance to this department is directly forward of the foremast.

At the bottom of the stairs, a little to the fore part of the ship is a small hatch, which leads to the magazines, two in number. The partition on each side of these magazines is of three thicknesses of oak; between each thickness is lined with lead. These magazines are under the main deck, of what I should call the men's berths in the fore part of the ship, about six or eight feet forward of the foremast. The canisters are fixtures on their sides, the screws lying one over the other. The magazines and the entrance to them, are filled with water during action, by a pipe on each side and by a pipe in the middle of the floor, the water descends to the bottom of the ship and is pumped out by steam power.

The entrance to the cabin is abaft the mizzenmast; each side is a brass ventilator, about twelve inches high. Forward of the mizzenmast is a skylight to the small saloon and forward of this skylight is a larger one, which gives light to the large saloon. The skylights do not stand more than a foot high on deck and which have iron bars across. Forward of this skylight and abaft the funnel, is a skylight 5 or 6 feet long, which gives light to the engine room. The base of the funnel forms a square, about 2 feet high; each corner is latticed with iron rails, to throw light and air into the stoke room.

Each side abaft the funnel, are two ventilators with round bell mouths and which stand about 5 or 6 feet high; more forward of the main mast are two more ventilators, of the same description. The entrance to the stoke hole is abaft the foremast. The entrance to the men's sleeping apartment is raised about 2 feet high. A small chimney or small brass or copper funnel, rises here from the cooking apparatus. Each side of the gangways is carved oak, with an anchor and rope carved on.

Commander Raphael Semmes rhapsodized on first seeing her that "her model was of the most perfect symmetry, and she sat upon the water with the lightness and grace of a swan." Undoubtedly, the *Alabama* was a superb example of the art of shipbuilding at the twilight of the age of sail, impeccably designed for her purpose.

Simon Waterlow, Publisher
November, 2003

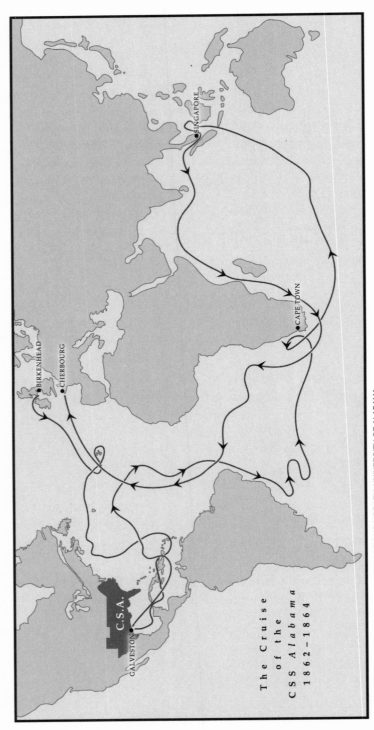

The Cruise of the CSS *Alabama* 1862–1864

BIRKENHEAD

CHERBOURG

C.S.A.

GALVESTON

CAPE TOWN

SINGAPORE

CHAPTER I

INTRODUCTORY

CAPTAIN RAPHAEL SEMMES'S account of the service of the *Alabama*, as the public probably observed, was most carefully confined within the limits of legal and professional statement. It was no part of his purpose to enter into the details of life on board, or to make any unnecessary confidences respecting himself or the officers and crew who shared his labors and successes. It is hardly necessary, therefore, to offer any apology for the matter contained in this volume. It will not be doubted that a cruise so unique and remarkable had its share of daily and hourly interests, and of manifestations of that human nature which is of the first consequence in all narrative.

It is certainly not a sense of peculiar fitness which determines the present writer to undertake to make a book from his recollections of the cruise. But those most interested have decided that his duty lies in that direction, and he would himself regret that the irresponsible romancer of the future should become sole heir to the *Alabama*'s traditions. Though in a minor sense, perhaps what he has in custody is history, and that requires reverent treatment. Truth, at least, he thinks he can promise, for he has spared no pains to verify through the testimony of others what he has herein set down.

Before and during the first year of the *Alabama*'s career, several Confederate cruisers raided the North Atlantic. The *Sumter* had fully demonstrated the tremendous damage which armed cruisers might effect upon the enemy's commerce, if they could be put on the high seas and maintained there. But the Confederate cruisers *Tallahassee*, *Georgia*, *Nashville*, *Chickamauga*, *Sallie*, and *Retribution* were not at all adapted to such a service and could add little substantial achievement. The *Florida* was unlucky from the first. She started from Nassau with the germs of yellow fever on board. The sickness and mortality among her crew were so great that she was quickly compelled to make port, and the blockading fleet at Mobile tore her literally to splinters. Months elapsed before she could be got to sea again, and then disaster after disaster beset her, until she was eventually captured at Bahia by the USS *Wachusett*.

Later in the war, and after the sinking of the *Alabama*, the *Shenandoah*, fitted out, like the *Florida* and *Alabama*, in England, made havoc among the American whaling fleets in the Pacific;[1] the respective results of her operations and

---

1. When it was determined to purchase and fit out the *Shenandoah*, the writer, being at the time in Paris and domiciled with Captain Waddell, her future commander, the latter confidentially disclosed the matter with the view of consultation in selecting some cruising ground where a good result in captures might be obtained. The recent cruise of the *Alabama* suggested no merchant industry undisturbed, save the whaling fleets of the Pacific; and after a most careful study of the charts before us, both came to the conclusion these were the points to strike, and with what marked results the reader is now fully apprised.

those of the *Florida* showing as great value in vessel property destroyed as was accomplished by the *Alabama*. But annihilation of American shipping interests was effected almost solely by the peculiar operations of the latter. It was not to good fortune alone that this distinction is due. The *Alabama* was fitted out with the most careful and astute prevision, commanded by a man of rare genius, and officered with special reference to the work in hand. It was to be, practically, one small, swift ship against the many which her enemy could send against her. Her itinerary was prearranged with exactness and carried out without any deviation. Mysterious and uncertain in her whereabouts to the foe, and for that reason a terror to his commerce in all seas, her movements could not be left to shape themselves upon events of the moment. The work to be done was definite; and the method must not leave Commander Semmes without suitable communications to inform him of the movements of the pursuers or to supply other emergencies.

At the same time, the *Alabama* had unusual resources within herself, such as no other man-of-war of her day could boast. She carried the means for making all ordinary repairs upon her machinery, spars, and armament while at sea or in ports where mechanical facilities could not be commanded. It was manifestly uncertain what influences might be excited by her powerful enemy in neutral ports against her. Of English sympathy alone she could be fairly assured; but that must be counted on only within the strict limit of neutrality laws peculiarly disadvantageous to a ship without consorts or home ports of entry.

The *Alabama*'s actual destructiveness to the commerce of the enemy was therefore out of all proportion to her force, or the actual number of her captures, or their money-value. Fifty-seven vessels of all sorts were burned—the value as estimated by the Geneva award being but $6,750,000. A large number were, however, released on ransom-bond, having neutral cargo on board, and hundreds of neutrals were brought-to and examined. In the meantime the *Alabama* sailed seventy-five thousand miles, or thrice the distance round the globe. Beginning her work in the North Atlantic, she shifted rapidly from place to place as the terror of her presence did its work—the West Indies, the Gulf of Mexico, back again to the West Indies, Brazil, Cape of Good Hope, China Seas, Strait of Malacca, Ceylon, Arabian Gulf, Strait of Madagascar, Cape Town, St. Helena, Brazil, the English Channel—this was her itinerary. For two years she preyed upon her enemy and set pursuers at defiance, accomplishing to the letter the mission upon which she was sent.

It is unnecessary as to those who have studied the sciences of war and statecraft to say anything respecting the moral quality of the *Alabama's* work. But from the fact that a fairly large and probably well-intentioned class among those who were suffering from her depredations got into the way of calling her a "pirate"—a circumstance entirely without the least shadow of legal justification, and which must therefore have been founded upon a misconception, not only of the necessities of war, but also of the spirit which animated her officers and crew—it may soften prejudices a little to call attention to a few facts.

The North was at the time pretty effectually blockading Southern ports and cutting off the Confederacy from all commercial advantages and resources, which were far more vital, not only to military power but to domestic comfort, than a similar blockade of Northern ports would have been. Reprisals were justified to a far greater extent than it was in the power of the South to inflict them. Retaliation upon noncombatants or private interests, especially when unlikely to effect political results or even to materially weaken a foe, is unchivalric and immoral. But it is evident that the operations of the *Alabama* were well calculated to draw away from Southern ports the swiftest and most effective ships of the enemy in order to protect his commerce; and thus, reducing the strength of the blockade, to procure relief both to the government and the people of the Confederacy. It could not be assumed that the North would certainly sacrifice its shipping interests. The South had also a fairly strong party of sympathizers in the North itself, which it was advisable to encourage and stimulate by striking blows, whenever practicable, at its all but omnipotent "business interests." Other considerations of policy might be cited to the same purpose. But it is chiefly in point to assure the reader that while the *Alabama's* main purpose was to threaten the shipping interests of her foe, neither her projectors, nor the officers and men who manned her, could possibly have foreseen that she would keep on for an extended period making audacious raids upon merchant vessels, without being overhauled and, if necessary, brought to bay by some of the numerous armed ships of her enemy. She was a fighting ship, and under no circumstances, within reasonable odds, contemplated avoiding battle. This is evident from what happened in the only two instances in which the opportunity was fairly presented, and should be admitted frankly.

The strict and firm discipline, the isolation, watchfulness, labor, and exposure which were concomitants of service on this lone cruiser demanded from her officers, at least, a strong sentiment of duty and patriotism not inferior to any manifested afloat or afield on either side of the great war-question pending. And quite apart from the English merchant and political policy, which to a certain extent favored the career of the *Alabama*, her officers received from the English authorities and naval officers a degree and kind of recognition which it is practically impossible for John Bull to extend to those he cannot approve as men of honor and principle.

Perhaps one thing more should be noted. The writer has had it suggested that inasmuch as the *Alabama* destroyed American prestige on the seas, a calamity to be deplored by all patriotism which now embraces a *whole* country, her exploits are rather to be forgotten as errors and sorrows than to be held up to admiration. But the writer, believing that the counsels of men can shape nothing contrary to the purposes of that Providence which is clearly manifest to reverent and thoughtful minds in history, and that acceptance of results (even to the extent of pleading guilty of treason) does not necessarily wipe out the moral value of heroism expended on the losing side, assumes that the *Alabama*, directed and controlled by American patriots, though of states'-rights persuasion, is pretty sure to remain a feature of American maritime history and a subject of legitimate interest to most Americans of generations present and to come.

This explanation to the general reader will not be construed, it is hoped, into apology. Whatever may be fitting for others, it would be at least highly indecorous for a person in the present writer's position to make excuses for a course of action on his own part or that of his fellow officers, which was prompted at the time by the highest motives and must therefore be remembered with many elements of satisfaction. At the same time, the statement may be added that a reunited country has, in the writer's judgment, no citizens more jealous of her unity and of the honor of her flag among the nations of the earth today, than the veterans of "The Lost Cause."

The necessity of possessing a navy appealed very early to the government of the Confederacy, as was natural enough in view of the distress caused by the blockade and the enormous advantages which Southern harbors and waterways afforded to the enemy. But the South had no shipyards or machine shops capable of building such vessels as were manifestly necessary to contend with the Northern armament. Only steam vessels could effectively overhaul the swift Baltimore and New York clippers which carried Northern commerce, or maneuver against Yankee gunboats.

The experience of the *Merrimac* had also shown that ironclads must be depended on for home defense, or for attack on Northern harbors. A number of the most efficient naval officers of the South were therefore sent abroad to seek facilities not to be had at home, and to contract on the basis of the South's cotton credit for such ships as were required. None of the ironclads contracted for were completed when the war closed. Of the "cruiser" class, the *Alabama*, the *Florida*, and the *Texas* reached completion, but only the first two in time for service. The *Texas* was ready about the date of the surrender. She was contracted for by Captain George T. Sinclair. The officer contracting for the *290* (*Alabama*) and the *Oreto* (*Florida*) was Captain James D. Bulloch, whose brain conceived and whose patience, caution, and executive ability, overcoming the most serious obstacles and discouragement, successfully materialized the "Scourge of the Seas." He arrived in Liverpool in the character of a private individual, and as such contracted with the Millers for the *Oreto*, and subsequently with the Lairds for the *290*; Fraser, Trenholm & Co., cotton merchants of Liverpool, assuming the responsibility of payment.

The whole transaction was as between private parties and so not liable to interference of the English authorities except upon proof of the violation of neutrality laws. But the obvious policy of the Confederacy was of course not overlooked by the United States government; and neither Bulloch's incognito, nor the utmost secrecy of all parties to the contracts, could prevent the watching of foreign shipyards by agents, and ultimate moral certainty as to the nature of the work in hand. But moral certainty and legally sufficient proof are separate things. And Captain Bulloch managed to push his affairs to completion before specific information, backed by the demands of the United States and passed upon by British red tape, could put a stop to proceedings.

The *Alabama* was a screw steamer with full sail-power. She measured 235 ft. overall, beam 32 ft., tonnage 1,000. Her draft with full coal bunkers was 15 ft. Her engines were two in number, horizontal, of 300 nominal, or 1,000 actual horsepower. She was barquentine-rigged, with very long lower masts, giving her principal sails an immense "drop" or surface. She was at the same time a perfect steamer and a perfect sailing-vessel, each entirely independent of the other. Her screw, which was a two-bladed one, hoisted in a propeller-well, and when triced up was quite clear of the water, hence no drag or impediment to her speed under sail-power alone. Kept constantly under banked fires, and with frequent hoisting and lowering of screw, her crew and engineers executed this maneuver with surprising alacrity and precision. Indeed, so rapidly could she be changed from sail to steam-power that no enemy, appearing on the horizon in clear weather, could surprise her under sail, nor could a sailing-vessel of superior speed escape her before getting her full steam-power.

The ship was rigged square at fore and main, and carried royals; also fore- and maintrysails, fore and foretop-mast staysails, jib, spanker, and gaff-topsail, and studding sails. The main-course set "flying," and was seldom used on account of its tendency to foul the smokestack. The standing rigging was of wire. The capacity of the coal bunkers was 375 tons, or sufficient for eighteen days' full steaming. Her speed under the most favorable conditions was 13–4 to 13–6 knots by actual observation, or fifteen and three-quarters statute miles—

about the extreme of speed attained in seagoing vessels of that day. The armament consisted of one 8-inch solid-shot or shell gun aft, one 7-inch 100-pounder rifle forward, six 32-pounders, weighing 5,700 lbs. each, in broadside. Eight guns in broadside was originally intended; but the battery seeming too heavy, one was omitted, and in action a gun could be shifted from side to side to effect the result required. The *Alabama* cost, complete, about $250,000. She was launched May 15, 1862, and July 29, without armament, stores, or a properly shipped crew, started on her "trial trip" down the Mersey. But from this trial trip she was already booked never to return to her moorings.

CHAPTER II

ESCAPE FROM THE MERSEY; FITTING OUT AT THE AZORES

IN SPITE OF THE utmost precaution, evidence of the real ownership and purpose of the *290* had been accumulated and formally lodged with Her Majesty's ministers, and the seizure and detention of the vessel was only a question of hours. But Bulloch had prepared for such a contingency. As she must leave England under the British flag, a British master must also be provided. This was itself a matter of no small delicacy; for a master once at sea is a power absolutely despotic, and the betrayal of this vessel into hostile hands would have been amply rewarded just then and could be managed without much evidence even of ill-faith. The gentleman chosen for this service was Captain Matthew J. Butcher of the Royal Naval Reserve, formerly first officer of the Cunarder Kamac—a fine sailor and the soul of honor. To him Bulloch confidently trusted, and his faith was not misplaced. But the public is already familiar with the events of the *Alabama*'s escape and safe arrival at Terceira in the Western Islands.

In the meantime, the officers detailed for the *Alabama* had met at Liverpool, most of them arriving from Nassau on the steamer *Bahama*, August 8, 1862. On the 13th, all embarked on same steamer for Terceira. It may well be imagined there was field for much thought as we steamed our way to the Western Islands. The career of the *Sumter*, though short-lived, had been eminently successful, and had taught us what a vast amount of destruction on the high seas was possible with a suitable cruiser under us. It had also impressed upon us that our enemy was not unappreciative of the situation and, knowing that our government had vessels under construction in England, would most likely cover each highway of commerce with swift and powerful pursuers. The familiar and significant term "pirates" applied to Southern cruisers would most likely be given a practical illustration, should defeat be our destiny. We found later the consensus of foreign opinion very emphatic, that had we been captured during the heyday of our raid we should have had meted out to us the full penalty. Butcher informed us he was somewhat uneasy upon making out a steamer (the *Bahama*) standing in for the anchorage, having visions of a United States cruiser. Work had already begun transferring stores to the *290* and so far all had gone merry as a marriage bell. Semmes at once relieved Butcher of his charge, and with his officers spent the first night on board the vessel that for two years was to be our home.

The *Alabama* had escaped from English waters a simple dispatch boat, so called, with nothing to indicate for what purpose designed; no guns or warlike implements of any kind on board. You can but faintly imagine the bustle and apparent confusion existing. The carpenter and mates assisted by the engineers were measuring and putting down the "circles" for the two pivot-guns. The boatswain and mates fitting train and side-tackles to the broadside guns. Gunner stowing the magazine, shot and shell lockers. Sailmaker looking after his spare sails and seeing them safely stored in the sailroom. All this with the three different crews of the *290*, *Bahama*, and *Agrippina*; men heretofore unknown to each other and in utter ignorance of the object of the expedition beyond what could be seen on the surface. It was essential we get to sea as soon as possible; for besides the danger of an enemy's cruiser happening in, the authorities might suspect something wrong and send notice to the mainland. Day and night on goes the work, each hour the *290* looking more like a man-of-war; but all this time there does not exist on board any authority or right to order these men to the guns should our enemy put in an appearance. They are British subjects, shipped for the voyage from Liverpool to the Azores. Their obligation ceases after transferring the cargoes of the two tenders to the cruiser, and they are at liberty to take return passage on their respective vessels back to Liverpool on full pay until arrival there.

Knowing the men were fully aware that to ship under any other flag would vitiate their claim to British protection was an element of great anxiety to us, and until a crew had been secured kept us on a terrible tension. We were helpless without a crew. While the preparation of our ship for sea was going on, no little annoyance and delay was caused by the officials of the island. Being so rarely visited by either naval or merchant vessels, they were seldom called upon to act in their official capacity and were but little versed in international law. Still, they knew enough to require our entering at the customhouse, and also insisted upon our changing our anchorage. This latter we did, being too well pleased to find so little required of us, though the change removed us from a still harbor to one of a rough character.

The status of the vessel was evidently a sealed book to them, else we should have had them about our ears like a swarm of hornets. Still, we have little doubt they afterward congratulated themselves that ignorance was bliss in their case; for had we been ordered from their waters before arming and getting ready for the cruise, the immigration which later poured on their shores from the captured whaling ships would never have occurred, and the rich trading with the officers and crews of burned prizes would never have fallen to their lot. Perhaps in its history the island has not experienced so lively a trade as the *Alabama* sent it. We landed a small regiment of men with much rich booty to dispose of; and no doubt the islanders were fully aware this plunder must change hands at some price, and secured good bargains in their barter. The whaleboats and their cargoes of provisions from the destroyed whaling fleet amounted to, in the aggregate, at least the value of any one of the destroyed vessels, and the whole of it passed into the hands of these islanders.

But we have strayed from the matter just now in hand. On the morning of the 21st, the *290*, accompanied by the *Bahama*, Captain Tessier; and *Agrippina*, Captain McQueen, steamed offshore to the leeward of the islands beyond the marine league and in smooth water, and hoisted on board her armament, placing it "in battery," reeving side- and train-tackles, stowing shot and shell rooms, filling shot-racks on deck, and putting ship generally in fighting trim. There was some swell on; and such work was not accomplished without danger and inconvenience, the pivot-guns being particularly dangerous to transfer as they weighed several tons each. Having managed this task by evening, we again hauled in under the lee of the land and anchored. The next morning we coaled ship from the transport. Thus, after several days of toil and deep anxiety, order is brought out of chaos, and the *290* is a fighting ship, *minus a crew.* All hands are "turned to," and the ship rid of coal dust, debris, etc., and put in first-class man-of-war shape. Holystones do their perfect work, and the brasswork and battery shine in the summer sun. Yards are then squared, rigging hauled taut and "flemished" down on deck, and we are ready for the sea.

On the morning of Sunday, August 24, 1862, in company with the *Bahama*, we again put to sea to unfurl for the first time at the peak of the *Alabama* the flag of the young Confederacy. The men of the two accompanying vessels, with the exception of working-crews, were transferred to the deck of the *290*. The officers were all in full uniform, of an attractive shade of gray, with a redundancy of gold lace, quite dressy, yet shockingly inappropriate to marine traditions, and which impressed our compeers of other navies, clothed in the regulation true blue, as at least a startling innovation. The crews of the several vessels are before us, dressed in every description of merchant-ship toggery. We may safely say the contrast of dress had much to do with winning the favor and respect of these waifs of ocean and securing the services of the pick of them.

Reaching the offing, both steamers are hove-to near each other. The officers and men are now mustered aft by "call" of boatswain (we had no boatswain's-mates as yet), and Semmes mounting a gun-carriage, first reads his commission from the President of the Confederate States as a commander of the Confederate States Navy, and the order of the Secretary of the Navy, directing him to assume command of this ship. The officers and men were grouped close around him in a semicircle, the former farthest aft, and all with uncovered heads. During the reading, the men, to whom especially it was a novel sight, seemed deeply moved. It was a grand subject for a painter. The reading over, the "stops" to the halyards at the peak and mainmasthead were broken, and the flag and pennant of the young nation floated to the breeze. At the same moment a gun booms from the weather quarter, and a quartermaster standing by the English colors (Henry Marmelstein, a Southern coast pilot and afterwards second officer of the *Tuscaloosa*) hauls them down, and the *290* becomes the CSS *Alabama*.

Our captain now addresses the men in a few curt but eloquent and persuasive words, making known to them the character of the vessel, her nationality, purpose of the cruise, and causes leading to it. He lays before them both the bright and dark sides of the venture, tells them they will receive double the wages paid by the English government, and in gold. Also an equivalent of one-half the value of the destroyed and bonded vessels as prize-money, this latter to be voted them by the Congress of the Confederate States. Dilates on the certainty of grog twice a day, as in the English navy (a strong inducement to Jack, as Semmes well knew), generous rations, much superior to that of any other navy, and good treatment generally, with incidentally the purpose to lay them alongside one of the enemy's cruisers, should one of about equal weight of metal be fallen in with, and their tastes tending this way.

On the other hand, he gives them to understand distinctly that the *Alabama* is no privateer or irresponsible nondescript to roam the ocean without discipline or order for the purpose of plunder, but a bona fide Confederate man-of-war commissioned by the President, flying the flag of the young Republic, and governed in her domestic life by certain rules and regulations of the Confederate Congress, to be referred to later; and to disobey these rules would subject them to certain and maybe severe punishment. The hardships of the cruise are portrayed, the constant cruising in all climes, toils of working ship and boarding vessels in all weather night and day, and possibly with but little respite; and to wind up, the quite possible chance of having a halter about their necks in case of capture and the nonsuccess of the cause in which they were asked to engage.

Now the bid for a crew had been made. Semmes dismounts from the gun-carriage and engages in a conversation with his executive, the boatswain "pipes down," and the men scatter forward in groups about the spar-deck, discussing the pros and cons of the situation. In the meantime, the paymaster has brought amidships, to the capstan, his shipping-list, and like the rest of us awaits the result of our gallant commander's speech. Momentous pause! For of what use are the heaviest guns, the fastest cruiser, the picked talent of a navy, without a crew. It is a beautiful day, the sun shining cheerfully through the thin broken clouds, the ship looking like a bride in her bright decorations. Surely these sailor lads must fall in love with her. That they are brave and resolute we do not wish to be told, and surely they will not abandon her to her officers alone to care for.

But the suspense is easing. One by one the groups dissolve, and Jack, hat in hand, presents himself at the capstan, and signs the "articles," till eighty-five men have been secured. SAFE NOW! The *Alabama* is able to man and fight nearly her entire battery! We have eighty-five less Englishmen on board than before. These men have forfeited the protection of the English government by this act of enlistment, and must now look to the brave young banner floating over them to carry them through. No little struggle it is to men to make the plunge, knowing as they do the perfect security abandoned by this act of enlistment; and that they *have* enlisted, fully realizing the gravity of the situation, binds them to their officers with hooks of steel. Nothing now remains but to arrange financial matters for the brave fellows. Our active paymaster, assisted by Bulloch, captain's clerk Smith, and others, are preparing half-pay tickets for such of the men as have mothers, wives, or sweethearts in England. It was far into the night before the labors of the paymaster and his assistants were wound up, and the *Alabama* ready for her grim work.

Bulloch had the whole creation as an entirety to look to, hence to him the whole credit. Further, it was a graceful act in him to accompany the vessel to Terceira and lend his invaluable aid in equipping her for sea. I can truly add that not even the most trifling article necessary to the efficiency of the vessel could be named as wanting. At the period of which we write, the *Alabama* was the most perfect cruiser of any nation afloat.

And a thing of beauty and a joy forever she was to us. And thus the christening of this vessel, destined to be the scourge of her enemy and the admiration of the world. So long as history is read will the tale of the exploits of the *Alabama* excite curiosity, and call forth notes of admiration and wonder. How strange the sensation created by the sight of this new, scarce recognized flag, floating at our peak. It was quite natural that the crew should gaze upon it with curiosity, "this banner with a strange device." Jack is just now drawing comparisons between Her Britannic Majesty's navy and this just-hatched bantam claiming and asserting an equality with the battle-worn monarchs of the sea, and doubtless somewhat staggered at the presumption, and with grave and serious doubts in his mind as to the ability to establish it.

CHAPTER III

GETTING ACQUAINTED WITH THE NEW SHIP; HER GOOD QUALITIES; PERSONNEL OF OFFICERS AND CREW; DRILLING; OUR FIRST PRIZE; THE OLD FLAG LOWERED

THE TIME HAS NOW arrived for good-byes. Look at her, reader, from the deck of the *Bahama*; a long, trim, black hull, elliptic stern, fiddlehead cutwater, long, raking lower masts, and you have the picture of the rover. Bulloch, with a hearty shake of the hand and a Godspeed to each of us, steps over the gangway. The *Bahama's* crew give us three cheers, which are answered by our gallant tars, the steamer turns her head for old England, and is soon lost on the horizon. And now for two long, weary, watchful years, in which the motto on our steering-wheel, *"Aide toi, et Dieu t'aidera,"* is to be tested.

> Our march is o'er the ocean wave,
> Our home is on the deep.

The representative of the Confederate States is now alone on the ocean, the last friend and companion ship having disappeared from our view.

We have been some days at sea, and have marked the speed and wonderful working qualities of our newly acquired cruiser. It will be fully appreciated by our sailor readers when we can say that the *Alabama* would go "in stays," and without fail, with a breeze giving her little more than steerage way; and in "working ship," later on around prizes, the captain of these vessels would be struck with the remarkable quickness and sureness with which she was handled. Frequently has the writer heard them to remark, upon hearing the orders given, "Ready about!" "Why, Lieutenant! You don't tell me this vessel will 'stay' in this light wind?" and have been lost in admiration upon witnessing the maneuver successfully accomplished. Indeed, she could be worked around a prize like a pilot-boat. There is nothing so excites Jack's pride and interest in his ship as to learn she can be depended upon in emergencies. It not only secures his confidence, but hints at much less brace-hauling of an unnecessary character.

The engine-room fires are banked, screw hoisted, and under easy canvas our head is turned to the northeast. This formidable engine of destruction is fairly launched on its mission, and we may speculate on the outcome of her efforts; but even with the acme of our wishes and expectations fully realized, how very far short shall we find them of results to be accomplished! That we look forward to seriously cripple and demoralize American commerce, unless promptly captured or sunk, goes without saying; but that a state of affairs bordering on total annihilation of it should have been the outcome of the *Alabama*'s cruise was more than the most sanguine of us hoped for, and many times surpassed our fondest daydreams. We can pardon fully the incredulity of the far future reader of history when he comes to study the career of this seemingly charmed cruiser (a venture, at that, of an agricultural race against a people cradled on the ocean), and note the result of the *Alabama*'s raid. But again is truth found stranger than fiction. A still more romantic and fuller history might have been hers, had not the *Alabama* voluntarily sought her doom in the historic English Channel. The grim work was still before her, had the election been to avoid conflict with the *Kearsarge*, and this without a stain clinging to her proud name, overmatched in every particular as she was. Better, however, as it is—her last effort sealing her title to lasting renown.

If one had the proper gift for description, something of great interest might be made of the individualities to be found among the officers and crew of the *Alabama*. In trying to convey any impression of our personnel, it is almost indispensable to draw some kind of a pen-picture of the more prominent personages who enter into the narrative. Of these our first "Luff," Mr. Kell, comes uppermost by a head and shoulders. He stands six feet two, and is of stalwart frame, lithe and straight as an Indian, with a fine head and a mild, benevolent, dark blue eye that can flash lightning all the same on occasion. His phenomenal mustache and beard, of auburn color, give him the very presence of an ancient viking. The former will meet behind his head, and the latter flows down to his hips.

The second lieutenant, Armstrong, is of more modern type, but also blue-eyed, straight, and fully a six-footer. He has an excitable temperament, is quick of impulse and speech, but always talks and acts to the purpose. He is a born ruler of men. The third lieutenant, Wilson, is shorter by a couple of inches, with dark complexion, eyes, and hair. He is very quick-tempered, and rather vindictive toward his foes, but otherwise a most generous and warmhearted man.

There are two other personages who cannot be omitted from this formal presentment. The first is Evans, our wonderful scout. Though a genuine salt, he, too, is erect on his pins as a drum-major, and quite as sensitive in the matter of personal dignity. I have often thought that Wilson was the most earnest fighter I ever saw; but Evans was brave to absolute recklessness. His steel-gray eye is like an eagle's in its concentration of energy. Evans is also a great yarn spinner, as you shall find when you catch him off duty and in the mood. His ability to determine the nationality of ships amounts to genius, and upon this point he cannot endure chaffing. Fulham, the prize-master, is a typical Englishman, five feet eight in height, broad-shouldered and muscular, with blue eyes, brown hair, and huge side whiskers. A typical sailor too, bighearted, full of animal spirits and fun. Fulham can spin the toughest yarn of any man on board; and with this quality, joined to his happy and magnetic disposition, he succeeds in keeping chipper even the captains of the prizes he calls upon in the way of duty. Withal, it may as well be said here, Fulham was a most competent officer and would have graced a lieutenant's commission. At the time of joining us, he was in the English Royal Naval Reserve.[1]

Our crew was in a sense "Hobson's choice," as has been seen. Pretty hard characters, some of them, no doubt; but all the same, a bronzed, stalwart, well-seasoned set of fellows who, now that they have exchanged their nondescript rags for our paymaster's nobby blue-and-white uniforms, look as promising as any set of men that ever went to sea. How this

---

1. The Royal Naval Reserve also gave us our fourth lieutenant, Low, who as a sailor ranked easily with Kell. His superb seamanship undoubtedly saved the *Alabama* from foundering when struck by the cyclone. He was officer of the deck at the time and wore ship on his own responsibility. Had he hesitated for an instant and allowed the tempest to catch him on the port-tack, there can be little question that this story would never have been written.

promise was fulfilled is now a matter of history, though we shall have occasion to speak of it as we go.

The writer has frequently been asked if he did not have "a good time" on the *Alabama*. Well, not by any means the sort of a time one usually proposes to himself by way of choice—if he likes comfort and ease. Taking the average, the work of the cruise was done by less than one hundred men; subtract boys and idlers, and the hard work fell upon a very few. And such work! The captures bear but a trifling proportion to the vessels boarded. With no night, Sunday, or holiday, sea-watches always, at sea or in port. Drill, drill, drill! Boarding, boarding, boarding, in all weather! Did men ever go through so much in the two years we were afloat? Talk about army life! Why, Jack's synonym for an easy life is "soldiering." The seaman of the present day very little resembles the bronzed, hardened, thoroughly trained salt Jack so fully represented on the *Alabama*. It is certain that no crew able to do the work ours did could be shipped in any port of the world today.

The watch-officers of the *Alabama* had all seen service in the United States Navy excepting one—Lieutenant John Low (who was an Englishman and trained in the merchant service)—and were thoroughly competent for the exceptional work required of them. The engineers were not only able to handle the engines in all emergencies, but to make the frequent and often difficult repairs that usually are intrusted only to machine shops. The master's-mates were thorough seamen, quite competent to take the deck and maneuver or navigate the ship. They were invaluable assistants in boarding and relieving the overworked watch-officers when bad weather made our duties arduous.

The midshipmen, as a matter of course, were little experienced except at gun-drill. But they were apt and intelligent, and they had rare opportunities for acquiring seamanship. Before many months they were all able to work the ship, and were handy with sextant and chronometer. We had, as will be guessed, some old man-of-war's men among the crew, competent to take the place of petty officers and to give instruction to the rest, as well as to set an example of submission to man-of-war discipline. This last, by the way, our Jack of the merchant service does not take to quite so naturally as he does to his abundant and well-cooked rations, or his allowance of grog. But with all our advantages, we needed time to organize and drill ere we were fit, not only to fight an enemy's cruiser, but even to capture and board a prize.

Our course lay for some days to the northeast rather out of the track of commerce. Our fires were banked and propeller hoisted, as coal was always to be most carefully economized, and we moved along under easy sail. In this way we burn but one ton of coal per day; and as the boilers are hot, we can always have steam in fifteen minutes when we need it. We are bound for no port, and while coal lasts we are not apt to seek one. The deep will tell no tales as to our whereabouts, and will offer our crew no opportunities for dissipation. The *Alabama* is also nearly as good under sail as steam, and it will be a swift clipper indeed that compels us to resort to the latter in chase, unless we are in a very great hurry. We expect to keep the ocean for many months at a stretch.

We have now been at sea for some days, no sail sighted, nothing to break the monotony but the blue broken clouds above and the lazy splash of the sea under our forefoot and propeller-well. But the deck is a beehive of industry. Here you will see a gun's crew under instruction of the lieutenant and midshipman of the division. At another point boatswain Mecaskey and his mates, marlinespikes in hand, deep in the mystery of a side- or train-tackle to be altered, and anon growling out an oath or two however the work is going on, a little more emphatic if a lubberly job meets his eye, but a swear or two anyhow, just to let his mates know he is boatswain Mecaskey. Now we have gunner Cuddy with his mates, polish in hand; for you must know that the battery is to be blacked, pumiced, and polished to a degree to put to blush a dude's patent leathers. We doubt not our capable gunner has already loaded his battery with blank cartridge, at least he should have done so; for if the enemy luffs alongside of us in the night, it takes less time to return his fire with only shot or shell to be rammed home. But we feel sure that everything is being put shipshape in the ordnance department. Sailmaker Alcott is on the verge of collapse with the importance of his trust; though the first set of sails has just been bent, and from present weather appearances is likely to do many a month's service. Still our "man of canvas" is casting an "eye to windward" for embryo squalls or blows and putting some spare sails in the locker. Who knows but in him we have a seer, and that is why he is now overhauling the storm maintrysail, which is to do such important work on the 16th of October next? Our carpenter, William Robinson, is perhaps the least-busy man to be found among our artisans; for unless the first lieutenant has some odd job on hand for him, it is more than likely he will have to "soldier" until some enemy's cruiser has knocked a plank or two off us, or old Boreas has embraced some spar.

Twelve o'clock now. We call it "eight bells." Who watches its advent with more thought and anxiety than Jack? He is impatient for rest and dinner, introduced by a little Jamaica for the thirsty soul. The sailing-master who, sextant in hand, has been "taking" the sun, touches his hat and reports to the captain standing by his side, "Twelve o'clock, sir—latitude so and so"; the answer comes, "Make it so, sir." The master now reports the time to the officer of the deck, who in turn directs the messenger boy to strike the bell. As the sound dies away, the boatswain and his mates pipe to dinner, and a sweeter sound than that from a boatswain's pipe one would not wish to listen to.

Jack now files around the grog-tub and, as his name is called crooks his elbow, throws back his head, and swallows felicity. Forward he rolls, rubbing his paunch and wishing he had it to do over again; and so he would if that vigilant officer had his eye off him for a moment. "Doubling on the grog-tub" is no crime, no, not even a misdemeanor, in Jack's eyes, so watch him well, Lieutenant! Let's go forward, even without an invitation, and see these late British subjects at dinner. A stiff "tot" of grog has cheered spirits and loosened tongue; and between chunks of salt horse and hardtack, he is eloquently expatiating on the events of the past few weeks and giving his opinion of matters general and particular. Jack is never modest in the forecastle, especially if he has doubled the "Horn." But we do not find much of an assortment of silverware decorating Jack's table. Seated on the deck, legs doubled under tailor-fashion, with a tablecloth of black painted canvas, and dishes and plates of tinware, sheath knife in hand he cuts a slab of salt beef or pork from the skid, and with a "hardtack" for a plate makes his attack, alternating with a pull at his coffee or tea dipper. But little time is consumed at the meal, for Jack is a rapid eater—considers time spent in eating almost wasted; pipe and tobacco is the goal of his desire, and he wants all the time possible for the enjoyment of it and for the inevitable yarn to be spun before the boatswain's whistle calls him to duty again.

We have now been twelve days on our cruise, and constant work getting our ship into fighting and sailing trim has almost banished from our thoughts the prime object of our adventure on the ocean. With constant drilling at great guns,

saber or pistol exercise, repelling boarders with pikes, etc.,
our crew have at last inspired confidence in their officers and
gained it for themselves.

On September 5, after dinner, a sail was made from the
masthead, hove-to, with her maintopsail aback. Wind light.
We approached her under the United States colors. She did
not move tack or sheet. No thought on her part of a Confederate cruiser! A little later the enemy did not tumble into
our arms so easily, for ill news travels apace. Still showing
United States colors we boarded her. She proved to be the
ship *Ocmulgee*. Alongside of her was a large sperm whale,
just captured, and being stripped of blubber and bone. A
prize-crew was thrown on board of her, her officers and men
transferred to the *Alabama*, and we lay all night in sight. We
were now on the whaling ground of the Western Islands; and
lest the bonfire should light up the night and stampede the
rest of the whaling fleet, we waited before firing her, in the
meantime transferring some provisions and small stores
from the prize.

Next morning our boarding-officer took his first lesson in
the art of firing a ship. Perhaps the reader may imagine there
is no art in it. Well, one way to do a thing well, another to
bungle, there always seems to be. We have many more to
send "where the woodbine twineth"; so listen to the modus
operandi (though we were not put to the trouble with this
whaler—inflammable enough without any preparation).
First, you cut up with your broadax the cabin and forecastle
bunks, generally of white pine lumber. You will find, doubtless, the mattresses stuffed with straw, and in the cabin
pantry part at least of a keg of butter and lard. Make a foundation of the splinters and straw, pour on top the lard and
butter. One pile in cabin, the other in forecastle. Get your
men in the boats, all but the incendiaries, and at the given
word—"Fire!"—shove off, and take it as truth that before

you have reached your own ship, the blaze is licking the topsails of the doomed ship.

We witness today for the first time the hauling down of the Stars and Stripes—to those of us who served in the old navy, a humbling of the emblem at our hands, carrying with it many a cruel wrench and sad retrospect. To men who in days gone by had stood on the quarterdeck, with the doff of cap, and amid the glitter of uniforms, presenting of arms, and strains of the national air, and daily witnessed the morning ceremony of hoisting this flag at the peak, it was difficult to disassociate the act with desecration.

The writer can never forget the feelings and impressions of this first capture, and the sight later on of the burning ship brought sorrow to the heart. I may almost say shame; but war! cruel, inhuman war! soon blunts the sentimental impulses, and what seemed at first sheer ruthlessness became in time a matter of course. It must be acknowledged that after a brief space of time the cry "Sail ho!" from aloft was received with the heartfelt wish she would prove a prize. The day after the capture of the *Ocmulgee* we made the Island of Flores, and being now on whaling ground the ship is "hove-to." We can here await the oil fleet. This is what may be styled "still hunting." Being quite near the land, the boats of the prize, which have been towing astern of us, are hauled alongside, and our prisoners, after being paroled, allowed to depart for the shore.

They were far from being destitute, having by permission secured full loads of provisions, all their whaling gear and other odds and ends, and would soon after landing be under the protection of the American consul. The plunder was to them clear gain and pocket-change. We have now been two weeks in commission, having changed colors on Sunday, August 24. Ten o'clock ("four bells") having arrived, we go to muster. Our former vagabonds, arrayed in all the colors of

Joseph's coat, would not be recognized just now. Standing in a group on the quarterdeck, the commander and his officers abaft of them, the "Articles of War" are read; and as the death penalty is frequently mentioned therein, Jack looks first up, then down, and at his mates most significantly. He is evidently coming to the conclusion there is something serious in this business. This ended, the muster roll is called; and as his name is reached, each man, now dressed in white frock and pants, pumps and sennit hat in hand, passes around the capstan and forward. "Inspection" is over, and the "pipe down" is "called."

It is wonderful what effect even just two weeks of soap and discipline have had on our crew. We had among them a few young boys who had smuggled themselves on board the *Bahama* at Liverpool, and had turned up on deck during our stay at Terceira. Being useful as messenger boys and "powder monkeys," they were signed and put to duty. Among them was one Egan, and a tougher case Liverpool could not produce. The sailors had brought from port a pet cat; and all who know a sailor will recognize the bond of affection existing between him and his pet, be it what species it may. The cat was missed a few days out of port, and faithful search having been made in vain, Egan was hauled up to the mast charged with knowing the fate or whereabouts of the animal. It seems he was suspected from some known circumstances, together with his reputation for mischief already established.

Egan was "spread-eagled" in the mizzen rigging barefooted, and was holding out well, denying all knowledge of the whereabouts of puss. In the meantime, a sail was made from aloft, the after pivot-gun cleared away for the purpose of heaving-to the vessel. One would suppose Egan to have been a student of Marryatt from his selection of queer pranks, when upon taking the tampion from the muzzle of the gun out jumps pussy. Egan soon after confessed judgment, being unable to stand the punishment longer, and upon being interrogated as to why he did it, replied, "Oh, to see what effect the firing would have on the cat!"

Soon after muster we have the cry from aloft, "Sail ho!" The two vessels now approach each other on opposite tacks and with a fresh breeze. The chase of the schooner was most exciting to us, and no doubt her skipper's nerves were on a tension—a touch-and-go capture, and will be to all time a memorable retrospect to him. This little schooner was bound from Fayal to Boston, via Flores, to land passengers, and, as we perceived upon getting within two or three miles, had some females on board. She declined showing colors in answer to our English flag flung to the breeze, well knowing her build and cut of sails stamped her American to us, and our blank cartridge significantly hinting our nationality. She had the land about six miles distant, a fresh breeze blowing, the wind abeam, her best point of sailing, and was evidently resolved on reaching the charmed marine league, if possible, before overhauled.

The presence of females on her deck precluded our firing a shot even near her if avoidable, but the indomitable pluck of her skipper forced the matter. A thirty-two shot was plunged a few feet ahead of her. Still the little captain had no idea of surrender. The breeze was too fresh and land too near. Evidently nothing entered into his calculation but the haven of rest and safety ahead. As usual in such cases, "the bull was taken by the horns," and another shot fired, passing just over his deck and between the fore- and mainsails. The jig was up. In a moment the graceful little craft luffed to the strong breeze, jib-sheet to windward.

Doubtless but for the lady passengers this typical specimen of a venturesome Yankee would have stood fire and escaped. We could but feel regret at his ill-luck. His pluck deserved success—a brighter fellow under adversity it would be difficult to find. Being now close aboard the islands, the crew of the prize are landed under parole. We are visited by a number of boats from the shore, and soon the mess caterers are bargaining for fish, turtles, fruit, etc. The governor and staff made us a visit, were entertained, and seemed favorably impressed.

The ship's head is now put offshore under easy sail (generally single-reefed topsails), for we are in no hurry—only on a loaf off the group of the Azores. The whaling fleet are to catch us rather than we them. Each day or so brings along the game; and by the 1st of October we have, in addition to the two captures already mentioned, boarded and burned the following eight vessels, all whalers: *Ocean Rover, Alert, Weathergauge, Altamaha, Ben Tucker, Courser, Virginia,* and *Elisha Dunbar.*

A small whaling vessel belonging to the island was cruising in company with the American whale fleet, and a witness to our work of destruction. We had captured a vessel, and an attempt had been made by our prize-crew to scuttle her, under orders, the idea being to destroy her without having the smoke of a conflagration to warn the enemy of our presence. As the reader can doubtless foresee, it proved a failure from the nature of the cargo, the result being simply that the oil-casks floating to the top forced off the hatches, and the vessel filling with water soon covered the ocean with barrels of oil. Our island whaling-skipper, permission being obtained, soon found himself possessed of a cargo without the risk of hunting. We need not inform you this mode of getting rid of a prize was not repeated. It was evidently conceived and acted on without due thought, and in the excitement and hurry of destruction. No doubt our "Dago" skipper was furnished for all time with a yarn to spin of how he filled up in one day on one of his whaling voyages. Still it was a case of reciprocity, the Portuguese skipper removing so much property that otherwise would most likely have been recovered by the enemy.

The skipper of the *Ocean Rover* brought on board of us an immense fruitcake put up in tin, the last of four, supplied by the good wife "to hum" to celebrate the wedding day—an old custom with the whalers. "Well," remarked the captain, "the wedding day is not at hand yet, but you had as well enjoy the cake, gentlemen." Little did the thoughtful and provident good wife imagine under what auspices and surroundings the ceremony of cutting this cake would take place! At the time this labor was undertaken, our land had not even the shadow of the coming eclipse resting over it. All the enjoyment of this rare treat was no doubt on our side; still we could spare our sympathies to the gallant but unfortunate fellow.

It would frequently suggest itself during our cruise in these latitudes why these skippers so readily hove-to at the suggestion of a rifle shell and allowed themselves to be boarded, the sea running high at the time, making the casting loose of a gun dangerous in the extreme and the lowering of a boat hazardous, the boarding of the enemy more so. Nothing was more practical than to refuse our commands, take our desultory and uncertain fire, and await night and fortune, in the way of a friendly rainstorm shutting in, when escape would be certain. Nothing was wanting to make it thoroughly practical and feasible but courage. It must have been ignorance of our comparative helplessness to act in a strong gale that guided these commanders. Surely coolness and courage are qualities not wanting in our average American skipper.

The *Elisha Dunbar* was boarded and fired in a gale of wind, and had her captain refused our blank cartridge or shot could easily have made his escape, the gale increasing each moment and rendering it most dangerous to cast loose a gun, and impossible to do execution with it in so heavy a sea. But her captain seemed to have lost his head, clewing up and heaving-to at the bid of our blank cartridge. The burning ship was a sublime spectacle—the flames leaping in mad play from spar to spar; her sails unfurled, burning from the yards and flying in huge fragments to leeward; while the lightning, darting from the angry dark clouds, seemed to mock the doomed ship in her misfortune. Her masts swayed and went by the board, and her hull, rocking on the seas and staggering like a drunken man, finally lurched to leeward and disappeared beneath the wild waves.

We have been but little inconvenienced with the crews of these prizes so far, having the land close aboard all the time so that we could run in under the lee and land them in their own boats. The pyrotechnic displays must have kept the islanders in constant excitement. For days together the heavens were lit up with these fierce bonfires. The whaler makes a grand blaze. I have no doubt, aside from the captains of the destroyed whalers, who in most cases are part owners, the men were well pleased with the adventure. They were given their boats, whaling gear, provisions, and traps, and indeed were allowed to help themselves to about whatever they fancied. We found no marked cases of excessive modesty on their part. The boats without exception were loaded, gunwales down to the water. These men, having their entire expenses paid by the United States government to their respective homes, through their consul, were no doubt rather benefited by the introduction to the *Alabama*.

We have by this time greatly increased the population of the islands, and to the decided gain of the latter; for unlike the mass of the immigrants to our own land, they have been put onshore with, in the estimation of these islanders, untold wealth. Doubtless a glimpse onshore after the landing of this horde would have furnished an interesting chapter. To this day, that ubiquitous individual, "the oldest inhabitant," causes the eyes of the rising generation to start with wonder as he dilates on the story of the raid of the *Alabama*, the army of people put onshore, and the good bargains had with the strangers.

Our prizes had also furnished us with every requisite for the comfort and health of both officers and crew. Whalers are the best provided in all particulars of any class of vessels, their cruises being of long duration and generally in parts of the world but little frequented. Our paymaster had laid in a carefully selected assortment of clothing, provisions, small stores, etc., and the writer will never forget (being a philosopher of the weed) a large lot of Virginia smoking and chewing tobaccos. The value of this "find" can only be fully appreciated by a fellow who has been without it for a long time. It is an expensive article at best in England, and the war had made it more scarce, hence a very limited supply had been included in our ship-stores at Liverpool. Jack for the rest of the cruise always had his cheek and pipe well filled.

The only articles saved from a prize, besides those before enumerated, are the flag of the vessel and her chronometers. The flags were consigned to the safekeeping of the signal quartermaster, though the sailing-master was held officially responsible for them. The chronometers were assigned a place in the cabin under the immediate eye of the captain, but under the care and in the keeping of the navigating officer. This duty devolved upon the writer; and as it was Semmes's orders they be wound up each day, a process necessary to their good order, it was already quite a task. We had about fifteen of them, requiring half an hour to wind up, with the prospect of a steady all-day job at it in the near future at the rate we were burning vessels. We had on hand at the end of the cruise, and landed at Cherbourg, seventy-five chronometers; and it need not be added the winding-up business soon came to an end, time being too valuable for expenditure on so many recording angels. The reason for saving these instruments was their portability as compared with their value.

It was highly amusing to note the inborn talent and taste of the genuine down-easter for a smart bargain. No sooner had the captures commenced than our Yankee skippers were concocting schemes to get to windward of Semmes. Without the shadow of a doubt as to the legality of the seizure of the foregoing vessels, some of the captains had the bold assurance to propose bonding their vessels, suggesting as an inducement that the bonded value would no doubt exceed that allowed by the Court of Condemnation. But this proposal did not work. Semmes no doubt considered the "bird in the hand."

We have been thirty-seven days in commission, most of the time weather moderate and suitable for the work. The last few days, however, have been ugly, reminding us that the season of storms is about on us. Now we are on our way to the Banks of Newfoundland, having effectually put a quietus on the whaling fleet. A great change has taken place in the appearance and discipline of our crew—the effects of the last shore debauch having worn out of their systems, replaced by bright eyes and ruddy complexions, the consequence of regular habits, hard work, and substantial rations.

We may safely say now we have a man-of-war under us; the men, from constant practice maneuvering about prizes, handling their vessel like a toy, and the faithful exercise of the gun-crews at quarters, by the lieutenants and petty officers, has taught them to flirt the battery in and out with most gratifying alacrity. But one chance has been afforded them thus far for exercise at great guns with shot and shell at a prize-vessel, and this was creditable for an introductory. We have also added to our crew somewhat since hunting among the whalers. We have secured fourteen additional men and have now a crew of ninety-nine men, or one hundred and twenty-five officers and men all told. We can meet the enemy now with a fair chance of success.

The reader may desire to know something about the morale of men so recently recruited from the enemy. Jack is a queer fellow, of a roving, restless disposition, fond of excitement and adventure, and loves the new ship and the new sweetheart best. So seeing this natty, trim, and saucy rover of the seas apparently having a good time of it, he falls head over heels in love with her and, presenting himself at the capstan, desires through the executive officer a few words with our skipper. The interview proving mutually satisfactory, our hero signs the articles, and presto! from being a prisoner in the lee scuppers has the privilege and comfort of sampling the *Alabama*'s "Old Jamaica." This is the way the complement of the cruiser was kept up during the cruise, the places of those left behind in port being supplied from fresh captures.

We will do our crew the credit to say of them we do not believe they actually deserted, in many cases, but were on shore hid away in some rum-hole or dance house, stupid from liquor and in ignorance that their ship was obliged to put to sea upon the expiration of the time allowed her in port. We may further add that Semmes would never ship from the captured vessels any seamen of North American nativity, and was most searching in his inquiries as to their place of birth. Among the prisoners shipping on the *Alabama* during the whaling raid off the Azores, we will call your attention to little David H. White. He became quite a marked character on our vessel. Dave was a Delaware slave, a boy about seventeen or eighteen years old; and wanting in the wardroom mess of our ship an efficient waiter-boy, the lot fell to Dave. He was not only willing but anxious to ship. The natural instincts of the lad told him we would be his friends. He knew Southern gentlemen on sight. Dave became a great favorite with the officers, his willing, obliging manners, cheerful disposition, and untiring attention winning for him the affection of not only the officers, but of the entire ship's company. Poor Dave! He was drowned in the engagement off Cherbourg. It was his privilege to go onshore with the wardroom steward to market; and on all occasions the American consul or his satellites would use all their eloquence to persuade Dave to desert his ship, reminding him of his present condition of slavery and the chance presented of throwing off his shackles, but Dave remained loyal in face of all temptation.

We are on the Banks of Newfoundland, in the Gulf Stream, as indicated by the temperature of the water, and directly in the track of vessels to and from Europe. This was one of the most trying portions of our cruise, dangerous beyond measure, hove-to or under very short sail all the time. We have not only the elements to contend with at this most stormy period of the year, but the hourly danger of being run down by some swift-passing steamer or grain-carrier, the nights being unusually dark and the fogs thick enough to cut with a knife.

We have also the danger of swamping when boarding vessels in heavy seas. Some of our officers had already had experience in this line in the last two captures, and did not look forward with a great deal of relish to the prospect ahead. Indeed, the cruise of our ship from this time forward to the day her prow was turned southward, was attended with as much hardship as ever fell to the lot of sailormen. We were constantly boarding vessels, the weather at all times vicious, often unable to remove anything from the prizes but the crews themselves, and this attended with the greatest possible risk of life. Still our captain and executive were incessant in their advice and caution, and through their watchful care we were enabled to finish up this raid on the grain fleet without the loss of one soul.

The plan of boarding vessels was very simple. The *Alabama* would luff to windward of the prize, allowing the boarding-officer to pull down to her before the wind. After seeing him safe alongside, our vessel would wear ship and take a position to leeward, thus allowing our boat to return in the same way. The cruise in this latitude was one constant succession of storms and boarding of vessels; and, as can well be imagined, both officers and crew were well nigh exhausted after a few weeks of such work.

We are now beginning to realize the hardships of our cruise; and anything but a boon would it be to be able to pierce the future and contemplate the two years of constant work of this character ahead of us. You have but just left the deck after a four-hour watch in villainous weather, perhaps working ship during the whole of it after some sail, and have begun to appreciate the warmth of your blankets, when the quartermaster flashes a bull's-eye lantern in your face and you are instanter wide awake to hear the cheerful intelligence you are wanted on deck at once to board a vessel just hove-to. You have ample time while bundling into your pea jacket to anticipate the weather you are to make the trip in, as oftentimes your boots, floating about on the wardroom deck, give the hint that you are not loafing around the tropics at present. If your wishes and inclinations could have full effect, the quartermaster would be in a most unenviable place. A more unwished-for visitor, or a more thankless job than his, does not exist on the *Alabama*. But as Jack says, "We've shipped for it," are "in for it," so must take it fair or foul. One redeeming feature displayed itself in the windup; it proved to he healthy. So the end justified the means. We were a lot of lightwood knots at the end of the cruise.

We have reached the 15th of October, and have since the last report captured the following seven vessels: *Brilliant, Wave Crest, Dunkirk, Manchester, Lamplighter, Emily Farnum,* and *Tonawanda.* The last two released on ransom-bond, one protected by neutral cargo, the other as cartel for the large number of prisoners captured on above vessels. On the *Dunkirk* we found a deserter from the *Sumter*, George Forrest, seaman, who was tried by court-martial and later on landed in irons and dismissed the service at Blanquilla, an island in the Carribean Sea (November 26, 1862). The penalty attached to his crime is death, but he had fallen into merciful hands. Lucky fellow! He was tried by a court composed of his old officers of the *Sumter*. Perhaps the recollections of common dangers and vicissitudes softened the hearts of his shipmates. Forrest joined an American fishing vessel found anchored off the island, and which we could not make a prize of, she being within Venezuelan territory.

It is to the credit of Semmes that he was at all times most punctilious in his respect for international law, as witnessed by his numerous decisions growing out of the capture of Northern vessels with quasi-neutral cargoes. Semmes always gave the benefit of the doubt in favor of the cargo, and released the ship under ransom-bond. The reader will notice the large number of vessels thus released by us as bearing out this statement.

CHAPTER IV

A STERN CHASE; ON NEWFOUNDLAND BANKS; THE CYCLONE; OFF NEW YORK; SOUTHWARD HO!; A NEW MAIN YARD; MARTINIQUE; ESCAPE FROM THE CRUISER *SAN JACINTO*; THE RUN TO BLANQUILLA; CRUISING AFTER THE CALIFORNIA TREASURE-STEAMER; CAPTURE OF THE *ARIEL*

THE CAPTURE OF THE brig *Dunkirk* was under beautiful conditions. The moon at near full, the chase a long and exciting one, with a strong breeze, both vessels going free, studding sails alow and aloft, fairly rushing before the rising gale. The chase was well in view, thanks to the bright night. She proved to be a very fast sailer; but, gaining on her slowly, we felt assured of final success, accident excepted, without use of steam. Towards morning, having the chase well in hand and wishing to drop the curtain on the scene, berth prisoners, and be ready for morning deck-cleaning, quarters, and inspection, we sent a "thirty-two persuader" after her. So rapidly did she respond and luff up, foretopsail to the mast, that our rapid headway rushed us far to the leeward of her. The breeze was now a sharp gale as we hauled on a wind, taking in all sail to topsails, and hove our maintopsail aback. Semmes had been up all night, legs astraddle the hammock-nettings, night-glasses in hand, and nursing his gratification at the business-like way in which the chase carried sail, endangering our spars to follow suit. The officer of the deck and men were worn out with trimming sail to the shifts of breeze.

However, the meeting between the two skippers turned out a pleasant one, the fine sailing qualities displayed by our ship keeping Semmes in a good humor, no doubt. He opened the conversation in a facetious vein, recently adopted, and which he seemed to nurse as a pretty good "get off." "Say, Captain, I should judge from the trouble you have put myself and lads to, you must have forgotten (canvas failing) my little 'teakettle' below." The old man rarely displayed temper, except when tangled ownership of cargo cloud ship's papers and set him overhauling his law library for "precedents." The skipper might look out for a blast, did Semmes in his search unearth a trick or subterfuge in "certificates." Then there's many a "d—n your eyes."

The weather from the *Dunkirk*'s capture onward was unsettled, moderate gales with but little intervening comfort of smooth sea. We had one day some strange visitors—a flock of curlew, blown off from land, settled in our port quarter-boat, wing-weary and starved. We captured them without an effort at escape. So poor in flesh were they as to offer no inducement to our steward. He declined upon inspection converting them into potpie. They must have been many days at sea. Our sympathies prompt us rather than our stomachs, the latter cutting no figure in it; so after refreshing them with fresh water and such suitable food as we had to offer, we launched them on the air to wing their way westward. We cannot say if they were Yankees or Johnny Rebs. Jack was pleased. His superstition as to harming birds is a strong feeling.

We are still on the Banks, the weather for the past few days villainous. If some good bird of that flock said to roost aloft and look out for poor Jack, had by his presence for the past week given us the warning, we undoubtedly should have put up our helm and under steam dodged the cyclone we are now on the edge of. The barometer has fallen to a point indicating not simply a severe storm such as heaves up the Atlantic each few days of this season but a veritable cyclone, that phenomenon of the Western Hemisphere all sailors not only dread but are appalled at. From its fearful vortex, should it be reached, not many vessels escape, and permit the witnesses to picture to owners and friends its awful sublimity.

The ship was put under very low sail, close-reefed topsails, forestaysail, and the main storm trysail gotten up and bent. All light yards were sent on deck, the quarter-boats swung in on their davits and secured, lifelines rove, the hatches battened down. All hands ordered on deck, and all fires put out but the binnacle light. The wind quickly increased to a hurricane. Men had been sent aloft, and the topsails furled and extra gaskets passed around the sails. Delayed until the storm struck, it would have been madness, if not murder, to have ordered the topmen aloft.

Still the blast increased, howling as if ten thousand demons had been loosed from Hades. Away goes the main yard parted in the slings, and in a twinkling the main- and maintopsails fly to leeward, torn from the gaskets and into shreds. In the meantime, the forestaysail has been blown to ribbons, and the ship lies to under only the main storm trysail, close-reefed, and not much larger than a lady's shawl. It soon went, and we were under bare poles.

To convey an idea of the force of the wind would beggar language. Its fury was so great that no sea could get up, the ocean surface having the appearance rather of a millstream. The air was white with "spoon-drift," giving the appearance of a heavy snowstorm. The officers and men were cowering under the weather bulwarks or lashed at important stations. The wheel doubly manned, and in spite of this precaution it at one time, during the violent laboring of the vessel, got away from control, and, with a whirl, threw a man completely over it to leeward.

For two hours this mad play of the ocean devils continued. The dark green clouds nearly met the water, twisting and squirming between each other like snakes or loathsome reptiles as the whirlwinds direct them in their play. In the meantime, our gallant boat was behaving nobly. Though pressed down by the force of the tempest so that her lee guns were quite hid by the water, and the lee quarter-boat twisted from the davits and floating alongside, she lay still and comfortably, but little sea boarding, though the deck was wet by the rain and spray. She was working in her deck seams from the fearful strain, but otherwise demonstrating that we had a gallant seaboat under us. She was making but little water in her hold.

One of the curiosities preserved, a souvenir of the cyclone, was the maintopsail-sheet, an iron chain of about two inches diameter, which was blown out to leeward as though a ship's pennant; the force of the wind whipping half-turns in it, and gradually tying it up into a solid mass. It was literally welded to such a degree as to require the use of tools in straightening it out.

As stated already, we had now been two hours exposed to the fearful sledgehammering of the wind, when suddenly, in a twinkling, it died away dead calm. Think not we are to be let off now; it is only a pause—a consultation, as it were, of the elements for our destruction. We are in that dreadful vortex. Our ship is now exposed to another danger. The removal of the pressure of the wind has allowed the sea to get up, and we are wallowing in it, the water swashing aboard, first in one gangway and then the other. It is all one can do to hold on to the bulwarks.

The seas are mounting to appalling heights, and the roll of our ship threatens to jerk the masts out of her; but they are of good Georgia pine and bend to the strain like willow branches. The barometer has been noted, and found to be more than one inch higher. Soon we see and hear the dread storm approaching again on the water, sounding in the distance like faraway thunder. The heavens seem, if anything, more threatening than before.

Butt-end first it strikes us, screeching and howling as though the air were filled with countless shot and shell in passage. The gallant boat again bows to its command, and with lee guns underwater seems to fairly struggle for breath and life, her timbers groaning and creaking as though suffering dying agonies. The clouds are lower than the mastheads and drawn into narrow ribbons of dark green color, whose writhing again makes the spectacle appalling. The spoon-drift nearly takes the breath away, the only relief being in burying the head in hands and turning the back to the blast.

Two hours more we hang between life and "Davy Jones's locker," when the storm breaks, though not so suddenly as when we entered the vortex, and once again our ship is staggering among the seas, jolting and butting against each other like sheep driven along a strange road. The barometer is again noted, and found to be rising rapidly. Sail is made to steady ship in the fearful sea, though there is but little wind to fill them. We have got a breathing spell and time to look about us.

Such a scene of wreck and confusion! We can promise our boatswain, gunner, sailmaker, and carpenter lots of business for some days to come. For a week or so we have dirty, unsettled weather, the effects of the late cyclone; and the ship is kept under close canvas, jogging in towards the enemy's coast. Meantime we capture the *Lafayette, Lauretta, Crenshaw,* and *Baron de Castile,* placing a ransom-bond on the latter, and transferring the crews of the prizes. None of these latter prizes had felt the cyclone, though captured just after it had left us.

We have now nearly completed the second act of the drama, namely, the destruction and demoralization of the "grain fleet"; for not much of anything but cereals comfort. It was a strange thing that the enemy's plan of pursuit was to look for us where last reported instead of studying the future probabilities. We are now bound to the West Indies. It would seem quite natural that the *Alabama* would turn her head in this direction after having stampeded the European grain fleet, and that we should find the West India Islands swarming with the enemy's gunboats—but we shall see.

Our vessel is once more shipshape, the damage of the late storms repaired, and we are standing south with the weather much improved. We are again rather out of the track of vessels, though we have boarded a number of sail proving to be neutral, and have been rewarded by the capture of the *Levi Starbuck,* whaler, outward bound. She proved a lawful prize, and was fired. Our next prize was the *T. B. Wales,* a splendid India clipper from Calcutta for Boston. This ship proved to be one of the most valuable, besides recruiting our crew to the extent of eleven first-class seamen.

The main yard of the prize, upon measurement, was found to be of the same dimensions as ours, which was crip-

pled in the cyclone, and which had been "fished" for temporary use. It was brought on board and slung instead of our
wounded one. Our young officers have now a lucky chance
for improving themselves in one line of their profession.
Boatswain Mecaskey and carpenter Robinson are hard at
work fitting the new main yard, and many a revelation in
spun yarn and knots will break upon their visions; and the
interest in the coming change of spars, the modus operandi
of sending down the crippled one and crossing the new one,
forms the current topic of conversation at mess-table and on
watch; and just now our active boatswain is by all odds the
most important character in the ship, not excepting scout
Evans. None of these middies have the faintest idea how it
is to be done, yet each has a commiserative look on his countenance for his brother middy's nautical ignorance. It was a
case where silence is golden with them. But Mecaskey will
get it there.

We have now a crew of one hundred and ten men and
twenty-six officers, or about fourteen short of a full complement. On the *Wales* we found, as passengers, an
ex–United States consul with his wife and family. Among
the effects of the consul's good wife were a number of very
handsome, elaborately carved ebony chairs. She was much
distressed upon learning they would have to be consigned to
the deep, owing to lack of room on a man-of-war. Her lady-
like resignation, however, to the inevitable was very sweet. It
has always dwelt in the memory of the writer; but such is
cruel war—no respecter of persons. I trust she bears us no ill
will.

It was the most unpleasant part of our boarding-duty, the
transfer of lady passengers to our ship. Not only the danger
and discomfort, but the awkward position forced upon them
while our guests in the wardroom. We always associate timidity with the ladies, but we must say it was not our experience

on the *Alabama*. There was never an instance of apparent fear on their part in all our transfers at sea; and frequently the weather was such as to drench them thoroughly in the passage to us, and requiring the use of whip-tackle and buckets to sling them over our side.

We are now running down for the Island of Martinique, where we expect to meet our transport, the *Agrippina*, which the reader will remember was the custodian of the *Alabama*'s armament and stores at Terceira. On the 18th of November we are off the port of Fort de France; and we find the *Agrippina*, laden with coal for us, lying at her anchor. After communicating with the governor and receiving permission, our prisoners of the *T. B. Wales* are landed, and we bid good-bye to the consul and his family, who had been with us nine days.

Our sailor-readers are the ones to fully appreciate the longing that comes over a fellow for fresh grub, after being on "salt horse" for many months. With the exception of one square meal of fresh food, we had been on ship's rations since leaving Terceira. Our wardroom steward, Parkinson, has carte blanche to supply the table. To say we breakfast, dine, and sup does not express it. It is eat all the time, fruits of all kinds between meals not counting. The crew, too, seem to be having a good time generally, but they have somehow managed to smuggle on board quite a lot of the "Oh be joyful." The main brace is spliced so often that soon our lads forget who commands the *Alabama*.

Matters getting serious, the beat to quarters is given; they recognize the sound and know they must go there, come what will or whatever their state, and Jack drunk and Jack sober answer to their names. Such the effect of discipline. The more mutinous ones are put in irons, the rest sent to their hammocks to sleep their drunk off. Poor Jack! He is in sense of responsibility a mere child, and with the disadvantage of neglect in early training. The *Agrippina* has been a number of days in port, quite long enough for the enemy, knowing her relations to us, to put in an appearance; so she is ordered at once to the Island of Blanquilla, off the coast of Venezuela, where we can join her and coal ship.

The wisdom of this appears the next morning. We are greeted with our first sight of one of the enemy's cruisers. The steam frigate *San Jacinto* lay on and off the mouth of the harbor; and judging from the extensive preparations she was making for battle, she must have had most exaggerated reports of our strength. All day her men were aloft, stoppering sheets, slinging yards, as if expecting a desperate fight. Our coal ship was off, and well on her way to our rendezvous, and this matter settled we cared nothing for the *San Jacinto*. We could steam around her.

At this port we were rather the victims of inordinate curiosity than the recipients of hospitality; for our decks were crowded with a promiscuous and impertinent lot of loungers and a few officials asking no questions of our officers and crew, but rather disposed to pry out their own conclusions. We were inclined to interpret our lukewarm and rude reception as the reflection of instructions from the French capital. The next night, rain and darkness favoring, we got under way, passed out at the southern channel, and saw nothing of the enemy. We afterwards heard she was at the other channel. There was a crestfallen set on the *San Jacinto* probably, when it was found out at dawn that we had given them the slip.

We are now off, and on our way to Blanquilla to join our old friend Captain McQueen and his gallant barque. Today finds the ship's company busy putting things to rights. Jack moves along with a listless roll; he feels dull, and disinclined for the routine of duty. The brig has been cleared of the delinquents; for Semmes is a kind and merciful superior, understanding the disposition of the sailor thoroughly, and ready to let bygones be bygones. And really we have as effi-

cient and happy a crew as could be picked up under most favorable circumstances. They are able, willing, obedient, and
cheerful, and attached to their ship by a feeling akin to idol-
atry. Amusements are allowed and encouraged. When free
from duty the evenings are spent on the forward deck; and
song and dance, improvised plays, yarn-spinning, etc., have
their turn. In this latter accomplishment Jack has no superior, if an equal. You have only to let off your story first, and
if he does not land you in the shade—well! you have evolved
a pretty tough one.

The young officers of the ship, with a view of passing the
off hours pleasantly, formed a glee club; and as we had some
charming voices among them, it was a real treat to both
wardroom and forecastle. Weather permitting and no vessels
to be boarded, at the approach of evening the audience gathers; the older officers occupy the "private boxes" (to wit,
campstools), the crew, the "gallery" (topgallant-forecastle);
and cigars and pipes being lighted by all who list, the program of the evening is in order. Songs sentimental, songs
nautical, and, last but not least, songs national, delight the
ears and hearts of all.

But it is eight bells (8 P.M.), and we must break up this
delightful party. The boatswain's-mate has piped "all the
starboard watch"; and while the lads of above are to watch
and ward over us, the other is to "turn in" to hammocks and
prepare for their turn. The watch is mustered and set, the
captain has passed his orders for the night to the officer of
the deck, directed what sail to put the ship under, and returned to his cabin, no doubt to hatch out some plan for
future tricks on the enemy. The "lookouts" have been stationed, the remainder of the watch, pea jackets under head,
lying down snug under the bulwarks. The quarter-master
stands by the wheel "conning" the helmsman. The officer of
the deck, stepping up to the wheel, passes the order just re-

ceived from the captain, "keep her north-northeast," or "full and by," as the case may be, then stepping to the weather-quarter mounts the "horse-block," trumpet and night-glasses in hand, on the lookout for sails and weather. Now should the wind be light, the silence is deathlike,

And all the air a solemn stillness holds.

Arriving duly at Blanquilla, we found our transport at anchor and also the American whaling-schooner *Northern Light*, which latter we simply detained until we were ready for sea lest she might report us. There was little of interest, you may imagine, at this point outside of fishing. This we indulged in to some extent, both with line trolling and the "grains," and turned over a few turtle for the messes. We found men on the island from the mainland of Venezuela who had cultivated the banana to some extent, it being their principal food, taking the place of bread—and by the way a most excellent substitute. Our men on their pleasure excursions had helped themselves to the fruit rather too bountifully, leaving the natives on rather short rations. Complaining to Semmes, the latter paid the bill with a plentiful supply of ship's rations, and the swap was most satisfactory to our islanders.

We found here in great abundance the iguana, a species of lizard much esteemed by the South Americans as an article of food; but though we captured quite a number we did not venture to test its toothsomeness, taking the natives' assurance as to its worth as a food product. It was sport to catch them, the modus being to creep up as they lay motionless in the bushes and lasso them with a long grass with a snood on the end. The reptiles are very watchful and wary.

Our young officers are having lots of fun at the expense of our temporary prisoner—the captain of the Yankee schooner.

He has become quite sociable since receiving assurance from Semmes that his little property will not be consigned to the flames, and visits our ship daily during spare hours. One fellow will say to him, "Say, Cap, did old Beeswax really tell you he should not burn your schooner?"—"Why, yes; of course he said so."—"It may be all in good faith, Cap," sighs the middy as he shakes his head, "but it's very like a joke of the old man"; and the skipper is again on the "ragged edge," and the youngster watching the anxious countenance is correspondingly happy.

Having coaled ship, the *Agrippina* is dispatched to the Arcas Islands in the Gulf of Mexico, there to await our arrival and fill our bunkers with the remainder of her cargo. Bidding Captain McQueen bon voyage, we are now on our way to the east end of Cuba, our object being to intercept the California mail steamer and handle a million or so of bright California gold. We coast along the south side of the island of Puerto Rico, pass through the Mona Passage, and skirt the coast of San Domingo.

It is now the 1st of December; and though we have boarded a number of vessels, we have not as yet had occasion to "strike a match," no enemy's vessel interrupting the sight of the horizon. We are beginning to think the *Alabama* has been well advertised in the United States. As we keep our lonely mid-watches in these calm and peaceful seas, our thoughts naturally stray to the past when these latitudes were the haunts of buccaneers, and in fancy picture them bound as we are after rich prizes. Indeed, aside from the legality attending our present mission, there *are* features to suggest a common occupation. There is no gossip or conversation, either forward or aft, that interests but of the California treasure-steamer. Whether convoyed or no; amount of bullion; speed we may expect in her. And every soul on board of us has become a self-appointed lookout. We are having, however, beautiful weather, and enjoying from the deck the exquisite tropical scenery as we lazily creep along the shores of these historic islands.

Meantime, although the *Alabama* has been loafing along lazily, she has kept her eyes about her; and as a result she has captured and burned the barque *Parker Cooke*, provision-laden. We had been for some days out of the latitude of a market-house, when our thoughtful purveyor put in an appearance. Evans, our factotum, whom we depend on for designating the nationality of a sail, had spent many weary and disappointing days aloft with the spyglass; and though sail after sail would peep up over the horizon, still nothing in the way of legitimate game passed the vision of his glass. So the visit of the *Cooke* was most apropos.

The wonderful ability of Evans to detect the nationality of a sail made him a very valuable man, aside from his other qualities. He had the eye of Hawk Eye of Cooper fame. It was simply a waste of time and useless labor on the crew working ship in pursuit of a vessel he had pronounced foreign. He could not always locate the stranger as to whether English, French, or what not; but that she was not Yankee you could make a book on it at large odds.

Having helped ourselves from this prize, secured her chronometer and instruments, the match was applied, and the crew of the *Parker Cooke* accept unsought hospitality. Lucky fellows in that the weather is grand, and sleeping on deck preferable anyway to a berth below. We may as well state here that all our prisoners were housed on deck from necessity, the berth-deck being crowded by our own men. But we made them as comfortable as we could under the circumstances, spreading awnings and tarpaulins over them in stormy weather, and in every way possible provided for their comfort. They were allowed full rations (less the spirit part), and their own cooks had the range of the galley in preparing their food to their taste. Indeed, when it is considered that our men had watch to keep and they none, they were better off for comfort than ourselves. We mention these facts as the prisoners, in some cases, reported to the Northern press cruel treatment on our part.

On every boarding occasion it was curious to note the wants that would suggest themselves to those of the officers whose duties never took them on board prizes. The commissions were as numerous as used to bother the head of a family, before railroads came along, going to a market-town. One would want a pocketknife, another a pipe, some light reading matter, anything and everything, really, but bonnets or ribbons. On one occasion a fellow wanted a warming pan, if the stewardess had such a thing. Sometimes they were made happy, sometimes the reverse. At least it was never the want of money that caused the disappointment, as is so often the case in this cold world of ours. Robinson Crusoe had about as much use for gold as we wanderers just now. Indeed, our sable peddler of the South could ever and anon have lightened our pockets of spare change with his cry of, "Oysters, oysters!" or "Buy a dozen quail, sir!" Beyond this the traps that might be set for our spare cash could never be sprung.

We are experiencing the most uneventful period of our cruise, most barren of solid results. We are still out of the track of vessels; and such as we may overhaul are likely to be of light tonnage and with cargoes of small value. When we consider that the plans cut out for this portion of our cruise, viz., the capture of the California treasure-steamer, and the destruction or scattering of the transport fleet of the Banks expedition to Texas, fail to materialize, we can but suffer some chagrin; still, some good comes out of it, for we are having a rest, and the time thus consumed enables the officers to become thoroughly acquainted with the men, to try them in experimental situations so that, emergencies arising, each man could be assigned to his best place.

We are out of late newspapers now, and most anxious to learn what is going on in Dixie—whether Lee has crossed the Potomac, or the enemy is still keeping our armies on the defensive and eating into our vitals. The capture of a vessel with late papers is an event with us—when it happens. First, they are carried to the cabin; and the skipper, assisted by his intelligent clerk, Mr. W. Breedlove Smith, cons them over carefully. They are looking for movements of the enemy's cruisers, first in importance, next as to how the tide of battle is flowing. This accomplished and noted, the lot is sent to the wardroom mess, thence to the steerage, finally reaching the forecastle. The stay in each department is brief, for the war news is about all we have time for, and Jack likes them to clean brasswork with. Certain sorts of bound literature fare much the same way; and Jack has to appeal to his imagination for the thread of a story, a fragment of which has captivated his interest.

We have entered the month of December and are stretching over to the east end of Cuba, occasionally boarding a vessel in the night. In the daytime friend Evans saves us the trouble by telling us at once that the ships we sight are neutrals. We take no prizes. On December 5, reaching our cruising ground, we captured the schooner *Union*, with neutral cargo, and released her on bond after transferring to her the prisoners of the *Cooke*.

The next day was Sunday, and a lovelier day is rarely experienced, even in this delicious climate. And the *Alabama* floats through it like a dandy arrayed for the eye of his best girl. The battery gets the best touches of gunner Cuddy's polish, and shines like patent leather. The decks you might pass your handkerchief over without soil, so perfect has been the work of the holystone. The brasswork rivals gold in its brilliancy. The crew are scattered about the spar-deck, their clothes-bags having been ordered up by the boatswain's and mates' pipe to the tune of, "All hands clean yourselves in white frocks and pants." The making of toilets proceeds apace—here a lad performing the tonsorial act on his chum, another elaborating a fancy knot for a messmate's neckwear or his own, with as interested and critical an audience as the same effort would secure among as many girls. Jack has all the instincts of a dude, though he is inclined to be more original in his style of elaborating his inspirations. On a man-of-war these have plenty of encouragement; and it is absolutely required of him that he shall be in a shape to pass the critical inspection of the captain and first "luff" at four bells (ten o'clock) on pain of having his grog stopped.

The crew are at last rigged out duly in their white duck uniforms and sennit hats. But the glory is not to them, nor to the official gray and gold aft. See the older salts eyeing the messenger boys, who, in ideal creations of nautical skill topped off with silk-embroidered collars and cuffs, strut the decks like young bantams under the proud gaze of their sea fathers. For time out of mind and in all navies has it been the custom for each youngster to have his proper and responsible relative of this sort, who makes his clothes and duly administers the ship's discipline with a cub of the famous ship's cat on occasion. The master-at-arms, under whose care the boys are supposed to rest, makes no scruple of delegating this duty with the rest; but you may be assured that the "chicken" gets no punishment that he has not well deserved, for no young mother is more jealous of the reputation of her bantling than is Jack.

But now, awaiting the muster hour, all hands are disposed about topgallant-forecastle and fore-rigging in a very unusual sort of way. We are on watch for the California mail steamer with its millions of gold. Everybody is sure of being rich before night—not on paper, in promises to pay of the Confederate Congress which may only be redeemed at best in shin-plasters, but in hard, shining, substantial gold! She is due hereabouts today, as our invaluable Yankee newspapers secured a few days since kindly inform us. But alas! Again is verified the song of the poet,

> Gold, gold, shining gold,
> Hard to get and hard to hold.

In spite of our diligence the masthead lookout has the best of it as usual, and from thence comes the expected hail, "Sail ho!" We could have forgiven that; but when in answer to the query "Where away?" the answer came, "On the port beam, sir," we understood that it could not be the steamer we were after. Steamer she was, though, a big side-wheeler, brig-rigged, and bound South. The treasure ship would be bound the other way and should have been sighted on the starboard bow. But she is our meat anyway.

All thoughts of Sunday muster are at once abandoned. Taking the deck, the first lieutenant orders the engine fires stirred, has the propeller lowered, clews up and furls all sail, and steaming slowly, places the *Alabama* in a position to have the stranger pass close to us. We know by this time she is not a man-of-war, from showing too much "top-hamper," so there is no necessity for going to quarters. She approaches us very fast, each vessel showing United States colors. We had gotten "athwart her hawse," to convey the idea we wished to communicate; but either we had no signals up to this effect or she was in a hurry. She sheered and passed us a biscuit's throw off. Perhaps she suspected us, even under our false colors. However, we had nothing left but to turn in pursuit, and in this maneuver some distance was lost.

By the time her stern was presented to us, she was a quarter of a mile ahead. There being no object in concealment now, our colors were changed. The *Alabama* had not as yet gotten the full benefit of her steam, and it was "nip and tuck" between us, rather, if any difference, in favor of the enemy who was now, we could see, doing her very best, her paddle wheels turning with great rapidity and dense smoke coming from the funnel. We could observe an immense crowd of passengers on her upper deck, principally women, interspersed with wearers of naval and military uniforms.

Wishing to cut the matter short, Lieutenant Armstrong is ordered to clear away the rifle pivot-gun of his division and give her a shot above deck, taking care to strike her masts well above the passengers' heads. The *Alabama* is now yawed; and the sea being perfectly smooth, a careful sight is taken, lock-string pulled, and in a moment splinters can be seen flying from the foremast about ten or twelve feet from the deck. Gallant shot! The mast is nearly cut in two, but holds on by the rigging.

It was a great relief, you may be sure, to Armstrong that he had taken no life, particularly as the passengers were principally women and children. In a moment the ponderous wheels of the steamer cease to revolve, and she lay motionless on the water, completely at the mercy of the enemy. We came up with the prize fast enough now. Upon being boarded, she proved to be the California mail boat *Ariel*, captain Jones, bound to the Isthmus with a passenger-list of five hundred and thirty-two, mostly women and children; a battalion of United States Marines under command of Captain David Cohen, numbering, rank and file, one hundred and forty-five; and several naval officers, all bound to the Pacific station. Quite an army all told. But it would have been as well had we kept out of her way. No chance now for the capture of a treasure boat, as the return steamer would not leave the Isthmus for New York until after the arrival of the

Ariel, so the "cat is out of the bag" as to the whereabouts of the *Alabama,* and we are not to have the pleasure of counting eagles and double eagles. Nor does the dilemma end here; we shall have to play nurse to several hundred women and children for some days. The passengers cannot be landed on any neutral territory, international law forbidding our taking the prize into port, nor are we likely, in this part of the world, to capture a vessel of sufficient tonnage to accommodate this army of people.

The boarding-officer having reported considerable consternation among the lady passengers, Lieutenant Armstrong and Midshipman Sinclair were sent on board to allay their fears and assure them of such treatment as Southern gentlemen and officers are accustomed to render to ladies. Arrayed in their bright, new, gray uniforms, swords, and caps, they looked natty indeed. The boat was manned by as handsome a lot of tars as you could wish to see, dressed in their white duck and sennit hats. Freemantle, the coxswain, was justly proud of his boat. We felt sure the appearance of this jaunty combination alongside the prize must dissipate the idea in the ladies' minds that we are ruthless pirates. For some time after boarding the prize, it looked like a hopeless task trying to convince the passengers they would not have to walk the plank. Many of the ladies were in hysterics, fearing the worst. But it did not take our gallants long to secure the confidence of one of the ladies braver than the rest. This accomplished, one by one they came forward, and soon our lucky boarding-officers were enjoying the effect of the reaction. A perfect understanding must have been arrived at between the fair ones and our "rascally" lieutenant and middy, for the latter were soon minus every button from their uniforms, not "for conduct unbecoming an officer and a gentleman," but as mementos of the meeting.

We may as well state just here that in no instance during

the entire cruise was private property of any description, cash or otherwise, taken from a prisoner. In many instances money in quite large quantities was found on the persons of prisoners, but oath that it was his personal property was all-sufficient with Semmes. Doubtless many a dollar of owners' money was denied our common prize-chest by false swearing, but that remained a matter between the oath-taker and his own conscience. In the case of the *Ariel* a considerable amount of money (greenbacks) was found in the iron safe; but Captain Jones promptly declared it ship's funds, without the necessity of inquiry. This sum was all that was transferred to our ship from her. The captain and engineers of the prize are removed to our vessel, and a number of our engineers sent on board the *Ariel* in their place to take charge of her engine.

In the meantime, Armstrong has had the marine battalion mustered on the quarterdeck of the prize, and proceeds to disarm and parole them. This was met by a vigorous protest on the part of Captain Cohen commanding, who, upon being ordered to have his men stack arms, hesitated for some time, but finally yielded to the gentle persuasion of the prize-master, upon having his attention recalled to the frowning ports of the *Alabama* only a few yards removed.

Many were the tales these lucky officers of ours had to tell after the bonding of the steamer and their return to their own ship. They had enjoyed a glorious "outing," occupying respectively the head and foot of the dining table. Champagne having been ordered up from the steward's wineroom, they had the audacity to propose the health of President Davis, which they *requested* should be drunk standing. Their request was complied with amid much merriment. And the saucy girls, not to be outdone, proposed the health of Mr. Lincoln, which was promptly drank amid hurrahs. Strange scene, reader! But we are an odd race—we Americans! sui generis.

We are now in company with the prize, and for some days steam side and side, our captain hoping to fall in with a vessel to transfer the passengers to, but in this we are doomed to disappointment. No prize comes along, and we are forced to release the *Ariel* under ransom-bond of $160,000. We had found Captain Jones, who was a guest with us in the wardroom, a modest and estimable gentleman. He had done all he could to save his vessel, and might have succeeded but for the passengers, whose lives he would not have been justified in exposing to our fire. We will do him the credit to relate that he spoke in high terms of the kind treatment received at our hands upon his arrival home.

As the two ships parted company the crew of the *Ariel* cheered, and the ladies waved their handkerchiefs. We fear our heroes of the boarding party will take unkindly to "salt horse" and rice after luxuriating on roast turkey and oysters on the half shell washed down with champagne—to say nothing of those aching voids in the region of the heart. But a sailor is like the lamp wicks they make of asbestos—easily inflamed, never consumed.

We ascertained afterwards that the California homebound steamer took the Florida passage, convoyed by a man-of-war.

CHAPTER V

INTO THE GULF OF MEXICO; AT THE ARCAS ISLANDS; OFF GALVESTON; THE *HATTERAS* FIGHT

THE EXCITEMENT OF THE last capture over, we allow steam to go down, hoist the propeller, and put the ship under sail. We stand along the north side of Jamaica; and after an uneventful run of some ten days without so much as a single prize, though we have passed a few neutrals, we enter the Yucatan passage and pass into the Gulf of Mexico. The sail through this strait was a reminder to such of our officers as had served on the *Sumter* of their exit here some eighteen months since. They at that time were fugitives from their homes. They are returning now to have another look at the land they love so well.

On the 23rd of December, standing in for the Arcas, we made a sail ahead, which proved upon overhauling her to be our coal transport, the barque *Agrippina*. She had made a tedious voyage from Blanquilla. We anchored together. The Arcas are of coral formation and almost barren, only a few stunted bushes and cactus giving the hint of vegetation. We were anchored in about eight fathoms, yet the water was so transparent the anchor could be plainly seen on the bottom; and about the coral branches, fish of varied hue lazily swam, secure in perpendicular distance from all surface foes. The fish found here are similar to those observed by the writer some years ago in Japan. They are of solid colors—blue, green, purple, red, and others of a combination of two or more colors. We speared numbers of them in the lake in the center of the largest of the three islands, and we caught many with lines and by trolling. These fish, however, do not compare in flavor to those of the Atlantic coast.

A most amusing episode on one of our fishing expeditions claimed chief engineer Freeman as the hero. The principal island is circular in shape, with a lake in the center connected with the sea by a narrow channel. At high water the fish would pass into the lake from the sea with ease, but they could not return if they lingered until the last of the ebb tide. There was always, however, plenty of water inside the lake— say, two and a half feet. Freeman was bathing and had waded to the center of the pond, about a hundred yards from the shore. A number of us were in the dingy spearing fish with the grains, when all at once we discovered a large shark swimming leisurely along, his dorsal fin exposed and evidently gorged with food, the pond being alive with fish of all sizes.

We at once put our worthy engineer on his guard. The shark was between Freeman and the boat, so there was nothing to do on his part but make for the shore—and such fun! I say fun, for the shark had no idea of attacking him. In his mad haste to reach the shore, Freeman first swam, and that not seeming very speedy, he would try wading. This was also found to be slow work, as the water was too deep, and so he alternated between wading and swimming, finding both modes most unsatisfactory under the circumstances. When the beach was gained, for some minutes he lay motionless for lack of breath. In the meantime the peals of laughter from our boats must have reached the ears of those on board ship. It was a side-splitting spectacle.

By this time Michael Mars, coxswain of the cutter, had made up his mind to have another sort of fun with the shark. Pushing the boat near, he jumped into the water and quickly plunged his sheath knife in the belly of the fish, giving him a fearful rip. The shark raised a terrible commotion, slapping the water with his tail and bringing his jaws together with a most uncomfortable snap. Mars was peremptorily ordered into the boat; but his Irish blood was up, and the fight was continued until the shark was vanquished. He was towed on-shore, and Jack was in high glee. Nothing so much pleases a sailor as dispatching a "man-eater."

We coaled from the transport, and giving the captain his instructions to report to Captain Bullock at Liverpool, saw him off. We shipped from the *Agrippina*, January 4, William Jones, seaman. Our attention is for a few days divided between putting the ship in order and getting all the fun there is to be had. The islands are the resort of innumerable sea-fowl, which come here to lay their eggs and hatch out their young. It is interesting to move up the "streets" between the line of nests and observe how curiously the mother bird will look up at you sideways. She will not leave the nest unless forced off with a club. At certain hours the parent birds, alternating, go to sea for food for self and young. Upon our arrival we first gathered bushels of these eggs from nests, in the absence of the old birds; but finding them stale in most cases, we had to resort to the plan of driving all the birds in a given space from the nests and breaking all the eggs, that on our return again we might find their place supplied with fresh-laid ones. These eggs are not delicate, and some kinds are even rank, yet the men ate and seemed to enjoy them. It was pitiable to see the old mother birds hover over the heads of the crew when driven from the nests, uttering their discordant cries of distress. They had no apparent fear of humanity, and would fly so close as to be easily hit with clubs.

On one occasion the captain and myself were about to take some "sights" onshore with the artificial horizon to verify the chronometers. Freemantle, the captain's coxswain, was pouring the quicksilver from the jug into the basin when a seagull, unobserved at first, waddled up to us, and after first interviewing us out of the corner of his eye, coolly put his bill into the mercury. Lest he should capsize it, Freemantle pushed him gently away, but to our intense amazement he returned to the charge, and finally we had to handle him quite roughly before he would desist.

The time passed rapidly here, one watch at a time at play, the other at work under our industrious and indefatigable executive. Our crew rapidly recuperated from the effects of arduous service and the monotonous sea diet; for if the islands gave us no vegetables, there was no lack of fish and fowl—the former in great variety and of excellent flavor, and turtle, curlew, plover, and sand-snipe in abundance. We had fine weather, and did not miss the opportunity for cleaning our ship's bottom by careening.

We are shipshape finally, and off for the coast of Texas, looking up Banks and his transport fleet. But "man proposes, but God disposes." We shall, instead of scattering the Banks transport fleet, find ourselves in a hornet's nest, and more than lucky to get out of it as well as we do. The fight we got on our hands might have turned out disastrously, for it was a matter of chance that the least powerful of the blockading fleet came out that night to battle with us.

The run up the Gulf was uneventful, giving all hands

ample time for recreation between duties. We have an excellent library of standard works for use of crew as well as officers, and have managed to add considerably to it from prizes. The bustle and constant business of man-of-war life materially interfere with satisfactory reading. The writer, time and weather permitting, preferred to take his book aloft and, straddling the topsail-yard and making the mast a rest for the back, vary the interest by occasionally casting his eye over the water in the hope of "getting to windward" of the masthead lookout in making out and reporting a sail to the officer of the deck.

In the wardroom and steerage, chess, backgammon, and other games are in full blast. Playing cards is positively prohibited. These mess-gatherings are the promoters of much that is entertaining, as also at times instructive, as when some intelligent messmate tells of his travels and observations or spreads himself in the sciences. At times a group will be all attention to a reading, lecture, or "yarn," when the uncanny wail of a violin in the hands of an amateur, the twang of a guitar, or some other distracting rhythmic monody proclaims right of free speech. Protests, and even strong language, in this case are often unavailing to support the majority rule. Your musical bore has no conscience and likes an audience, willing or unwilling, like a youngster in pinafores.

A favorite amusement was keeping a set of books containing an account of the owner's share of prize-money. The value of the manifest of each prize was of course carefully recorded, as was the finding of a court composed of a number of the commissioned officers. This record was intended as a memorandum or guide for the Confederate government, which had voted to officers and crew a sum equal to one-half the value of the vessels of the enemy, destroyed or bonded. This division of prize-money was to be made on a sliding scale proportional to rank, and was to the commander and commissioned officers, at the end of the cruise, a large fortune. Hence the deep interest taken in the book. As each vessel would be condemned and burned or bonded, the entry would be copied in the individual ledgers, each officer and man knowing his pro rata of the whole.

So, as with the people on shore, we have our days of active and also of dull trade. These carefully kept accounts can be bought cheap now, but there is a melancholy satisfaction in feeling that one has once made a fortune. Only one of the *Alabama*'s officers ever realized anything. This young gentleman transferred his interest, right, and title to his prize-money to a speculative London Hebrew for about five percent of its face, just after the sinking of the *Alabama*. This seemed to us a reckless extravagance at the time, but it did not prove so. As the poor fellow was lost at sea soon afterward, leaving no heirs, it is to be hoped the fun he got out of his few thousands left no regrets to be reaped.

Some fine fishing for the past few days, the wind being light and the ship under easy sail. We had good luck with both trolling lines and grains. The fun was the most of it, though, for the Arcas had given us a surfeit of this sort of food. On the afternoon of the 11th, the masthead gave us the familiar hail, "Sail ho!" and then promptly following it, "Land ho!" The shore off Galveston is so flat and low that a vessel would be made sooner than the land. In this case the lookout reported a number of ships at anchor having the appearance of men-of-war, but no transport fleet. It was soon apparent that the craft were all steamers, and then a shell from one of them was seen to burst over the city. This made the case as plain to us as a Quakeress's bonnet. It seemed to strike all hands at once and in the same way—Galveston had been retaken by our forces, and the enemy's fleet driven outside the bar. Hence the shelling of the city.

It must not be thought that because the *Alabama* was mainly confined to the high seas by the operation of international law that the world and its doings were entirely shut out from her. The newspapers of the North were allowed an astonishing latitude in dispensing news of the movements of armies and fleets; and the captured vessels frequently supplied us, through copies of these newspapers, with information of the greatest consequence, enabling us to avoid cruisers and to learn of the movements of armies and transport ships destined to points of attack on the Southern coast. It was information received in this manner that determined Semmes to attempt the destruction of a transport fleet destined for the invasion of Texas through the port of Galveston, then in the possession of the United States forces. General Banks fitted out this expedition and was expected off Galveston about January 10. Semmes, surmising that the expedition would not be convoyed by men-of-war, the South having no navy to attack it, judged that it would be an easy matter for a smart and powerful ship of our class to destroy or disperse it. But it had happened in the meantime that Galveston was recaptured by the river gunboats supported by the land forces of the Confederacy; and this had broken into General Banks's plans, turning his fleet by New Orleans and the Red River upon Texas, and the blockade was resumed off the harbor. Of this we had of course no knowledge.

Our situation was critical. Very soon the smoke from the stack of one of the steamers apprised us that she was getting under way, and soon she was bowling along, steering right for us. We had been under sail all the while. At once the fires are stirred, the propeller lowered, and the ship's head put offshore, steaming slowly. Blake signals the admiral as we plainly see; and before the darkness shuts out the view, it is evident that the whole fleet is preparing to get under way.

This to us is certainly an ominous sight. We must make a close, quick, yardarm fight, and if successful stand not on the order of our going but GO! For to nautical experience it is well known that the Gulf of Mexico is a dangerous trap, with only two passages for escape. We could not tell what facilities the admiral off Galveston might have for speedily closing these against us.

But it was necessary to get the enemy now approaching as far from the rest of the fleet as possible, and also to allow night to set in before engaging him. We succeed in putting about fifteen miles between us and the fleet, then with canvas furled, steam by this time being sufficient, the engines are stopped, and with officers and men at quarters we await the result. It is now dark, the enemy being but indistinctly seen. Many are the conjectures as to his strength and class, and opinions as to whether the rest of the fleet is on its way out. The concensus of opinion is emphatic that what we do must be done quickly, and that the captain ought to lay us alongside her if she does not prove too heavy.

The enemy has now come up. We have been standing in shore while awaiting her, but now our head is turned offshore again. Then comes the hail, "*What ship is that?*"—"*This is her Britannic Majesty's steamer* Petrel," is the reply. The two vessels are now nearly motionless, and both of course at quarters. Our men are wild with excitement and expectation. In the darkness it is impossible to make out her class except that she is a side-wheeler. Our crew have lock-strings in hand, keeping the gun trained on her and awaiting the command to fire. The two vessels are so near that conversation in ordinary tones can be easily heard from one to the other.

For a time the *Hatteras* people seem to be consulting. Finally they hailed again, "*If you please, I'll send a boat on board of you,*" to which our executive officer replied, "Certainly, we shall be pleased to receive your boat." The boat was soon lowered from the davits and began pulling towards us. All occasion for subterfuge being now at an end, word was immediately passed to the divisions that the signal to fire would be *"Alabama."* When the boat was about halfway between the two vessels, Lieutenant Kell hailed, "This is the Confederate States steamer *Alabama*!"

The last word had barely passed his lips when sky and water are lighted up by the flash of our broadside, instantly followed as it seemed by that of the enemy. A running fight was now kept up, the *Alabama* fighting her starboard and the *Hatteras* her port battery, both vessels gathering headway rapidly.

Never did a crew handle a battery more deftly than ours. About six broadsides were fired by us. The enemy replied irregularly, and the action only lasted thirteen minutes. It was evident to us from the trifling nature of the wounds to our hull and rigging that the *Hatteras* was being whipped. A crash among her machinery soon settled the business. Then she fired a lee gun, and we heard the quick, sharp hail of surrender, accompanied by the request that our boats be sent to her immediately as she was sinking.

The whole thing had passed so quickly that it seemed to us like a dream. Our battery was hastily secured, and then our boats started for her at lightning speed. The daily practice of our crew in handling boats and boarding vessels now served the enemy in good stead. A few strokes of the oars put us alongside, and none too soon. In two minutes after we cleared her sides only her mastheads were showing above the water; and in just nineteen minutes from the opening broadside, the officers and crew of the *Hatteras*, wounded included, were on our decks, and the *Alabama* was steaming away at her best speed for the Yucatan passage.

This is probably one of the quickest naval duels on record. But it was none too quick for our safety; for as we laid our course their lights were to be plainly seen coming up rapidly in our wake. But there was now no danger, for the *Alabama* was at that time more than a match in speed for any vessel in the admiral's fleet. By the following evening shot-plugs and paint had obliterated nearly all marks of the engagement from the *Alabama*.

It is illustrative of the uncertainties attending naval engagements that the shot of the *Hatteras* should have expended itself so entirely upon the upper works of the *Alabama* where the damage would be but slight, while our shots with depressed guns almost invariably struck her in vital places. The two vessels were so close that frequently their yardarms could have been locked by a turn of the helm. There was no chance for a shot to miss. The mortality on the *Hatteras* was astonishingly slight in view of the damage inflicted on the vessel. Only two were killed and five wounded. The wounded men subsequently all recovered. And it is scarcely less remarkable that on board the *Alabama*, though her bulwarks were riddled with shot-holes, there was but one casualty, George Addison, carpenter's mate, receiving a slight wound in the cheek from a fragment of a shell.

Captain Blake afterwards said that his purpose had been to run down and board us; but as the *Alabama* had the speed of him his program could hardly be carried out. It must have been a hot place for the *Hatteras's* boat, between two fires with only twenty-five or thirty yards intervening. As the boat escaped, the officer in charge of her must have made a sharp move out of the way. Probably the mastheads of the *Hatteras* sticking up out of the water were discovered by the fleet on their return from the chase, and anticipated the news conveyed by the escaped boat. But it is improbable that the name of the *Hatteras's* antagonist transpired until the news was received from Kingston.

CHAPTER VI

THE *HATTERAS* PRISONERS ON BOARD;
AT KINGSTON, JAMAICA; TROUBLE
WITH JACK; ADIEU TO FORT ROYAL;
FORAGING FOR PROVISIONS; BAFFLING
WINDS; A CARGO OF WINES AND
LIQUORS; ENEMIES' SHIPS GETTING
SCARCE; DISPOSING OF PRISONERS AT
SEA; IN THE BRAZILIAN HIGH ROAD;
WASHING DAYS FOR JACK

WE ARE NOW BOWLING along, steam and sail, for
Kingston, Jamaica, where it is proposed to land the officers
and crew of the *Hatteras*. The weather soon after leaving the
coast sets in squally with rain, the wind veering ahead. We let
steam go down and battle with it under sail. This is bad, as
we have in prisoners a force fully equal to our own, and
though on parole, we are anxious to land them as quickly as

possible. The strict watch kept over them is very wearing to officers and men, who must sleep at all times on their arms.

We were ten days on the passage to Kingston. Captain Blake was the guest of Semmes, and the remainder of the officers of the *Hatteras* were distributed as to rank in the wardroom and two steerages. We found our prisoner officers a rather jolly set; and the time passed very pleasantly, barring the villainous weather. Porter, the *Hatteras*'s executive officer, seemed to take quite a fancy to me, having known my father intimately. He would keep nearly all my watches with me, pacing the deck and talking of old times. I did everything possible to cheer and reassure him, giving his officers and crew full credit for doing all they could under the circumstances, having to contend against a ship much more powerful than theirs and from constant practice more efficient in handling her battery. I was amused to observe the blank surprise of Porter when informed that grog was only served to the seamen on our vessel, the officers being positively disallowed it. However, upon being informed that *his* officers were not included in the list, and that our captain had plenty of it for entertaining purposes, he laughingly said, "Well, I suppose we must play the *role* of apparent selfishness."

Porter greatly admired the speed and seaworthy qualities of our ship and thought she would cause the shipowners of the North immense direct as well as indirect loss; and he looked for bitter disappointment, if not censure, from the country at the result of the late engagement—the *Hatteras* not even being able to cripple us—and thought it would be no enviable position to command any vessel sent in pursuit of us. He considered the *Alabama* the most complete ship afloat, all and all, for the purpose in hand.

The paymaster of the *Hatteras* was most excellent company. He was my roommate. I remember his first remark as he was ushered into our wardroom. "Well," he said, "boys,

I'll be d—d if we hadn't a cast-iron atmosphere in our engine room! I was stationed there, and shell after shell exploded until the air smelt of iron fragments! I don't want any more of it; I'm going home right away, and don't you stop to fight any more cruisers until you land me." Again, pulling some gold pieces from his pocket and shaking them at me, he remarked, "Say, Johnny, ain't there a sight good for any fellow's sore eyes? Don't you want to handle some of them?" But we had the joke on him as he afterwards confessed upon learning that our salaries were paid in sterling.

During the passage we made a sail ahead, and upon overhauling her she showed English colors. We recognized in her our transport, the *Agrippina*. She, like ourselves, had experienced head winds and rough weather. Of course we kept mum as to any previous knowledge of her to our prisoners.

One day, the grog being served out, Kell was standing near and observing an old "barnacle-back" among the prisoners, eyeing our men as they passed around the grog-tub and brought their inclined plane in contact with the contents of the cup, asked the old fellow if he would like a "tot." Touching his hat quickly with both hands, for he was ironed, the answer came, "Your Honor—thanks." Receiving the tin measure from the "captain of the hold" in charge of the grog-tub, he slowly and carefully raised it with his teeth, and at the same time throwing back his head with a dexterous jerk, he emptied it without the spilling of a drop. Soon after, many of the prisoners asked permission to ship with us, which was of course refused. The matter was kept from the knowledge of their officers. Such the power of grog over a sailor. These men were not allowed grog in United States service.

But we must now get ready to say good-bye to our friends of the *Hatteras*. We have made the lighthouse of Fort Royal. The 21st of January we drop anchor. We find several vessels of the British squadron on this station—flagship *Jason*, also the *Challenger* and *Greyhound*, and, as we found it ever after in English colonies, a hearty welcome awaiting us. Civilities are exchanged with the governor of the island and the commanding fleet officer. Upon being apprised of the recent engagement and the presence of the prisoners on our ship, the town was of course in a state of excitement beyond description. Everything in the way of a boat that would float was in requisition, and the boatmen probably never in their experience reaped such a harvest of fares. They were many yards deep around our vessel, each struggling to get their passengers to the gangway.

At no time during the cruise was our ship in such a state of confusion as during our stay at Kingston. The prisoners were to be landed; and meantime our decks and officers' quarters were besieged with officials and citizens from the shore, besides officers from the fleet and garrison, and these all to be entertained. Ship-coaling, and ship's mechanics engaged in repairing damages of the late fight, stopping shot holes in the hull and replacing damaged rigging. Officers with manifold duties suddenly thrust upon them.

The most important and onerous service of all was that of a watch to keep, if possible, liquor out of the ship. Having no marine guard to call into service, we could only command the personal services of our lieutenant of marines, Mr. Beckett K. Howell, assisted by the master-at-arms. These officers kept alert, first with an eye on this and now on that bumboat, wherever a suspicious movement on the part of Jack or the bumboatmen pointed to a mutual understanding. Our ubiquitous first lieutenant, assisted by the officer of the deck and midshipman of the forecastle, also had an eye to the same subject. We miss a marine guard sadly in port; but it must be confessed "a sogger" at sea is a fish out of water, in everybody's mess and nobody's watch. However, in spite of the most rigid espionage, some confusion is soon observed, and one by one our fellows begin to be hustled in irons to the brig. But by this time the prisoners have been landed and are under the protection of the United States consul, so that half our crew are sent ashore on liberty.

The presence of a large fleet of English men-of-war giving a feeling of perfect security in the event of one or more of the enemy's cruisers putting in an appearance, Semmes, who felt the want of quiet and removal from the scene of confusion and uproar, the unavoidable condition of our present situation, had accepted the invitation of an English gentleman, a merchant of the place, to visit his country-seat in the mountains for a few days. Kell was left in command. His position was surely anything but a bed of roses; but as usual, he managed to fill it with dignity and credit. It was a trying time for us all. Cruising and boarding vessels we had got used to, and we knew pretty well what we could depend on, and what bodily and mental strain we should have to meet; here the unexpected beset us like the troubles of Pandora's box, and there was no such thing as dogwatch or watch below. Every man-Jack of the crew was in for a lark, and discipline had to be relaxed without being quite allowed to "go by the run." We were beset at all hours with visitors of high and low degree, and the courtesies of the ship must not be neglected. Among the officers permission to visit the shore on pleasure was not even thought of.

A serious mortification came to us in the misbehavior of our paymaster, Clarence R. Yonge. Visiting the shore on duty, he was reported to be guilty of traitorous communication with the United States consul and of drunken consort with paroled seamen of the enemy. Kell at once sent an armed party ashore, arrested him, and kept him under arrest on board until Captain Semmes's return, when he was at once dismissed the service and drummed out of the ship. This is the only case of discipline we have to record as regards the officers of the *Alabama*, but one dose of this sort was surely enough. Through this man's influence with our crew, backed by the persuasions of the United States consul, we lost several valuable seamen. He was afterward a secret agent of the enemy's diplomatic corps in London—but that has nothing to do with the present story.

Before leaving Kingston, it was my good fortune to meet Lieutenant Cardale of Her Britannic Majesty's ship *Greyhound*, recently from Norfolk, Virginia, where he had met and been entertained by members of my family. This brought home news down to within ten days. And only those who have suffered from this banishment—without mails—so rare in modern life, can realize the value of such a happening. In the meantime, Jack is having a good time onshore. Sailor-like, he is hobnobbing with the liberty men from the British ships as well as his late opponents of the *Hatteras*, and supplying funds to the latter, who are broke. Groups of them may be encountered at every turn of sailor-town, arm in arm, and in every stage of intoxication, from hilarity to fighting humor.

When the time arrives to scoop them up and give the other watch a chance at the sport so-called, officers in uniform with armed boats' crews are scouring the streets and dens. One is reminded of the old problem of ferrying over the river the goose, the fox, and the bag of corn; for no sooner is one lot delivered at the boat and another raid made uptown than the prisoners break guard somehow and are uptown again. The writer, visiting a dance hall after dark with a boat's crew in quest of delinquents, was met at the threshold by a body of men from the English squadron backed by the lady participants in the ball, and good-naturedly but firmly informed that he could not come in, the visit being quite malapropos. One of the ladies remarked, "Say, middy, come some other time. The tickets are limited at this ball;

and besides, the company is select!" "Tell old 'Beeswax,'" said another persuasive maiden, "your old piratical skipper, to go to sea, burn some more Yankee ships, and come back. We'll give up the boys then, and you shall have your turn." It took much diplomacy to carry our point; and it was only accomplished by reasoning most earnestly with the soberer of the crew, and a generous amount (on my part) of treating among the fair hosts.

Returning with this party to the ship, it was found necessary to put some of the most drunken fellows in irons. And while this was going on, two seamen managed to call alongside a boat in which two negroes were prowling about the harbor. Taking possession of the oars, they put off for shore at a great rate. We started a boat promptly in chase, and were just about to overhaul them when overboard went one of the negroes. Of course we had to stop and pick the poor fellow up, and this gave the fugitives quite a start. Again, just as we were upon them, they shoved the other negro into the water. However, as they were now out of this sort of amunition, we got them finally before they reached shore. When brought to the mainmast on charge of attempting to desert, they pleaded not guilty. "No idea of deserting, Your Honor," they declared. "We are part owners of this craft. We only wanted to say good-bye to the girls."

We are coaled, the crew has been scraped together as thoroughly as possible, and we are ready for sea, minus seven men. The reader will fail to fully realize the import of the loss. These men have been drilled and educated for the work in hand; and their place must be supplied by volunteers from future prizes, who in turn, however capable as seamen, will require months of drill to bring them up to the standard of the rest of the crew. Besides, we had been all along short of our full complement of men. But for coaling and other unavoidable needs, the voice of our officers would have been

never to enter port during the cruise. To us a port was anything but a recreation or pleasure. Our missing men are described on the ship's books as "deserters." This, however, is a
misnomer. Jack has been kept drunk and hid away in some
den until the sailing of his ship. He will wake up, poor de-
luded child of Poseidon, to find his home swept from him,
accumulation of pay sacrificed, and quasi friends knowing
him no more.

The delinquents are now released from the brig. We bid
adieu to Fort Royal, and are soon outside of the lightship
and on our way to the coast of Brazil. It takes some time to
get discipline back to the old high standard, and we are crippled by the loss of our runaways. Time heals all calamities,
however. The routine of cruising life is promptly resumed,
working ship after "sails," and the everlasting drill, drill, drill!
If the officers find *playing fighting* tedious and monotonous,
how must Jack look at it? But it is important, yea, indispensable; and wrestle with it we must. We are running down the
coast of Haiti; have made two captures since leaving Fort
Royal, the *Golden Rule* and *Chastelaine*, both with food products principally. (A majority of the United States vessels we
shall overhaul in these latitudes are provision-laden.) Both
of them are fired, after removing such stores and provisions
as our ship departments have need of, and transshipping the
crews, bags, and hammocks to our decks.

The reader by this time must have observed that our
prizes furnish all departments of our ship—canvas and twine
for the sailmaker, cordage and naval stores for the boatswain,
lumber for the carpenter, with but little, however, for the
gunner, unless he comes across a can or two of material for
the composition of his gun polish. Our paymaster, however,
is *the grand* freebooter of the ship, taking in provisions, small
stores, tobacco, and whatever he lusts after, never crying
hold! enough! so long as patience, time, and plunder hold

out. The search continues until night, bad weather, or some unlooked-for intervention puts a stop to the raid. But we always manage to find use for everything transferred to our several departments, and then comes the paymaster's chance to return in kind the jokes poked at him by messmates as to his "Mrs. Toodles" proclivities. "There!" will come from "Old Cheese," "didn't I tell you we should find it useful?" We may as well state here for the enlightenment of the reader that no one, officer or man, was allowed to take from the stores or cargo of a prize for personal use the smallest article, even of the most insignificant value. All articles removed were transferred to the respective departments of our ship, under the care and responsibility of the head of the bureau, and issued only upon requisition, being charged to the account of the officer or man requiring it. A careful account of everything is kept, as representing a part of the prize-money.

This rule also had the effect of keeping up discipline, as nothing so demoralizes a crew as being allowed to plunder ad libitum. And again, Jack is much like his namesake the jackdaw, with a most decided aptitude for stowing away slyly any and every thing having an unknown value that may come in his way. Indeed, he will hide, in the lockers and hammock nettings, old shoes, dilapidated hats, and other rubbish, thinking and hoping the day will arrive when he can produce them for an emergency. It is amusing to observe the old salts on a Sunday morning, watching the first lieutenant in his rounds of the vessel before reporting the ship to the captain as ready for inspection. Old barnacle-back has some treasures, in the above line, stored away, and keeps a keen eye on the officer as he orders some man to throw off the hammock cloths. He knows well his toys are in danger, and he is all expectation and anxiety. Should the executive trust to the carrying out of his order and the report "nothing contraband," all serene; but should the distrustful Kell mount a gun-carriage and glance his own lynx eyes inside, good-bye to the traps, and the owner sneaks forward, brokenhearted at the loss of his *penates*—for overboard they go to "Davy Jones's locker." The mortification must be accepted without sign or sorrow; for to acknowledge ownership would not save the trash, but only bring the self-condemned culprit into trouble, or at least stoppage of a day's grog.

We coast along the shores of Haiti, and stand in for the town of St. Domingo. We communicate with the Spanish government, receiving permission to land our prisoners of the *Golden Rule* and *Chastelaine*; and having made as usual some purchases of fruit and fresh provisions, the next day we are under way, and leaving the historic shores of the old town point eastward. We are in a hurry now, having wasted much time with but little achievement on our western trip, to reach the coast of Brazil, where lots of plunder await us. There is much of interest to be seen and pondered over by a visitor to these shores, but we anticipate seeing little of it but what goes afloat. We coast St. Domingo and enter the Mona Passage, an occasional sail in sight but all reported neutral by Evans. We are in a comparatively unfrequented latitude for *brisk* trade in our line; still, we make a capture today (February 3, 1863), the *Palmetto*. Inappropriate name, we reflect, for a Yankee vessel. She proves a lawful prize, though, and is "looted" of what we require of her stores and cargo, crew transferred, and then burned.

We had now been nine days out of port. Three vessels burned, but of insignificant value. We shall not make big hauls until the track of East India–bound vessels is reached in Maury's "road of the ocean," a road all vessels *must* follow, cruisers or no cruisers. Navigators have only the choice of some sixty miles of width at one point off the Brazil coast. Neglect warning, stray from the milestones, and head or baffling winds and currents will waft you hither and thither, any

way but the one wished. So here is the place for us to stand
by, and *also* the place for Uncle Sam's cruisers to hold argument with us. It will therefore be understood why anticipa-
tion of another fight on our hands off the Brazilian coast
makes much of the evening and mess talk. Not that Jack
worries about it much. His mourning eye has resumed its
dignity, his sore head has healed, and his spirits have their
sea legs on.

Song and dance and the glee club's melodious strains take
the deck as of yore; and Semmes himself lights his evening
cigar on the bridge, where not only these things may be
viewed and listened to but also the private sentiments of
Jack, freely spoken to his messmate in plain English or in
subtlety of yarn or witticism. Semmes understands just how
to keep himself near to the hearts and in the confidence of
his men, without in the slightest degree descending from his
dignity or permitting direct approach. He does not seem to
pay the slightest attention to what is going on below him.
But Jack knows well enough that he is taking it all in infor-
mally. Individually and collectively, Jack has taken soundings
of the "old man," and knows pretty well how to steer and
where an anchor will hold. The men feel no restraint from
his presence—rather they enjoy it. In their way they love him
and are proud of him, and he returns the sentiments—in his
way.

We have been slowly working along to the eastward, baffled by variable winds and dirty weather for some days. Sight
a few sail, but easily make them out to be neutrals. Approaching the last days of February the sky clears up. And
then the masthead hails and hails again, and to the query,
"Where away?" reports vessels here, there, and everywhere—
all around the compass. As there is but little wind, we have
only to pick out our victims. Evans is sent aloft and soon reports several "Yankees," and says they are changing their

courses as if they smelt a rat. This is soon evident enough. They are separating as much as possible, so as to give us a long chase in detail. There is nothing for it but to steam up and make sharp work. We do not make chase with steam except in rare cases. Semmes well knows that he cannot enter port for coal without advertising his whereabouts and subjecting his crew to the demoralizing effects so lately noted.

The power of our engines soon puts us alongside the first prize; without a moment's delay a prize-crew is thrown on board under command of master's-mate Fulham, with orders to follow us as closely as possible, and we are after the next, already well down on the horizon. She also proves to be a lawful prize, barque *Olive Jane* from Bordeaux, bound to New York with wines, brandies, sardines, olives, etc. In the meantime the prize in charge of Fulham was hull down in the distance, standing towards us as ordered.

The character of cargo on board the *Olive Jane*, consisting as it did mostly of liquors, made the "looting" of her for needed supplies for our vessel dangerous to the morals of our boarding-crews. The writer, in command of the captain's gig, with faithful Freemantle as coxswain, had charge of the breaking out of the hold of the prize, with strict orders to hurry up the work, and above all things to keep the boat's crew from grog and see that they did not bring any on board their own vessel. Reader, if you know a sailor, you understand the gravity of the present trust; otherwise you fail to realize the weight of responsibility on the officer's shoulders.

Calling Freemantle aside, after taking off the hatches, I explained to him the nature of the cargo and the strict orders received, at the same time hinting at the utter impossibility of keeping the men from the tempting fluids; and added my determination, arrived at after mature thought, to spread a lunch on the cabin table, furnished from the cargo and ship-stores of sardines, olives, cheese, etc., flanked by sundry bottles of brandy, burgundy, and claret, that the men would be required while working in breaking out the hold to abstain from opening the casks or cases, but might quench their thirst in an orderly manner from the cabin set-out.

The scheme worked to a charm. Jack had no incentive to disobey orders and get into trouble in consequence, and doubtless also felt thrown upon his honor not to get his officer into "hot water." From time to time the cabin was visited for a bite and a nip. And now observe the self-constituted guests at the cabin table of the *Olive Jane*, luxuriating in the comfort of a chair, a snow-white cloth, and verily a four-prong fork—the table groaning under the weight of luxuries! Surely Jack could be in no better luck, even as the guest of a Friar Tuck. And you have only to watch narrowly these waifs of the world, and draw for yourself a moral of life. One fellow but yesterday you noted at his forecastle-deck dinner, a hardtack for his plate, a slab of salt pork on it cut with his sheath knife, handled with greasy fingers to the mouth; the old boyhood training asserts itself, and as he wipes his mustache with his napkin he has given his heart's secret away. A broken-down gentleman with a story! What a storeroom of tragedy, comedy, and heartache the forecastle of a man-of-war frequently is! Material for an army of novelists.

Not a bottle of liquor reached our ship; and the boat's crew under my command returned in a *good humor* only, no more. The prize was fired in cabin and forecastle and made a grand blaze, owing to the highly inflammable character of her cargo. We were not many hundred yards off when the flames could be seen licking the topsails. We secured a quantity of sardines among other delicacies; and if you have never added heretofore to your menu *fried* sardines, reader, do so.

We now overhaul the first prize under the charge of Fulham. She proved to be the *Golden Eagle*. It is late when we get alongside of her, the *Olive Jane* having drawn us hull-down away. We find her, upon examination of papers, a lawful prize, and transferring her crew, and adding her chronometers and flag, fire her.

Allowing steam to go down, and putting the *Alabama* under short sail, we loaf along. The wind is light; but we are now in "the road," and in no hurry, hence the reduced sail. Single-reefed topsails alone, merely enough to steady the ship. On one beam is the *Olive Jane*, on the other the *Golden Eagle*, both wrapped in flames from spar-deck to masthead, the sea and heavens glowing in the red glare, the flames varying in brilliancy, as the material for the time being is supplied or denied, suggesting the phenomenon of the aurora borealis. On the rail in groups may be seen the officers and crews of the burning prizes, conversing in subdued whispers—we cannot flatter ourselves in complimentary terms of us; so, as listeners rarely hear good of themselves, we will not invade the sanctity of their circle. One cannot but admire the nonchalant manner of the American sailor when confronted with danger or disaster, and it makes our hearts go out to him as we mark the cool bearing hiding the avalanche of conflicting emotions. You may not know it, boys, but a sympathy for you dwells in us. We are all of us but the victims of circumstance. But we must smother these feelings—at least for the present. We are here for duty, and must strain our efforts to the utmost, and tread the path resolutely.

We should make many captures in this fashionable highway of commerce—at least, we shall have the opportunity to judge the extent of demoralization produced by our past efforts. We are now having a surfeit of chronometers. The winding of them still continues, under orders from Semmes; and a precious lot of time is consumed at it. It was a joyous day to the writer when the time came to rescind the order, and let them take care of themselves till overhauled by a maker. By the way, they supplied the only prize-money ever realized by the custodian. Just before leaving Cherbourg for the fight, the chronometers, some seventy-odd in number, were transferred to the British yacht *Hornet*, Captain Hewitt, and eventually landed at Liverpool. In the year 1867 or 1868 the writer was handed a sterling check by a member of a Baltimore banking-house, as coming from Captain Semmes, with the remark, "Semmes desires me to say this is your share of the sale of the chronometers abroad, and also requests you to give him the address of Lieutenants Armstrong and Wilson." The request was also made that the transaction be kept shady. The reasons for silence have happily passed away, as also my old friend the banker. Between us we held for many years the secret of this, the only prize-money from the *Alabama*. A small dividend compared to outlay.

The next day we have sails in sight constantly, and Evans is kept busy at the masthead; but he never squeals at the duty, indeed, the contrary—he is quite proud of his importance. From time to time he reports neutrals, now English, now Northcountrymen, etc., but none, so far, "contraband," as Ben Butler would have dubbed them. Evans's shipmates are never so pleased as when they can guy him. One middy would say, "Look here, Evans, you are playing the devil with your reports! This won't do, see? The skipper has turned our head from the chase, and I'd swear she's Yankee!"—"What do you know about the rig of a craft?" growls Evans, his eyes snapping in anger at the insinuation; "I made out vessels in the offing when you were sucking sugar rags." And turning his back in contempt, he mounts the rigging for another scout. The middy signals his chum with a wink of the eye, and rolls forward in imitation of the boatswain's-mate. He has had his fun "nagging" Evans.

Several days elapse with only neutrals in view. Our past

industry is beginning to tell. The enemy's ships are getting scarce. Later in the cruise the reader will witness at times all hands sorely disappointed in their hopes of a prize, though Evans has put his endorsement on the back that the sail is "Yank." His judgment is true; but upon being boarded, the vessel, though American-built, is found to be under foreign papers, having been sold and transferred to some other flag. Thus gradually sinks the proud carrying-trade of the North American Republic. We have at last, however, found the Stars and Stripes at the peak of the ship *Washington*; but her cargo (guano) being entirely on neutral account, and not contraband of war, she is bonded and released.

The *John A. Parks* next requires our polite attention. Her cargo proving to be enemy's property, her officers and crew are transferred to our ship, the usual removal of nautical instruments made, and the *Parks* is fired. We are experiencing all the same an active, stirring, and exciting life. The ship under close-reefed topsails in the strong "trades," sauntering along in this busy pathway of commerce, the diverging point to the many quarters of the globe, both north and south. The *Alabama*, like a beast of prey crouching on the crossroads, is wide awake and alert. It is a dark night, and the usual "trade" mist spreading out over the water and dimming the sight. The clear, sharp hail comes from a lookout, "Sail ho!" "Close aboard"; and looming up out of the mist a great ship is seen like a ghost rising from a graveyard—a cloud of canvas alow and aloft, bounding by as though perceiving and appreciating the danger.

In a twinkling the dead quiet on our deck gives place to bustle and stir. The quick, sharp orders through the deck-officer's trumpet, the shrill pipe of the boatswain's-mate's whistle, the rattle of running rigging, the topmen and sail-loosers springing up the ratlines, and in a flash the rover is under a cloud of light-kites and studding sails, and you realize the magic of the maneuver. The wild beast is making his spring. Before the trade-gale the two racers are rushing, feeling "the thrill of life along the keel." Now a flash, lighting up the racecourse, a BOOM! and a screech of the rifle-shell; the chase luffs up, and shivers her canvas in the strong breeze—a tremor of surrender and despair.

No wonder Jack has become a revelation of quick and methodical motion. Without boast, just now the *Alabama's* hearties have no equals in ship maneuvers. But he is a cheerful fellow under it—indeed, enjoys it to the point of physical exhaustion, as preferable to otherwise languishing under ennui; nor does he fail to keep in mind a prospect of fresh grub possibly from the stranger, prize-money, and the inevitable—"All hands splice the main brace!"

Now it is quiet again. The *Alabama* is disrobed to close reefs, the prisoners under guard in the "waist," the burning ship in the distance lighting up the lea and sky, a beacon of warning to the close-hunted foe; the watch again coiled up under the weather bulwarks, snug in their pea jackets, the insatiate rover stealing along to a next victim.

No chance for stagnant blood in this. A wild western hunting-ground offers no more excitement than this promenade of commerce for the next few weeks. The caravans of merchant-traders, passing this narrow belt of ocean travel, bound both north and south, to the United States and Europe, the Pacific, East Indies, China, and Japan, had reason enough for surmise and conjecture in the long line of wreckage encountered day by day—a puzzle doubtless to the mass of them, as there had been no severe weather to propose a solution of the unusual sight. Frequently, many hours' labor were required in the effort to reach certain articles of cargo required in one or more departments of our vessel, necessitating the throwing overboard of a heterogeneous mass of boxes, bales, and casks. Could some rascally North Sea or

Hatteras wrecker have these scenes presented to him in a dream, he would awake from a nightmare of grief that such valuable plunder should float so free and far from his rapacious grasp.

A novel but interesting sight it is to watch the curious faces of all hands as the skipper of a detained vessel emerges from the *Alabama*'s cabin. It is the question whether a bonfire or otherwise is the result of the legal examination just completed below. You are not kept long in suspense. Simply note that the skipper, minus his ship's papers, with downcast eyes and lugubrious countenance, saunters aft, and the tale is told. And now our boats leave the side for the work of breaking out cargo and securing articles manifested on the prize for which requisitions have been filled out. Sometimes, as the boats return after many hours of hard labor, the squeal of pigs and cackle of fowls strike the ear, and the sight of hampers of potatoes and onions the eye; then, not only Jack all smiles, bustles about to "whip" them over the side, but wardroom and steerage descend from their dignity and, with jokes and commendations, reward the returned purveyors. More importance, for the time being, is attached to the improved condition of the commissary than to the prize-money secured by the capture. The one is practical and tangible, the other in the dim future. You may rest assured all thoughts, fore and aft, tend towards the next meal. It would require a phethoric pocketbook to purchase any fellow's seat at table or mess-cloth for the next day or two. We have by this time learned also in what latitudes to look for these windfalls. In cruising off the Brazils, an inward- or outward-bound East Indiaman will never satisfy your cravings for fresh grub. You must find a purveyor from some near port.

We are by this time in the "middle of the road"; and a British vessel passing, bound to London, her captain was induced for a consideration to take our prisoners to port.

Paroling them, they were transferred to the barque. Perhaps the reader would like an insight into the modus operandi of getting rid of a lot of prisoners, and troubling our English cousins with their care. The inducement is, first, ample rations for the prisoners to tide over even an unusually long passage, with the addition of sundry barrels of salt beef and pork, equal perhaps in value to half a year's pay to her captain. Sometimes it takes a chronometer to tempt the skipper's cupidity. This is the bait thrown out; and as it is a personal matter between the two captains, the owners have no cause to protest or claim any share of the reward. You will see that the *Alabama* is equal to any emergency. Being thrown on his own resources, Semmes has often to work "Tom Cox's traverse" in getting rid of his prisoners.

Our vessel is today in an uproar of excitement—the capture and burning of a prize is but a calm to it. Johnny Raw happened under the lee of the mainsail, and, being caught in the eddy, was dashed in the sea to leeward. He was a poor sailor at swimming, and was making bad weather of it. A request from a boat's crew is complied with, the maintopsail hove to the mast, a boat lowered, and Johnny is brought on board wet, cold, and shivering, and forlorn-looking indeed. But we must introduce you to the subject of this stir-up. Johnny Raw is a bird, raw by name, but not otherwise; he has outlived on board our ship the appropriate cognomen allowed at the time of his first rescue, for his late associations have made him a rascal. Johnny reached our quarter-boat at sea one lucky morning (for him) in an exhausted state, wing-weary and starved, and was taken in and cared for by Jack. The poor orphan soon came about and got his sea legs on. A great pet he was, black as a raven, about the size of a field lark, and with a noble carriage. Johnny had a most remarkable gait, hopping, both legs together, rapidly and with giant leaps. He would cover several feet at each hop. When the boatswain and mates piped to dinner he recognized the call, was the first on hand, and moving over the mess-cloths helped himself to the choice bits, wandering from mess to mess and disputing with the mess-cooks. He was literally like the marine sogger, in "everybody's mess." Johnny soon recovers from the present exciting adventure and returns to his piratical expeditions to the mess-cloths. To complete his history, now we have been obliged to begin it, he did not survive the cruise, eventually meeting his fate by being blown to leeward in a gale of wind.

We are now jogging along towards the equator—weather good, with a clear horizon, enabling the "masthead" to see what is to be seen. But strange to say only a few vessels appear. We have boarded one American ship, the *Bethiah Thayer*; but she had to be bonded, her cargo being all neutral and non-contraband. To illustrate the constant danger of being run down by passing vessels, "lying to" as we now are, under only topsails, across the path of travel. Near midnight in the first watch, the writer having the deck, and standing on the horse-block beating the rail with his trumpet for want of something better to do, the outlook sang out, "Sail ho! Close aboard!" We were on opposite tacks. As rapidly as thought the sail has passed astern, so near it looked as though you could throw a biscuit on board. She was under full sail and bowling along at a lively rate.

In a jiffy the reefs are shaken out, helm-put up, and soon we are under full sail. The hound is after the fox. As a matter of course the chase is a long one—all stern chases are—but the *Alabama* has her seven-league boots on, and time at last is called. Getting within gun range, she answers to the warning of a blank cartridge, gracefully luffing to the breeze, and lays her maintopsail to the mast.

Reader, it is a beautiful sight—that of a gallant ship, her

light-kites spread to the breeze, and careening under the press of canvas, dashing the spray from her cutwater, as a noble steed the foam from his curb. The writer would involuntarily be reminded of the flutter of a bird brought wounded to the ground by the shot of the sportsman, as at the report of our gun the split sails flutter in the breeze. She proves upon being boarded the American ship *Punjaub*. Her cargo is neutral (guano). She is released on bond, and the *Alabama* again under low sail saunters along.

We have run, you will say, many miles out of our way and wasted time. But no! Any way is our way, so "it's in the road." We are as likely to make a haul here as at the spot left at midnight. We are now in the doldrums, approaching the equator, light airs and calms, with frequent and heavy tropical showers. The officers and men are paddling about the decks in bare feet, indulging in a freshwater corn-soak, and the stewards and mess-boys filling the officers' washtubs preparatory to the luxury of a bath of a sort not to be had every day. Our condenser supplies commonly the fresh water used; but the allowance is just one gallon per day, per capita, and deducting the portion needed for the cook's use but little is left for drinking purposes and ablutions. One reason for this economy of water is the possible danger of accident to the condenser, in which case we should have only enough to last to the nearest port.

During this drift in the light airs and currents, our worthy and thoughtful boatswain has improvised a bathhouse for officers and crew, a safe asylum from that aggressive hunter, the shark. From the lower studding-sailboom, rigged out, Mecaskey has spread a large square sail, sunk some feet under the surface of the water and kept beneath by solid shot in the center, the foot, head, and leach of the sail triced up, forming a huge bag. In this contrivance you may sport in comfort and safety, and it is no slight luxury under this scorching tropical sun.

Two vessels of the enemy's fleet have drifted to us, or rather we have drifted together in the light airs, the ship *Morning Star* and the schooner *Kingfisher*. The first is released on bond, cargo being neutral and non-contraband of war; the latter, a whaling schooner, is condemned and burned. In the meantime we are busy enough boarding vessels, but nearly all neutrals. Evans is constantly aloft, at one moment nearly drowned by a passing torrent of rain, and anon scorched by the blazing sun. And though it is a post of duty which none other of us would like to fill under present conditions, I verily think Evans likes it. It possesses the same excitement that hunting the ostrich on the desert plain does to the African sportsman.

On March 23, about on the "line," we fired the whaling schooner *Kingfisher* at nightfall, an equatorial rain and thunderstorm of unusual severity prevailing at the time. The little craft, though oil-soaked, blazed by fits and starts. In the lull of passing rainsqualls, the flames would shoot masthead high, seeming to play at hide-and-seek with the vivid lightning, anon shrinking beneath a drenching shower, leaving nature to keep up the pyrotechnic display—a weirdlike spectacle. To the returning boarding party, the *Alabama*, hove-to in wait, silhouetted in sharp outline against the horizon, lay pictured, "a painted ship upon a painted ocean." A wilder scene it would be difficult to imagine, and one of the many of our cruise offering a fine chance for the artist's brush. We are constantly, just now, on the qui vive for an enemy's cruiser. The belt of ocean travel is very narrow at this latitude; and our beacon fires are daily and nightly lighting up the waste and sky for at least half its width, inviting a clash if we are destined to have one.

The boarding work is quite arduous. Our scout reports many American rigs among the vast fleet drifting lazily in the light, variable airs, and the boats are kept constantly at work overhauling and examining. Where transfer papers occur, and they are quite frequent now, the master of the suspect is requested (we cannot order) to take his papers to the "court room" (our ship); so far a mere form. They are invariably found to be correct. So Evans is exonerated, and struts to the main-rigging bound aloft for another investigation. We are finding transferred ships plentiful.

Rain! Rain! Rain! We are paddling in it all day, and give us time, we shall become web-footed. However, it is equatorial weather, and, to be frank, we have no good clothes on to spoil in wet; Jack is making himself comfortable in raiment washed in fresh water, free from the sticky and clammy feeling which is the inevitable result of saltwater scrubbing.

We now approach two ships singled out by Evans as American. We soon come up with them under increased sail. They are the *Charles Hill* and *Nora*. Both proving lawful prizes, their crews are removed, and vessels fired. We received a welcome addition to our crew list from these latter vessels—nine men.

It is interesting and significant to note the zeal with which our crew enter into the task of gathering recruits from the prisoners. Nor is the motive altogether a patriotic or unselfish one. Our men have realized that a full complement means much less labor to themselves, to say nothing of the security of a full-manned battery. Observe a group of stalwart, lithe, and active North Country and English sailor-prisoners, lounging in the lee-gangway.

Our "hearties," enjoying the after-dinner pipe, have insinuated themselves in their midst. We are still short of men. Semmes and Kell are aft in deep consultation over the group forward, anxious and impatient to have them step to the mainmast and request an interview. It would be beneath Semmes's dignity to take the initiative. Casting their eyes forward, they take in the situation. They know our self-constituted shipping-masters are plying all their arts and wiles to secure these halting, hesitating adventurers. Kell telegraphs Semmes a significant look and smile, as much as to say, "Those lads of ours are steering it OK"; and they part—our captain to his cabin and international law, the first "luff" to his daily round of duties.

Now stray forward, and take a stand near the hunters of men and their game. It is easy to guess the line of persuasion and seduction that is employed to secure the services of these picked sailor lads. The items are most alluring—double pay, *in gold;* generous rations; tobacco *ad libitum;* grog twice a day and in generous quantity; prospective prize-money; and last, but not least, kind and sympathetic officers over them. The bid has been made. Our worthies of the lee-scuppers are lost in revery. They are thinking of the character attached to this lone rover by her enemy (pirate), what might be their fate if captured, and of other consequences of casting off home protection by the act of enlistment. There is an ominous silence on the group for a while. Our men have thoughtfully and judiciously retired to their several tasks, leaving them untrammeled. All at once a concerted move is made for the mainmast, the captain and first "luff" sent for, and shortly the interview is over, and we have secured half a dozen splendid specimens of old Neptune's bantlings. The very danger of the venture has appealed to their instincts; and the romance of the situation, fully as much as other considerations, has captured them, hearts and hands. Jack's very soul loves daring and adventure.

We have for the first time our full complement of men; and take them all round, they are as select and competent a lot as could be picked from the crew of any English man-of-war. Just now some of them need a thorough course of drill at the great guns and at other exercises; but as we shall buckle down to this daily, they will soon be up to the standard. Besides, we usually find in every batch of recruits some who have served in one or the other of the navies, and their former experience at the gunnery schools enables them to materially assist the officer of division in the training of the raws.

Our middies are having a circus today with their sextants. We happen to be crossing the equator in company with the sun (it is March 29, 1863). It is rather funny to watch them shifting about from point to point, now on the quarterdeck, and then on the forecastle, trying to fathom the unusual behavior of the chariot of Phoebus, which seems for a second time to have fallen into the hands of inexperience (which is in a sense true enough this time). They are in a state of great perplexity, and furtively watch the writer until he turns to the captain at his side with the unusual report, "About twelve o'clock, sir—no latitude—about on the equator, sir." This time there is no calculating to be done, no altitude to calculate from. The young gentlemen avoid each other's eyes as they gravely put up their instruments, and then saunter off to mess-quarters without handing in their reports. Something has dawned upon them, but they are sedulously careful not to invite sympathy.

We are still about helpless, under sail, with the lightest of zephyrs drawing, now from southeast and anon northeast, then breathless calm with a saturation of solar fervency that is almost intolerable, relieved by a sudden forming of the blackest of clouds and a downpour of rain such as the dweller in regions of moderate evaporation has no conception of. A rain that in ten minutes floods the decks so that the swash of the torrent as we roll on the gentle swell would be dangerous to life and limb if the side ports were not left open to facilitate its escape. In the meantime one is constantly kept in remembrance of Mother Goose's pathetic ballad,

>The maid was in the garden
>Hanging out the clothes,

for from mast to mast and from all convenient points stretches a web of clotheslines laden with Jack's *annual* wash. His clothes-bag and his person are, for the present at least, immaculate.

But presently a sail drifts in sight, and Evans, between showers, pronounces her American. A boat is lowered, and an officer sent to board her. She cannot escape, and elbow grease is cheaper than coal. But could we only have guessed the character of this vessel's cargo, the *Alabama* might very economically have used up her whole remaining stock of fuel to get alongside. She was shortly reported to be the *Louisa Hatch* from Cardiff to the East Indies, and a lawful prize. She had all the coal we needed and tons to spare; and it was the very quality we preferred, being nearly smokeless, not likely to attract the attention of our prey when out of our sight, and free from the dust and smut which we disliked so much on our decks.

We are bound just now to the Island of Fernando de Naronha off the coast of Brazil, where we expect to meet our old transport the *Agrippina*. It will be remembered that we relieved her of her cargo of coals at the Arcas some time since, and sent her back to report to Captain Bulloch for another load. But we have always felt doubts of Captain McQueen. He has the Scotch vices, with a very sparing allowance of the Scotch virtues, especially those of loyalty and temperance; and many indications have led us to suspect that honor would not weigh much with him if the interests of McQueen happened to fall into the wrong scale. As he did not keep his engagement with us at Naronha, we were particularly pleased to be rid of him under circumstances so satisfactory. He might have sold us to the enemy's cruisers had the opportunity come in his way. We afterward learned that he sold our coal for his own account on the way to join us. It is therefore hardly needful to add that he took good care to keep out of our possible vicinity during the rest of the cruise.

Necessity very often compelled us to repose confidence where there was considerably less than a perfectly trustful feeling in our own breasts to warrant it. We have as a rule been agreeably disappointed to find so many, not to the manor born, so faithful to their pledges to our struggling young Republic. It is to the credit of human nature that the instances in which we were betrayed were so few; and it is curious, almost to the extent of the marvelous, unless we may say that it was providential, how systematically we were saved from disastrous and even unpleasant consequences as a result of them.

In the doldrums we have little trouble in keeping company with the *Hatch*. Her officers and crew are transferred to our decks, and a prize-crew put on board. So for some days we continue boxing about, meeting with no further luck in the way of captures. At last Semmes appears to be tired of it and, as we have coal to burn, clews up the useless canvas and puts her for the coast under steam, with the *Hatch* in tow. The run is uneventful. On the 9th of April, 1863, we are at anchor under the lee of the Island of Fernando de Naronha, our prize-transport alongside, and we proceed to open communications with the governor. We have now been just eight months in commission.

CHAPTER VII

AT FERNANDO DE NARONHA; A COAL SHIP; BAHIA; IN THE TRADE WINDS; SOWING THE SEA WITH PIANOS; CAPTURE OF THE *CONRAD*; COMMISSIONING OF THE *TUSCALOOSA*; VOYAGE TO THE CAPE OF GOOD HOPE

FERNANDO DE NARONHA is of volcanic origin, springing perpendicularly from the ocean, and rock-bound. It is the penal colony of Brazil, a governor and staff keeping order among the convicts with a battalion of troops. Our commander addresses a letter to the governor, of course chiefly in the diplomatic line. No doubt it was most eloquent and persuasive, fully packed with notes from the international code; for the next morning two officials came on board with a communication from the governor, granting permission to come in with the *Hatch*, to coal ship from her, and to secure fresh provisions from the shore. If the matter had been settled by the inexorable code under the usual interpretation, we should have had a rough experience, coaling from the *Hatch* in mid-ocean. But the governor turns out to be a first-class fellow. I trust he will excuse the familiarity, if these lines should ever meet his eye. International law doesn't bother him—indeed, it is doubtful if he has ever given it a thought. We are in high luck. However, it is the governor's lookout, not ours. He seems to be monarch of all he surveys—a quasi emperor.

The two vessels are now hauled close under the land, and the *Hatch* warped alongside, and the coaling begun. The quietest we are ever to experience. We shall have no jail-loosing after leaving this lone isle of the sea. We feel now, as never before, confidence in our fighting power, having a full complement of men. The day after making port, Semmes and Gait, our surgeon and paymaster, pay a visit to the governor onshore; the former in an official capacity, the latter to look out for Jack's gastronomic wants. Meats, poultry, and fruits are in abundance here, and the latter most delicious. The landing on the island is not unattended with danger, the surf is heavy at times, the coast being most precipitous. The boat is first beached going in on a high breaker, and as the wave recedes a native has you on his back, and at a trot places you beyond the return wave. We experienced in all our landings, however, only a slight sprinkling of salt water. The natives are experts in handling the surfboats.

Intercourse with the governor, staff, and prison islanders is now established, and a more democratic state of affairs cannot possibly be imagined than exists here. As a penal colony it is surely not paralleled on our habitable globe. Hundreds of convicts are sent here from the Brazils for serious crimes; and, as is always the case, they are from every class of society. Having no chance or hope of escape, the main shore of Brazil being too distant and the small boats of the island carefully looked after, the convicts roam the island ad libitum. They have their own huts and in many cases caves in the rock constructed by themselves, and are divided into messes, congenial company amalgamating as fellows. It seems strange to see them saunter into the veranda of the governor's house, bow a good morning, and taking a seat enter into an animated conversation with any of the household happening to be present—and even socially on the best of terms with the governor himself.

Indeed, the latter had as guests at his table a father and daughter, the former a most notorious forger, the latter, however, a sweet, innocent girl, her misfortune being that she was the daughter of such a man. She was a voluntary exile with him. One of the convicts invited the writer and others of the liberty party to his home, a cave in the rock fitted up nicely and cozily. He had been sent here for counterfeiting the notes of the bank of Brazil. His sentence was, as he informed us, for eight years, and he had served six of them to date.

To illustrate the state of his feelings we will give the substance of his story. He was an engraver by trade, and had turned his steps to the paths that are crooked. Having finished the plate of a banknote of large denomination, some minor finishing touches only being required, in an unlucky moment he printed one of them, presented it at the counter of a fashionable café at Rio de Janeiro in payment of his score, was arrested, tried, and convicted. The result, as he stated, "of being in too great a hurry." He went on to say (by-the-by, he must have placed great confidence in our fellowship) that his time was nearly out, and upon his return he should "*not be in so great a hurry*"; and freely admitted that he looked forward to a glorious time, with pockets full of bank bills. He claimed that the execution of his plate was marvelous in exactness. So you see the fresh air and generous food of the island were keeping up the courage and spirits of our host, whether he was bragging or only lying. Perhaps eight years in Albany prison would have taken the buoyancy out of him. His home was hung with musical instruments of different kinds, upon many of which he performed for our entertainment, and I must say his skill was far above mediocre. Take him altogether, he was a brick in his way, only he had a bad way.

Ships rarely stop at this point, simply sight the island to verify their chronometers. Occasionally a Brazilian man-of-war puts in to see if there has been a revolution.

We are disposed to pronounce the governor a whole-souled gentleman; for he is every day sending presents, not only to Captain Semmes (which, as he has sampled Semmes's champagne and cigars freely, is not so surprising), but to all the other messes. We are also made free of the island, but Jack does not seem to appreciate shore liberty where there is neither a grog shop nor a dance house—not even a theater. Jack isn't fond of dry land for its own sake, even when it is covered with tropical foliage.

We finished coaling in about five days; and notwithstanding the advantages given us by the governor, the job was not an easy one. There is no harbor, only an open roadstead, with at most times quite a heavy swell; and we had to keep the vessels riding to spars lashed between them to prevent them from grinding each other dangerously. But still we are waiting in expectation of the *Agrippina*'s arrival. The story of Circe's enchanted island must have taken its rise from conditions much like these we are experiencing. Languor and laziness breathe out upon us as we rise and fall with the lullaby motion of the tropic sea. We have no thought of prizes to be won and battles to be fought. We idly cultivate our hospitable friends the jailbirds, with whose etiquette no introductions are required—they are not exclusive, though they have the air and manner of lords. And if living in a paradise of nature without labor and on terms of equality with everybody isn't lordship, it is certainly a very rational substitute. A philosopher he, who, having been banished from this island by expiration of sentence, straightway commits another crime to obtain another season of residence here. Nothing is compulsory in this prison except virtue. The only wonder is that the island is not overpopulated.

We had saved from the conflagrations all the whaleboats of the *Lafayette* and *Kate Cory*, intending them as a present in return for sundry kindnesses and attentions extended us by the governor's surfmen, who had daily carried our shore parties on their backs to and fro through the surf. As we passed out of the roadstead, one by one the boats were cut adrift from our stern. Such an excitement was never before witnessed at this island. All the surfboats were in the grab race, their crews stripped for the scramble. They had gotten the hint of what was to follow from some of our young officers. Huzzahs would ring out on the air, from shore and boats, as a boat's crew would make a capture. As well as we could judge, the prizes were about equally divided, the capture of one whaleboat minimizing the captor's chances of another haul. These whaleboats made a royal addition to the surfmen's equipment, being vastly superior in every respect to their own.

Our *dolice far niente* life is at last broken in on by the appearance alongside of the *Hatch* of two whaleboats, evidently American, as also their crews. They pulled in from the offing to ascertain if repairs they were in need of could be made here, and came alongside the *Hatch* on a visit, seeing that she was an American from her build. Fulham, the prize-master, invited them on board; but just as they hesitated, a small Confederate boat's ensign was observed by them on board the ship, and quicker than lightning the two skippers had backed off and were pulling for dear life to their vessels. We had been so wrapped up in other matters that the two whalers had approached within six or seven miles of the island, and but for the visit from their captains might have escaped our notice until within the charmed marine league. No time was to be lost. Steam was ordered, and soon the *Alabama* is at her old tricks. The captains are making a useless retreat in their boats, for nothing can save their vessels but a fine breeze, and that at once, to run them within the magic line. As this was possible, the part of prudence was being taken by both sides. The *Alabama* throws "three sixes" with fortune's dice, and closes with the vessels about five miles from the land. We hoist Confederate colors; they United States bunting. No occasion for guile or coquetry. They proved the barque *Lafayette* and the brig *Kate Cory*, both whalers. We burned the *Lafayette*. This is the second vessel of this name we have burned, the first being a ship.

The *Kate Cory* was held a while; but a Brazilian vessel happening in, our prisoners were turned over to her and the *Cory* burned. We had intended bonding the latter and sending the prisoners to the coast in her. Having finished with the *Hatch*, we tow her outside the charmed distance and make a bonfire of her also. We are sorry to destroy so much coal. We have got to place more value on good coals than on gold. Fernando de Naronha was never so lit up before, and great was the excitement of the convicts over the spectacle. We ship from these prizes five picked men. We are now quite independent in the way of seamen. We are full up in complement and over. It would require a heavy premium to secure a position on our payroll. We refused a number who requested to be allowed to enlist, taking only the very desirable.

On the 22d of April we go to sea, giving up the *Agrippina*. We are tired of waiting for her. We have had a glorious outing, are fat and saucy, and ready for spoils. What an empire that island would make for some nabob, though! At no time during the cruise did we have a better time; and as for our table, it fairly groaned under the weight of turtle, fish, meats, fruits, and vegetables, even the toothsome turkey being included in our menu. Bartelli and Parkinson, stewards respectively of the cabin and wardroom, are in their glory. Even Kell has enjoyed a quiet life at the island, the men being unable to obtain grog. A little *aguardiente* is distilled, but evidently under the eye of the governor, who takes care that it does not reach the convicts. No luckier epoch of our cruise than this of our stay at the Brazilian penal colony. We had captured all the coals needed and to spare, stowing a day's steaming of it in bags on deck; had recruited our force five men, and recuperated all hands fore and aft. We are departing in the best possible order for business.

I forgot to mention that we had a little break in the monotony of daily life before sailing—a sparring match between two of the powder monkeys, Egan and Parker. It was to work off an old grudge, and gotten up by the men. Not many rounds were fought before Kell took a hand, elbowing through the crowd into the ring and calling *"time."* No bones were broken, only a little *"claret spilt,"* as the professionals would say. Egan was the culprit as usual, and is given a taste of the usual punishment served out to the boys—"spread-eagled" in the mizzen-rigging. This boy afterwards deserted at the Cape of Good Hope, and I can't say but we were pleased to get rid of him.

What a capital idea this on the part of Brazil and some other powers—the establishment of penal colonies. The advantages are so numerous, both to the government and the prisoners, as to be worthy the careful consideration of our own country. On the part of the latter, the life of close confinement in cells, constant contact with gloomy and revolting prison scenes, unnatural discipline and degrading oversight all tend to produce prostitution of whatever of manhood and regret for past crimes remain. To the contrary, fresh air, liberty to choose companionship, moderate agricultural employment, liberty of recreation at appointed hours, and means for the cultivation of cleanly habits must tend to elevate if not to refine the prisoners. On the part of the government, some advantages would be the slight chance of escape of prisoners, greater economy in all departments of the system, and removal of prison buildings from public view. Islands in the ocean are to be had for the taking, or may be cheaply purchased.

We are now catching the southeast trade winds in south latitude, though they are light as yet. The writer is engaged these fine days, when off watch, fishing for dolphin, large schools of them playing around the ship, and remaining while the weather is fine. As a rule, the men trick them with a bit of white cloth or bright metal attached on the hook, playing the line on the water. It is more successful than spearing them, but not so exciting or scientific. The manner of fishing with the "grains" is as follows: Standing in the chains with a waist-belt on for support and leaning forward over the water, the staff of the grains grasped and the coil of the line in your left hand, you await the approach of the fish in their trip around the ship. The habits of the dolphin lead him to circumnavigate the vessel continuously for hours and hours. Should the sun be unobscured by clouds, the fish is wary, and seeing you or your shadow swims deep upon arriving in your wake; but otherwise comes near to the surface, two to four feet under. At this depth you are sure of the grains reaching him. The instrument used is five-pronged and barbed, what we are familiar with as Neptune's trident, only with the addition of two prongs at right angles with the others. The object is to strike the fish in the head, it being the most likely part to give you a hold. The refraction of the water is a factor to be considered, so you can guess what there is of skill and practice required for the successful prosecution of the sport. The writer has spent hours at it unrewarded by a single strike. At another time (as in matter of capturing prizes) all would go merry as a marriage bell, and the deck be spattered with the blood of many a victim.

It is a strange phenomenon of nature, the rapid changes of color in the dying dolphin. I do not know if scientists explain it. Care must be observed in eating this, as well as other deep-sea fish. Should the fish have recently fed on barnacles from the bottom of coppered ships, the meat is dangerous, producing high fever. Its unfitness for food can be ascertained by placing a silver coin with it in the frying pan. Should the coin be turned black, avoid eating the fish.

We are having now from time to time flying fish on our table, at present in all cases from the men, their game preserves being by custom exclusively their own. We allude to the extreme forepart of the deck. The manner of securing these little rice-birds of the deep is as follows: A net is suspended from the head-booms perpendicularly, another below it horizontally as a receptacle, and a lantern hung in the center. The fish, flushed either by the passage of the ship through their midst or stampeded by their relentless enemy the dolphin, make the rise from the water, and blinded or attracted by the light are trapped into the net. "A winged mullet" is a good description of the appearance and shape of the fish. The muscular power required to propel these creatures through the air for so long a distance, say one hundred yards or more, is marvelous, and must approach, in comparison to that of larger life, the proportion assigned by scientists to the flea in his jump. The flying fish does not appear, when in motion in the air, to use his wings, except as a rudder or guide; hence, we take it, the propulsion is in the force of the spring from the water.

We have the ship under sail, steam down and propeller

up. The usual routine is broken into by the masthead cry, "Sail ho!" and without the slightest excitement and with only the notice of a blank cartridge, the sail is lying quiet near us with maintopsail to the mast. She proves the whaling barque *Nye*, with part cargo of oil. As in the case of all whalers, the captain cannot dodge behind forged papers as to ownership of cargo, hence Semmes has not to look up the code. After looting her and removing prisoners and chronometers, she is fired. These whalers make a fierce conflagration and dense smoke, and it may be taken as a certainty that scores of vessels have been warned by this sign and escaped capture. Indeed, in heaping all the opprobrium possible on us, it was given out by the Northern press that we stood by the burning ships in order to capture others, who, mistaking the cause of the fire and actuated by the impulse of common humanity, would bear down to save life; and continuing, these newspapers would picture, as a result, vessels actually taking fire at sea accidentally being left to their fate. Disingenuous! though a somewhat plausible statement at the first blush, it will not stand the crucial test of analysis. Prudence on our part would suggest leaving the burning prize at once, for fear of the enemy's cruiser, and common sense would suggest that the merchant fleet *of the enemy* would severely avoid these burning signposts on the ocean. Humanity would be smothered up in this case in self-interest. But a very decided majority of the vessels on the ocean are other than American, and without fail *they* would stand down to any burning vessel to ascertain the cause. We found they always did so, night or day.

We have before referred to the usefulness of the whaler as a supply ship. We got from the *Nye* a choice lot of good old Virginia tobacco. Next to the sight of rum, this pleases Jack most. Lots of comfort to him in it. We have been furnished through late newspapers with the description of a large clipper vessel, the *Ino*, purchased by the United States Navy Department from the merchant fleet, strengthened, armed with a heavy battery, and stationed now on this coast "to look out for the *Alabama*." We are pleased to learn it. For besides furnishing the officers and crew with food for conversation and gossip, it has increased the interest of the masthead lookout, as well as of Evans. A sharper (if possible) watch is kept especially for her. We want to find her badly, yea, are pining for her. What chance would the heaviest armed sailing ship have with a fast steam cruiser under her stern raking her? Particularly if she was caught in the light airs prevailing in this latitude. Wise Secretary of the Navy! But we never had the chance of changing her flag, and cruising in her against the old one.

We are now in a narrow belt of ocean travel and should run across an enemy's cruiser at any time. Day by day we expect it. We cannot imagine they are not hereabouts. It would seem a schoolboy could arrange a plan of pursuit. Yet we raid this pathway of commerce, scattering American shipping as chaff before the wind, and the only cruisers we come up with are the *Florida* and *Georgia*, our own ships. The best display of judgment falling under our observation was that of Captain Baldwin of the United States steamer *Vanderbilt*, whose unerring judgment led him, as the hound after the fox, to follow us from point to point without a loss of the scent at any time, until he had tracked us from the West India Islands to the Brazil thoroughfare, thence to the Cape of Good Hope; where he on one occasion came out of the port of Simon's Town a few days before our arrival, and must have at times been close aboard of us. Nothing but his enormous consumption of coal, some eighty tons per day, compelled him to take the back track to Brazil. Coals increase in value in almost geometrical progression as you get away from the coal fields of Europe and North America. Had this vessel kept on and stationed herself in the Straits of Sunda, the fight off Cherbourg might never have taken place, and many an American vessel rotting at anchor in the Eastern ports might have been released and once more homeward bound with flowing sheets and plethoric cargoes. So far as the writer can judge, Baldwin displayed better judgment than any of his compeers sent in pursuit of the *Alabama*. It has often occurred to the writer to marvel why each narrow strait of commerce was not watched constantly, instead of patroling the open ocean in search of us.

We are in the trade winds fairly, and the breeze has freshened, making the meeting of vessels more likely. "Sail ho!" again, with a report soon from aloft that she is Yankee. She is southern bound. Not much trouble or waste of time with her. A blank cartridge heaves her to. We seldom have to use a shot or shell now. Our enemy has found out we have them if required. Upon being boarded, she proved the ship *Dorcas Prince* for Shanghai. Prisoners are transferred and torch applied.

We have now been cruising ten days. Luck has not been poor, still not what it should be. We are on the best hunting ground on the map, excepting some of the narrow straits leading into open oceans, and we should be driving a brisk trade. It looks as though the ubiquitous Yankee skipper had sold out to John Bull and gone out of business. We are having lots of talk from the masthead lookout, but we can draw no comfort from Evans. The monotonous answer to the deck hail being "English, sir," or such.

At last a bird is flushed from the covey. Soon the hail from Evans comes to the officer of the deck, "Yankee, sir." That settles it. We soon near each other, and a cartridge brings her maintopsail to the mast and United States colors to the peak. She proves, upon boarding, to be the *Union Jack* for Shanghai from Boston. While the prize-officer is on board of her, and before sending, as usual, the captain of the enemy's ship on board our vessel with his papers, "Sail ho!" comes again from the masthead. Leaving this vessel to follow with the prize-crew in charge, we make sail, and putting on our race boots start to overhaul the stranger. A fine breeze blowing, we are soon near the sail, and a blank cartridge heaves her to. This latter vessel also proves to be a prize, the clipper ship *Sea Lark* of New York, bound to San Francisco. You see we take them here, bound to every quarter of the globe.

The boarding-officer of the *Union Jack* has now run down to us. Removing such provisions and other stores as are required and sending to our ship the prisoners and chronometers of both vessels, they are ready for the torch. The caravan of boats from the two doomed ships have deposited their human freight on our decks, and soon the prize-masters may be seen tumbling over the sides. Marvelous the rapidity with which the flames burst out from the cabin and forecastle and envelop the ship, leaping the masts and licking the sails. Say what you will, we experience deep feelings of regret at this wholesale destruction of splendid ships and valuable cargoes. But as we peruse a batch of Northern newspapers and learn of the devastation going on in our own dear land, we laugh at our mourning with a heart steeled and embittered over again.

We are much inconvenienced in the wardroom. The last three prizes have given us a number of female passengers. We do not designate them prisoners, and the officers have been turned out of their staterooms to accommodate them. This situation settles it that Semmes must board some foreign vessel and make a bargain to transfer this army, or put the ship into port. We had quite an excitement today. Made a steamer under sail to windward of us, and from the rake of her masts and two funnels had no difficulty in recognizing the Confederate States steamer *Florida*. We would, if we could, have spoken her; but she had the advantage of a windward position, hence no unusual effort was made to communicate with her. That she recognized us as a man-of-war seems quite likely; but whether she was busy at the time overhauling some enemy to windward of herself, and consequently below our horizon, or what not, we never knew.

Upon going into Bahia a few days after to land our passengers, we had a telegram from Pernambuco, stating the *Florida* had just arrived to land prisoners and coal ship. I have frequently since twitted one or two of the officers of the *Florida* with sighting us and taking advantage of the weather-gauge to run away. But my fun was understood. They stated afterwards that they did not recognize us. We are now in the country of the wardroom (that is the mess room proper) wanderers and tramps, no staterooms to loaf and sleep in, and the wardroom floor for a bunk. The ladies, bless their sweet hearts, are desirable company at all times and all places with but few exceptions; one of the exceptions is the crowded wardroom of a man-of-war. I often had the thought present itself, in this situation, what would become of these women if we should get alongside of an enemy's cruiser.

We are now heading under full sail for the coast of Brazil, and from the steady course given the officer of the deck, not deviated from except to note the rig and nationality of a passing sail, feel sure we are bound for Bahia. Perhaps there may be some surprise that I speak of the officers as only surmising where the ship is going. But it is a fact, reader, never during the cruise did any soul on board (to my knowledge) receive information respecting her destination, present or future. As sailing-master, determining and picking off the position of the ship on the chart from day to day, I could often make a reasonably close guess as to the objective point. But in answer to the question from my brother officers as to where we were bound, my answer had always to be that I could only guess. If a still tongue makes a wise head, our skipper was a Solomon or two.

The wind is light again, and ship jogging along. A strange sight now, the deck of the *Alabama*. It is early evening. Ladies are gracing its promenades, and the hush incident to strict discipline is broken by the gentle laughter of the new, and to us strange, companions. They have recovered from the excitement and fright of the capture, have learned that the supposed shot sent after their vessel was an innocent blank cartridge, and are reassured and fast becoming sociable. One of them soon lays a grievance before me. Among the nautical instruments removed from the prizes was a pair of opera or sea glasses which she claimed as private property, and learning they were under my charge asked that they be restored. The matter was referred to the captain, and they were promptly returned. A number of our wardroom mess, the writer included, were rather surprised the day after our arrival at Bahia by the receipt of a nicely perfumed note from the fair party, containing an invitation to a *déjeuner a la fourchette* at the hotel on shore. The occasion was one of real pleasure, and marked an episode in our eventful lives. So it may be suspected that some sly fellow of our mess had been exchanging soft glances over the mess-table, or abaft the wheel, behind the back of the officer of the deck.

We had the other side of the matter to look upon for variety. An Irish stewardess was brought on board from one of the prizes, and sad to relate, a little "how came you so." This charmer was given a free ride over the side, it being necessary to rig a "whip" from the yardarm for her accommodation. She was particularly severe upon our gallant though modest commander, applying to him epithets of so emphatic a character that we omit them mostly, but "pirate, rebel, free-booter," etc., were the mild ones.

Standing to the south and westward, still with light airs, and weather fine. The deck reminds one of an emigrant vessel, our prisoners, some under the awning spread for them and others in the open, sleeping quietly, having adapted themselves to the sudden change of surroundings. The ladies have retired to the wardroom, "and all the air a solemn stillness holds." It is near eight bells of the midnight watch. The officer of the deck is on the horse-block, one leg easing the other by turns, elbow resting on the hammock rail, trumpet in hand, and night-glasses near. The quartermaster with folded arm is "conning" the man at the wheel, and from time to time shifting the quid in his mouth. The slow turning of the spokes of the wheel conveys the fact that the wind is steady, and but little effort required to keep the ship on her course. A gentle heave in of the topsails as we roll to leeward hints to you the lightness of the breeze. Nothing breaks the quiet but occasionally the strike of the bell and the cry from the lookout accompanying, "Starboard cathead!" "Starboard quarter!" or the opposite.

If there is a place on earth where communication with one's thoughts is especially apt to master one's senses, it is the deck of a ship in the quiet mid-watch, upon a calm, still night. Jack is coiled up under the weather bulwarks, dreaming perhaps of days long gone by, when a little tot he was the idol of his island home, naught crossing his childhood path to bring a tear—all sunshine. The love for mother dear, long since dead, sends memories flitting through the uneasy brain; and as remembrances of her love, since outraged and crucified by a life of waywardness and dissipation, stride in vivid reality upon him, he starts, sighs, and turns uneasily on the deck. What experiences the floating home of the sailor keeps hidden away! Could the tale of each and every one of these gallant—perhaps wayward—fellows be unveiled, what a romance! what a revelation! what a tragedy! And the best of us has enough to reflect upon in the presence of night and silence upon the great deep.

We have reached the month of May, and captured and burned a few days since the whaler *Nye* of New Bedford and clipper ship *Dorcas Prince* of New York, coals for Shanghai. Today, May 3, we have unusual luck, capturing first the clipper ship *Union Jack*, Boston to Shanghai. We hastily threw a prize-crew on board of her, the lookout having another American-rigged sail well in sight. Within two hours we have fastened our talons into the clipper ship *Sea Lark*, New York to San Francisco—both with general cargoes of high value. Quick work. These captures are made in a fine, smashing trade. Both prizes have numerous articles, manifested in cargo, needed for our ship's use. We lay, hove-to, near them for some hours, breaking out cargo and covering the ocean for miles with a miscellaneous assortment of boxes, bales, and cases, containing articles of great value in the aggregate but of no use to us, and cast on the waters as being in the way of the despoilers, delving under hatches to fill an order received from our paymaster, maybe for soap, candles, or some other stores invaluable to us but of trifling pecuniary worth. In the meantime we have sent to the *Alabama*, from the two prizes with our compliments, a colony of one hundred or more souls to be cared for, which, with the crews of the *Nye* and *Dorcas Prince*, means crowded spardeck and mess quarters.

Included in the shipment is a consul bound to China and quite a number of ladies. We can, from the deck of the *Sea Lark*, study, in fancy, the lugubrious countenances of our swell lieutenants as they peer over our gangway and detect the crinoline coming alongside. It means to them they are to empty, for the use of the ladies, or lock up their bureau drawers and join the juniors of the "country," who have no state-rooms, in hammocks. The dear girls have engaged the best rooms. Get your tin basin and campstool ready now, fastidi-ous lieutenants, and pray for fair winds and a port close aboard. The writer, although a looker-on from afar, may be one of the lugubrious victims, and may find upon his return to the *Alabama*, weary and pining for his bunk, some most nec-essary of his toilet articles chucked in a corner awaiting him, and, upon visiting his stateroom, the exclamation thrust upon him on finding a pretty girl in possession, doing up her hair, "Oh! beg your pardon! but you are quite welcome. Make your-self at home." Now, gentle reader, you must determine for yourself in these remarks of the lieutenant the amount of sin-cerity to be allowed this "forced volunteer," as Pat would put it. But candidly, we willingly accept the temporary incon-venience in exchange for the refreshing presence of bright eyes and smiling faces, an oasis in the desert of our surroundings.

We enter the Port of Bahia today (May 11, 1863), and a beautiful harbor it is. The city is snugly embosomed in handsome trees on the side of a hill. The deep green of the tropical foliage contrasts sharply with the snow-white houses. The waterfront is lined with warehouses. As usual, the first matter to dispose of is the landing of the prisoners. This has been accomplished, and they are safe under the of-ficial wings of the American consul. We need no coal, hav-ing just filled our bunkers at the islands, and so amusement and sightseeing are to be the order of our stay. Our crew are allowed liberty in watches, and soon the streets of the town are enlivened with the bright uniforms of officers and men. At every turn we are "the observed of all observers," shop-keepers leaving their yardsticks and measures, clerks their desks, ladies shyly peeping through the lattices of the ver-andas, and the more enthusiastic flirting their handkerchiefs.

We had a slight diplomatic muddle soon after anchoring, in

relation to our recent visit to Fernando de Naronha; the president of this province thinking we had been too careless with international law—bringing our prize into Brazilian waters, coaling ship from her, and then towing to sea and burning her. But we could claim the permission of the governor of the island as sufficient excuse for our action. He was the proper person to answer for it and shoulder the responsibility. However, his error was quite overlooked, and ours forgiven. We had the pleasure of attending a ball given in our honor by Mr. Ogilvie, an English merchant, which was honored by the presence of the elite of the town, and at which we danced and flirted until the "wee small hours of the morn," carrying on board with us no few souvenirs of the charming evening, many of which survived to the day of the fight off Cherbourg.

We had a surprise in store. In the early morn a man-of-war steamer was observed at anchor near us. She had arrived during the night. You may imagine our astonishment when she exchanged the same colors with us. Rare flag to see in this region. It was the Confederate States steamer *Georgia*, Captain Lewis F. Maury. She had made port for coal and provisions. It was a joyous reunion for many of our officers; Chapman and Evans, who were serving on board of her as lieutenants, having made the cruise in the *Sumter* with Semmes, Kell, Armstrong, Wilson, Galt, Howell, Freeman, O'Brien, Brooks, Cummings, Cuddy, Mecaskey, Robinson, and Smith of our ship. Pleasure parties onshore and on the two ships result; and, with the attentions of our foreign friends time flies swiftly. We learn while here of the arrival of Confederate States steamer *Florida* at Pernambuco. We can straighten up now and put on airs, boast of the "Confederate squadron of the South American station," and await the arrival of any vessel of the enemy's navy in perfect security.

Herein the ludicrous side of the picture presents itself. The *Alabama* is supposed to be dodging the United States

cruisers, yet now the *Georgia* is in port with us, and the
Florida within telegraphic communication and two days'
steaming, it would be tough luck for the enemy should one
of his cruisers happen to stumble in. We cannot avoid the
feeling of pride and satisfaction that our struggling little
Confederacy has actually been able to overmatch the enemy
in cruisers, at least for the time being, and put them on the
defensive so far as the Brazilian coast goes. We were much
gratified that the fact was commented on by both the Brazilian and English naval officers. It was at this time that our
hopes for foreign intervention were brightest, and it pleased
us that the South was presenting no mean showing in the
cruiser line. The attentions and willingness of Brazilian officials to grant our requests was no doubt due in a measure to
the fact that the favors asked for were backed by plenty of
heavy guns. Through all time nothing is so successful as success, which always commands respect.[1]

Our men have behaved well onshore, seeming to have
made up their minds to wipe out the recollection of their late

1. Later on this port is the scene of a desperate and determined attack of
the enemy on one of our cruisers. The *Florida* had put into Bahia for coal
and refreshments; and feeling the neutrality of the port a thorough protec-
tive and safeguard, her captain, Charles Manigault Morris, gave liberty to
his men, and with a number of his officers was also onshore. In the night
the United States steamer *Wachusett*, advised by the American consul as to
particulars, steamed alongside the partially helpless vessel, boarded, and
passing a hawser, towed her to sea. At the time of the attack the officers and
crew on her were principally asleep below, and one would suppose, under the
circumstances, the resistance would have been feeble; yet the writer learned
from several officers of the *Florida* present and captured at the time, that the
resistance was stubborn, and most creditable to the defenders. The *Florida*
was taken to Hampton Roads, Virginia, and *accidentally* sunk by collision,
thus preventing her return intact to the waters of Brazil and restoration to
her own sovereignty, which had been acquiesced in by the United States
government. An apology and salute to the Brazilian flag followed, and there
the matter ended.

hilarity at Martinique and Kingston, and enjoying rather sightseeing on the promenades and in the attractive shops. Perhaps their fear of falling into a blissful state of oblivion under the influence of John Barleycorn and being left behind has its weight with them. Our crew are sincerely attached to their ship and justly proud of her.

The advantages of protracted cruises, consequent removal of all hurtful indulgences, regular hours, generous rations, and last but not the least important factor, constant activity of mind and limb in working ship and boarding vessels, had brought the condition of the ship up to a standard difficult to equal, almost impossible to excel.

We have not so many visitors to the ship at Bahia as at Martinique or Kingston. Probably the absence of curiosity to see the ship is the result of general indifference to all sur-roundings peculiar to this race. But in time we have squeezed all there is of pleasure from this incident of our cruise and must up anchor and away to the work. Overhauling and burning vessels has passed out of the category of excitement and become an everyday, matter-of-fact business. The sight of a whale or school of porpoises at play, the chance of strik-ing the latter, produces more excitement and comment than the cry, "Sail ho!" from aloft. Evans is not of the same im-portance as formerly; indeed, it is not infrequent, upon the report that the strange sail is "Yank," to hear a growl go up, "D—n the sail; I wish the fellow was Dutch! What are you monkeying aloft for, Evans? Why don't you let the masthead lookout attend to his business, and you go below and read your book!" Verily a luff alongside of an enemy's cruiser might be of service, awaking the senses and stirring the blood, and we were never better prepared for one.

It has so often been asked the writer how the *Alabama* re-couped herself in stores and how she managed as to funds or credit, that an explanation may be in order and prove interesting. The credit of the Confederate government, based upon its cotton purchased and shipped per blockade-runners, was upon more solid foundation abroad than even that of the enemy based upon promises to pay (greenbacks). Our commander was clothed with authority to draw bills on Liverpool to the extent of his requirements, and never during our cruise was there the slightest hesitancy on the part of merchants or others in accepting Semmes's "sterling bills" on England, though amounting generally to about ten thousand dollars at each coaling port. A considerable sum in gold was also at all times kept in the strongbox for emergencies and tendered in payment of ship's bills if wanted; but invariably it was refused, merchants preferring the more convenient form of bills. Indeed, the credit of the *Alabama* was, as they have it in commercial parlance, "A1." The stock of gold on hand at the end of the cruise was much larger than at the outset, being recruited by sale of the prize *Sea Bride* and cargo,[1] and also by smaller sums secured from prizes at sundry times.

We are at once, after leaving port, in the track of both outward- and homeward-bound vessels, and the cry of "Sail ho!" is frequent; but the spyglass of our expert seldom eliminates an American. It is the latter part of May before the enemy is rendered poorer at our hands. With a fresh breeze we are well in the trades. We approach the two vessels, reported from aloft as game, at a sharp angle, not a dead stern chase; and after some hours crowding of sail bring them within the sight and sound of a blank cartridge. Luffing up and bringing their maintopsails to the mast, they prove the ships *Gilderslieve* and *Justina*, the former of New York, the latter of Baltimore. The first was burned, the latter released under ransom-bond. This is the first vessel we have captured

---

1. At Angra Pequeña, in the latter part of August.

hailing from Baltimore, and we are overjoyed at being able to release her; for while Maryland had not the chance to join her sister states of the South, still her gallant sons were breasting the fight on Virginia soil. The prisoners as usual are put on board of the bonded vessel, and again our decks are free and clear.

Boarding vessels is heavy work in these fresh trades, blowing at times a full gale of wind, and dangerous work too. It seems almost a miracle that we escape all accident, engaged as we are both by day and night in this risky business. At times it is so rough that the boarding boat alongside the prize lifts on a sea above her spar-deck, and descending in the trough falls far below the copper line. The least carelessness or unskillfulness would swamp us. The officer is often obliged to reach the deck by an active spring from the boat as she rides up on the sea. The return from the prize to the boat is even more hazardous than the boarding, and the transfer of the prisoners, if possible, more delicate still.

But it has become a mere routine matter. We sometimes at night, the cover of darkness preventing the recognition of the rig, give chase to a vessel in a strong breeze. The watch on duty are constantly kept at it by the officer of the deck, bracing up a yard a pull or two, or hoisting a topsail to a taut leach in the hopes of getting an extra half-knot out of our racer. Blank cartridges are also called into requisition, and maybe a shot or shell. The intimation at the breakfast table next morning that a vessel had been overhauled, boarded, and burned during the night, and numerous guns fired to heave her to, would be received with surprise and sometimes doubt by the "idlers" of the mess, until verified by the appearance on deck of the prisoners in the weather waist.

We are now near the first summer month, or rather in this latitude winter month, and but two prizes captured and only one burned since leaving Bahia. "Sail ho!" Here she comes, borne over the blue waters by the glorious trades. Again is our scout Evans a prophet; and after a long chase the hint sent over the waters is heeded, and the graceful model luffs up in the wind and awaits the arrival of the boarding-officer. The vessel proves the *Jabez Snow* of Bucksport, Maine; a clipper ship, graceful as a swan on the water, and with her snow-white canvas and long, taut skysail masts a thing of beauty. Well, the matchsafe is brought into requisition, and away she goes, less a quantity of ship-stores and her chronometer and flag. We are again playing host and have a small colony on deck in the way of prisoners. The weather being fine, the quartermaster has broken out his signal lockers and is airing his signal flags—the captured ensigns as well—and such a sight! A stranger happening on our deck, and in ignorance of the character of the ship, would be puzzled to account for this display. Most likely in the absence of explanation the idea might present itself to him that the skipper is a monomaniac on the subject of United States flags, much as persons are in the accumulation of postage stamps or other odds and ends. We might have supplied the entire United States Navy, without exaggeration; and as for quadrants and sextants, even Jack can be seen forward at midday, instrument in hand, "taking the sun" for the benefit of the forecastle. Some days again pass without a bite, naught but neutrals, though the gallant trades are bringing them to us and we to them by the scores.

At last! Here we are! "Sail ho!" "Where away?" from the deck. "On the lee bow! On the starboard tack!" The sail is approaching us. No occasion for Evans aloft, however, for she has "gone in stays" and is soon running away, evidently suspicious of a vessel under low canvas in the glorious trades, where if a fellow were not the "flying Dutchman" and bound everywhere and nowhere at the same time, he would be a mass of canvas alow and aloft, speeding along at best. This sail gives us a long chase and is only overhauled after repeated warnings in the way of blank cartridges, and finally the ominous screech of a rifle shell.

The wind has been strong, necessitating, as usual, a long chase, and, as usual, working "Old Beeswax" into a temper, which later will expend itself on the unfortunate skipper of the prize, if not in a manner serious, at least facetious; for Semmes sometimes lets off the explosion in some such words as, "Well, Captain! So you wanted to be unsociable! Didn't want to call to see me! Well, never mind, I've come to you. By the way, Captain, you had probably forgotten my 'little teakettle' below, where I get my hot water. No use, Skipper—running. Steam will fetch you when canvas fails."

The screech of the rifle shell seeming to say, "Where are you? Where are you?" has had its effect; and the vessels are within a stone's throw of each other, motionless, held in by the backing of the after sail. Speculation is rife as to whether neutral cargo or otherwise. Our sea lawyer will soon settle this point, for here comes the boarding-master back with the skipper of our victim bringing along the vessel's papers. The suspense is soon over, and we need not ask any questions. The visiting captain is making no motion to leave the side of our ship as he comes up the companion ladder from the cabin minus his ship's papers, and Fulham returns to the prize with orders to apply the torch.

She is the barque *Amazonian* of Boston or Montevideo. Some queer pranks are cut up now on board of the captured vessel. We are in need of small stores, soap, candles, etc., and the articles are described by the first mate of the prize as being under such and such cargo. Overboard go pianos, pier glasses, cases of fine boots and shoes, etc., articles of high value, for what? Why, to get a few boxes of soap, of more value to us at present than all the pianos in Boston. It frequently reminded me of the soliloquy of Robinson Crusoe upon finding in the cabin of his wreck an assortment of garden seed. There is much of apparent vandalism in this wholesale destruction of beautiful articles, monuments of man's ingenuity and skill. Oh! War is the most deplorable misfortune that can overtake a people, and senseless in that the final arrangement has to be reached after all by peaceful methods. We have transferred the crew of the *Amazonian*, relieved her of such stores as were needed in our several departments, applied the torch, and are now standing along under reduced sail in the strong breeze. We are lucky again in finding the captain of a British brig willing to take our prisoners to port. So paroling them, and transferring the necessary provisions for their care and rewarding her captain in kind, we fill away, our decks clear of alien people once again.

Boarding neutrals again the order of the night. Incessant work now. We are in the most *fashionable* highway of commerce on the globe, and are beginning to realize how swiftly the carrying trade of the world is slipping away from the United States and casting its responsibilities on the shoulders of John Bull and other peacefully disposed nationalities. Still we get a prize now and then, just to keep our hands in.

"Sail ho!" We are under low canvas, and she is approaching us rapidly, but smelling a rat refuses our blank cartridge and passes on. We are in the race saddle at once after her. She answers to the second gun, and heaves-to, showing her colors without hesitation, knowing well her doom is sealed. She proves the clipper ship *Talisman*, from New York for Shanghai. Her cargo being per manifest American property, she is condemned; and prisoners, nautical instruments, and needed stores removed, she is committed to the flames. We secured from this vessel two twelve-pounder brass guns, with fixed ammunition to suit. At the time it was the subject of much comment what use these could possibly be put to. Semmes had an idea in connection with this *find*, though he kept his own counsel; like Mrs. Toodles's coffin plate, these things will come handy by and by.

We run through the trades and are having variable winds, still boarding numbers of neutrals and otherwise keeping busy, particularly in making the ship snug for bad weather. We are about to stretch over for the Cape of Good Hope, a long, dreary road, and shall soon be out of the way of commerce until we reach the pitch of the Cape. Albatross and gulls are putting in an appearance, which gives us hints of overcoats and pea jackets, and to Jack, notice that snoozing under the weather bulwarks on watch at night will soon be among the things of the past. We are just about ready for a long interregnum of boarding ships, and settling down to yarn-spinning, draughts, etc., pending the harvest of captures anticipated off the Cape, when, "Sail ho!" and we know the stranger is American, her long tapering masts and flaring bow telling the tale before her ensign is hoisted to the peak.

She proved the barque *Conrad* of Philadelphia, for New York from Buenos Aires, with wool. A lawful prize. A more beautiful specimen of an American clipper could not be produced—new, well-found, and fast, and, being barque-rigged, easy to handle with a small crew. Semmes determined to fit her out as a temporary cruiser. We had now a use for the guns captured on the ship *Talisman*—two brass twelve-pounders, battery enough to tackle the heaviest merchant ship, even with a crew inferior in numbers. These guns transferred to the *Conrad* and mounted in battery, Lieutenant John Low was assigned the command, with Midshipman William H. Sinclair as first lieutenant under an acting commission from Semmes. Twelve men were selected for the crew of the new ship, to be the Confederate States cruiser *Tuscaloosa*: Henry Marmelstein, second officer; James F. Minor, third officer (watch officers); Henry Legris, Edwin

Jones, William Rinton, Robert P. Williams, Thomas Williams, Martin Molk, Samuel Brown, Robert Owens, Thomas I. Altman, John Duggan. All is now ready for the christening; but this is so simple you would hardly suspect it a ceremony of such deep importance. A short document had been penned by Semmes and handed the future commander of the *Tuscaloosa*,[1] simple, yet of grave import. It was no less than a license to roam the seas, sink, burn, and destroy—and all in due form of law. A legal document none had the right to gainsay. What a vast power to place in the hands of any one man. Truly we may say the power of the commander of a man-of-war in times of war is the embodiment of President and Congress. Is it any wonder the simple children of the ocean—our crew—should look up to Semmes as an (almost) emperor?

The *Tuscaloosa* runs the colors of the Republic to the peak, the pennant to the mainmasthead. The crew of the *Alabama* man the rigging and cheer, the crew of the fledgling answer, and we have a new instrument of destruction afloat

---

1. Thus in twelve short hours we have commissioned, armed, officered, and provisioned another engine of war, and have thrust her out on her pilgrimage of destruction. Evening is now on us, the *Tuscaloosa* lost to us on the vast deep, and as we gather about the bridge and the glee club forms its circle for song, we first begin to miss the bright, cheery face of our tenor, Mid Sinclair, and later on, as the night-watches pass, the strong, firm countenance of our late-watch relief, Lieutenant Low. A gloom pervades the ship somewhat akin to that experienced when death has strode into your midst. It is by no means an exultant feeling that catches hold of our messmates, as they gather tonight about the mess-table. We appreciate that we have sent abroad a most insignificant representative on the ocean—one that, with a prize-crew on an enemy's deck, has left the bantam cruiser quite helpless. Our grave fears seem almost a forecast of facts to be. We can only record the *Tuscaloosa*'s cruise barren of results, our ship crippled in numbers, and her officers and crew denied the opportunity of participation in the *Alabama*'s glorious future career—a disappointment none but a naval man can fully appreciate.

on the 21st day of June, 1863. Both vessels fill away, and are soon lost to each other in the waste of waters.

What rapid changes! We are now ready for our cruise off the Cape, and are fortunate, in our daily boarding of neutrals, to find a vessel willing to take our prisoners to the Brazilian coast. Our decks are again clear, and we settle to the daily round of duties. Our worthy captain's secretary, Mr. W. B. Smith, will now for a time be continually sought out for reading matter by the officers and crew. He has charge of the library of the ship, and dull, uneventful days are ahead of us, stretching over for South Africa outside the beaten track of vessels; the return India and China traders rounding the Cape, and with the wind right astern making their way homeward via the historic Island of St. Helena, which they all sight if possible for a new departure.

The discovery has just been made after cutting adrift from the Brazilian coast that our ship's supply of hardbread has been attacked by the weevil and rendered useless. It being out of the question to continue our cruise without a fresh supply, the ship's head is turned for the near coast again. We soon find ourselves in the "variables"; and as the name indicates, we are recipients of all sorts of weather—much such as Mark Twain describes New England weather, thirty kinds in twenty-four hours, and "a great deal of it."

It is now the close of June; many, many neutrals boarded, but no prize; nor do we seem likely to get that ship's bread wanted but by a visit to Rio de Janeiro. "Sail ho!" and at last an American hull in sight. Chase is given in earnest, the stranger not liking the appearance of things and crowding sail. She refuses the order of a blank cartridge and continues obstinate, hoping some lucky turn may come in the way of a thick squall passing and shutting her in. But we are gaining on her rapidly; and after tiring of her obstinacy, being in a hurry to reach the coast and port, a hundred-pounder rifle shell is sent on a message to her, about three miles distant. As usual, the hint is taken, and the enemy luffs to the wind, and backing her after sail hoists her colors to the peak and awaits events.

We have an ugly sea on to board in, but the vessel is reached in safety. Her captain coming on board with his papers, it is soon assured that she is a prize—ship *Anna F. Schmidt*, from Boston to San Francisco, and has among her cargo the very description of bread we want and are on our way to Rio for, also the most welcome item of boots and shoes. In short, the cargo is a general one—just what we should have requested our Boston friends to put on board had we known they were sending to interview us.

Such a looting as now goes on, and throwing overboard of articles—with utter disregard of value—which happen to be in the way of our search. We are breaking out the hold to get at the much-needed ship's bread. Officers and men are also badly in need of shoes, and next Sunday all hands may appear at muster with fine new calfskin adorning their pedal extremities. The *Schmidt* is looted with an industry commensurate with our delight. The ocean is fairly covered with floating wealth; that is, from a money standpoint, though it is as valueless to us as so much gulfweed. We remove prisoners, chronometers, and flags, and apply the match, turning our head to the eastward again. A sudden change of destination for the officers and crew of the now burning ship. But lately bound to San Francisco, and now to Cape Town.

During the night we make a fine taut ship standing to the northeast and having the appearance of an American clipper, as well as we could judge through the darkness. Steam is given the ship, and we fairly fly after her, canvas assisting. It was a beautiful sight, the race of two greyhounds of the ocean. It proves a long chase, though we overhaul her not slowly, but at best a stern chase is a long one. All things have an end, and this may be the end of us. We are now close enough to discover in the sail a heavy man-of-war, and as always happens in such cases we both beat to quarters. She had made us out a cruiser. Our suspense was short. Upon being hailed, she reported herself Her Britannic Majesty's *Diomede*, homeward-bound to Plymouth. Through the trumpet comes the query from him, "I suppose that is some of your work?" alluding to the burning prize in the distance, "I saw you leaving her." Offers to take a mail for us, which was declined with thanks; we only desire to be reported "all well." We dropped astern of the *Diomede*; she was soon lost to sight. Hoisting propeller and letting steam go down, we are again on our way to the Cape.

Several days go by without event of moment, vessels passing but neutral. Just as we are again departing from the track of commerce, a sail is made from the masthead, pronounced by Evans "Yank," and no doubt. It required a succession of reminders in the way of blank cartridges, and finally the never-failing persuader, before she would luff up to the strong breeze. You can't but admire the pluck and never-say-fail disposition of the American skipper. So long as there is the least chance he holds on. You cannot tell: A United States cruiser may put in an appearance, or a friendly rain-squall shut him in, or the pursuer lose a mast in the strong breeze under a press of canvas.

Often the unexpected happens, so he trusts and hopes. The sail, upon examination of papers, proves the clipper ship *Empress* of Boston, from Callao to Antwerp. She is condemned and her officers and crew being removed, with such stores as we can find use for, the torch is applied; the last boat leaving her with one more chronometer for the sailing-master to care for and wind up.

We are now considerably crowded and inconvenienced with prisoners. It is impossible to make them decently comfortable in such weather as we are having, for it is the dead of winter. And they are in the way of working ship and washing decks. As to other work, it is not even attempted; which, by the way, is decidedly a compensation to Jack for the inconvenience of crowded decks. It is all dogwatch. There is an occasional exception, due to the sense of parental obligation. The group referred to is seated in a convenient spot under the weather bulwarks, the younger faces more or less lugubrious, the elder reflective, and yet beaming with that spontaneous benevolence which is such a reward to the possessor. The sea father is teaching his bantling to make sennit hats, to point ropes, tie matthew-walker, diamond, or other knots useful in nautical life, and his delight in the occupation is evidently in direct proportion to the thick headedness of the pupil; for the delay in realizing results considerably enhances the triumph when it does come; and the pleasure, after all, is not in the accomplishment but in its ardent pursuit.

The little chap, as a rule, is not ardent but decidedly reluctant; this only enhances Jack's sense of responsibility and gives opportunity for exercise of his talent as a lecturer and disciplinarian, which gives variety to the occupation. The youngster finds something in it at the end, unless he is especially unlucky, either in the way of pleasure or pain. His reward may be a bunch of raisins or it may be a taste of the "kitten," which is not, on the whole, any great improvement on the sorrows of pupilage. But when the feat is accomplished, the small chap finds lots of fun in it and soon becomes proficient through his disposition to show off among his own sort.

Farther aft in the waist, there is fun of another sort, but as certainly it has its victim. Somebody is badgering Evans, possibly Fulham, whose hard service is largely built on Evans's prophesying. The middies are represented pretty fully in this case. Maffitt, with mild, observant blue eye and those incipient side whiskers—very English "don't yer know"—which he is perpetually petting with one hand or the other; Anderson, professedly scornful of such facial ornaments but none the less a notable dandy, who is Semmes's reliance when we have to board a ship with lady passengers to be soothed and reassured and has reached the dignity of officer of the forecastle; and then, by way of contrast, boatswain's-mate Brosman, with a skin like a shark, and a quid in his jaw that has to be kept carefully to windward in a squall; or Johnson, of similar rank, who restively strokes his luxuriant beard like a pasha impatient to sentence his latest favorite to the sack, only restrained by deference to superiors from drawing upon himself the full blaze of ire which Fulham has aroused. But whoever may be for the nonce of the party, there has been no trouble about starting the fun. As usual, the only thing necessary is to express a doubt of Evans's infallibility in the matter of spotting Yankee ships. It makes no difference that the scene has been played before fifty or a hundred times. There is no such thing as joking with Evans on this subject. Start it when you will, and he is mad in a minute. But for their own satisfaction the jokers vary the style of attack. The assertion has just taken effect that there is evidence enough of his errors among the officers, though "Old Beeswax" has become fatuous in his confidence.

"I'll b-b-bet two sovs n-not one man here can p-p-prove a single mistake on me!" stutters Evans, too much excited to control his utterance.

"Done!" shouts Maffitt, who has been waiting his chance, "but what's the use of putting up on a fact that everybody knows? I say, Evans, you may as well come down gracefully, you know. Once in a way you can hit it off, and the rest of the time all you have to do is to say 'Neutral' and let it go so. Almost any of us could do that."

"Just tell me when I ever made a mistake!" foams Evans. "J-j-just one single time! I defy you t-t-to!"

Fulham calls order, and after a little more solemn chaff cites the case of a Nova Scotia barque that once on a time Evans said was a "Yank," while King, who was quizzing her through his glass, had pronounced her British.

"That all came of King's d—d foolishness," shouts Evans, infuriated at what he conceives to be the stupidity of his tormentors. "Everybody knows that a Province ship has the rig and cut of a Yankee, and if King had known anything, he would never have said she was British!"

"All the same," persists Fulham, "I understand from Anderson that 'Old Bim' is seriously thinking of sending you back into your watch and letting King do the scouting in future. Seems to be getting onto your lines. You'd better look sharp!"

This finishes Evans, who is just able to stagger out of the crowd, which by this time is laughing without restraint. He is only able to mutter as he retires, "When Old Bim puts that d—d shoal-water coast pilot in the crosstrees, you can have all my share of the prize-money he brings you for a five-pound note!"

This makes tame enough reading; but to those who saw this stalwart giant under the kidding of his messmates, the memory will always bring a smile.

The cape pigeon and albatross now warn us that we are approaching the stormy cape. The flight of these birds gives a curious substance and perspective to the blue, cloud-flecked sky and huge, foam-capped seas of this latitude. The idea of vast space is inseparable from the motions of the albatross. How effortless and sweeping his flight, now up and now down the gale to the limits of vision, and from the utmost distance suddenly returning to a position just above the decks where, balanced on his wide, snowy pinions, he slowly turns his head from side to side, a good deal after the manner of the first luff at inspection; and then, satisfied apparently with our makeup, wheels away to the weather-quarter, where he takes position and proceeds to act as escort. He regards us as some kind of a cousin, no doubt, and wonders why he cannot tempt us to rise and take a flight with him in the upper air. But anyway he means to be social.

The pigeons, on the other hand, do not venture away from the stern once they have got a sight of it, but with their soft, plaintive cry circle perpetually from quarter to quarter until twelve o'clock comes and the refuse from the galley is dumped from the lee shoot. Then they settle down to the feast and let the ship go on for a while without their attendance. But in a very few minutes they have returned to their play. No trouble to them either to find the ship or to catch her. They are greedy little wretches, though, and you can pull them aboard, as indeed you can the albatross, by trailing a baited line and hook over the stern. Once on deck they cannot rise without a helping hand, and they are anything but good sailors on shipboard, the motion of the ship making them seasick in short order. There is some fun in fishing for them, and there is no cruelty in the sport, for the hook does not hurt their bony bills. You will notice, though, that while you keep one of them captive Jack's lee eye is on you. His firm belief is that bad weather and bad luck will surely attend the harming of any of these creatures; and you can see, whatever his confidence in your humanity, he feels more comfortable when he sees it back again among its mates.

> They all averred, he'd killed the bird
> That made the winds to blow.

It is not really essential to bait for the cape pigeon; a black linen thread from a spool trailed astern will sooner or later get him tangled up, wings and feet, so you can haul him aboard. Albatross and cape pigeons are not fair-weather birds, though, by any means. You only see them in the region of storm and gale. So by this time we are having a touch of cape weather. At the same time, the menu at the mess-table is pleasantly varied with the fish we catch by trolling. They make a delicious chowder.

We are having a dull time, though, on the whole. Gather around the wardroom table and listen to one of the old officers as he relates, to pass the evening away, a few of his recollections of past days in the old navy. This relater had the advantage of many years' service, and knew by heart the jokes on the oldsters of past naval days.

"Well, it was on an East India cruise. The squadron was laying in Yeddo Bay. One of the vessels was commanded by as able an officer and seaman as we had in the United States Navy, but rather too fond of 'crooking his elbow.' The habit was so strong on him, and so widely known in the fleet, that it was impossible for the fact not to reach the knowledge of the commodore. Our hero was a great favorite with him, indeed with all, who admired the commander for his many fine personal qualities and remarkable ability as an officer. Still, the commodore could not shut his eyes to the unfortunate failing. He must either take official notice of it by preferring charges against the offender or remove him so that he could not see it. His regard for his subordinate suggested a method, which materialized in an order to proceed to a group of islands some hundreds of miles to the southward and make an extended inquiry as to the 'manners and customs of the natives,' and make a full report of same; the idea being that ere the commander returned, the squadron would be well on its way home. The trip was made, and the sloop returned after many months' cruise but to find the squadron (unfortunately for the commodore) still on the station.

There can be but little doubt our hero well knew the true intent of his banishment and mission, as the following official report will suggest. 'In obedience to your order of _____ date, I have the honor to report: Having visited the southern group of islands to inquire into the "manners and customs" of the natives, I have to submit; their customs are scandalous, and manners—they have none at all. Respectfully your Obedient Servant.' The squadron soon after dispersed without this case taking a serious turn.

"I can give you another good story on the same commander," says our yarn-spinner. "The squadron, consisting of a number of steam frigates, sailing sloops, and supply vessels, was at anchor. Our hero commanded one of the sailing vessels. A signal was hoisted from the flagship for the squadron to get up steam, when to the surprise and indignation of the commodore, at once from the masthead of the sailing vessel the signal was made out, 'My steam is up.' Instanter a signal from the flagship ordered her commander to 'repair on board.' Upon being ushered into his presence, the commodore reprimanded him quite severely, remarking, 'You are constantly making light of serious matters, sir! Indeed, you are drunk now, sir.' 'Well, Commodore!' was the reply. 'You made signal to—hic! get up steam, and I did it at once.'"

"Now give us some yarns of the war of 1812–1815."

"Well, here's a characteristic story on old Hull of frigate *Constitution* memory. Hull was noted for having the bump of official economy developed to that degree that it amounted to a mania. The first lieutenant of his ship had very frequently presented, for signature, requisitions for bass drumheads for use of the frigate's band. Hull had conceived the idea that a leak existed in this department. Determined to satisfy himself, he watched the band closely at play. He made the discovery, to his own satisfaction at least. Calling the bass drummer to his side, he interviewed him as follows:

'You d—d scoundrel! I've been watching you closely, and now know why you have been making so many requisitions for new drumheads. You keep beating the drum on the same spot in the middle. That's why you wear them out so fast! You beat your drum all around the sides in future, or, d—n you, I'll give you a dozen of the "cats."'

"Another story on old Hull would intimate a lack of music in his soul, however good a fighter he was. He was listening to his band playing a difficult piece of music, when his attention was all at once riveted on one of the musicians, who from time to time ceased to play, and then again resumed his part. With an excited air and manner, Hull beckoned to the man to approach him. 'You rascal, you!' said Hull, 'I've been watching you skulking at your play! Now, you go back and play all the time! I'll have no d—d skulkers in my band, and if I catch you at it again, your grog shall be stopped a week.'"

And now four bells (ten o'clock P.M.) has sounded. "All lights out," and Kell is off to report to the captain, "Ten o'clock, sir, and all secure for the night." All but the spar-deck is now hushed in silence.

CHAPTER VIII

SALDANHA BAY; REPAIRING SHIP; DEATH OF CUMMINGS; CAPTURE OF THE *SEA BRIDE*; RECEPTION AT CAPE TOWN; THE CRUISER *VANDERBILT*; NASTY WEATHER

IT IS THE LATTER PART of July when we make the land. Sails being clewed up and furled, we proceed under steam to the anchorage of Saldanha Bay on the west side of the coast of Africa, a British possession about sixty miles from Cape Town. We anchor in as beautiful and safe a harbor as a sailor could desire. The first thought suggests fresh provisions; and our reliable paymaster Gait soon negotiates the arrangements, and the gastronomic longings are satisfied. Beef, mutton, fish, and game are plenty, and the latter in great variety—deer, antelope, pheasant, hare, and quail, and on the seashore snipe, plover, and curlew. In the bay we notice wild duck and geese in immense flocks, surpassing even the renowned Chesapeake Bay.

But the romance chiefly lies in the fastnesses of the interior, where the lion and tiger may be hunted, and on the plains, where the ostrich and springbok are to be found in quantities. Naturally there is much excitement at the prospect of unlimited sport with rifles, guns, and fishing lines; and the sense of full protection from the cruisers of the enemy leaves us free to cast aside care and enter heart and soul into the enjoyments of the passing hours. Many are the expeditions planned and carried out. In the meantime, our commander has communicated with the governor of Cape Town, advising him of the arrival of the *Alabama* in British waters and requesting, as customary, the hospitalities of the colony. A matter of ceremony merely, this; for we had already experienced the hospitality of John Bull and knew we could depend on it.

We soon found our decks crowded with people from the shore, many of them from long distances in the interior. These people had heard of the *Alabama*, and the playful pranks indulged in by her on the ocean, and had come, bag, baggage, and tents, to make a stay and see all there was to see. They are Dutch, descendants of the first settlers of this portion of South Africa, though the colony has long since passed into the possession of the English. They are a simple, hardy, and brave race, hospitable to a fault. Although these people appear on the surface to have accepted the inevitable—the transfer of their country to British rule—and seem happy and prosperous under the present status, it is more than probable, the opportunity presenting itself and England being hard-pressed, they would throw their strength against their conquerors. In this event they would prove troublesome foes, being hardy, brave, and superb soldiers. In general physique and bearing they remind one of the Scottish household troops.

Long wagon trains followed each other in quick succession, coming from interior points to view the remarkable ship, visitors tumbling on board in an ever-flowing stream. They were in family parties, from the venerable grandfather and grandmother to the little tot carried in the arms. Verily the farmhouses must have been left to the faithful care of the house dog ad interim. Many and pressing were their invitations to visit the back country with them and enjoy the chase after big game. They had evidently observed our extensive preparations for the hunt. Some of our officers accepted and went; but as we saw no evidences of success, in the way of ostrich plumes or tiger skins, upon their return, and as we were oppressed by an ominous silence on their part as to where the wagons with the game had been left, the rest of us contained our eagerness and satisfied ourselves with more modest sport. Our guests were most curious and observant, watching each move of our crew engaged in the daily routine of duty, and handling each article carefully and critically, asking its use, and in the matter of the shot and battery the weight of each, range, etc.; indeed, it can be safely affirmed that upon the return home of these people, by comparing notes, all there was to be known of the *Alabama* could be learned in the colony.

The men are fine, stalwart specimens, dressed principally in corduroy knee breeches and hunting shirts, having, with their rifles slung over their shoulders and hunting knives in their belts, the appearance rather of pioneers and hunters than plain farmers from way back. A more frank, open-hearted lot it would be difficult to find. Offers pour in fast to guide us to the different hunting grounds, and presents of game brought on board to that extent as to amount to surfeit; indeed, it was everywhere, game to shoot, game to receive, but none to purchase. We are truly in a land flowing with milk and honey. And all this the property of our English cousins, just had for the taking.

John Bull is a remarkable fellow. Speak of the ubiquitous

Yankee, he is far in the shade as compared with his neighbor over the ocean. It is true he is to be found here and there scattered over the earth, but not everywhere as is the Englishman. Visit, as we are doing, the uttermost parts of the globe, wind with your ship into some intricate nook or channel, and behold, upon the flagstaff floats that flag; and investigate farther and you will find the land "good to behold," and that Johnny has appropriated it, or as he puts it, is exercising a fatherly care over it and establishing an outlet for the overproduction of the Manchester and Oldham mills and foundries. Still, none can gainsay that, with an occasional blunder now and then, Johnny is an advantage to the comparatively helpless peoples of the world, and improves their condition at once on coming into contact with them. His method is law, order, conservatism, but trade first and last.

We must not neglect an introduction to the fair lassies of the South African Colony. Buxom they are, brown and rosy, and with the assurance in their makeup of intimate acquaintance with the flail, churn, and washtub; yet, moreover, a delightful womanly grace diffusing itself through every movement. If our gallants of the *Alabama* prove as apt at carrying hearts by storm as at boarding with cutlass, we shall have here prisoners by the score. Our lady friends, true to their instincts and taste, are carried captive by the neat and orderly appearance of the steward's pantry, its complete methods. These matters appeal directly to their tastes, and elicit their approbation. You must know these people have, the large majority of them, never visited a ship before, and the order and neatness of a well-equipped man-of-war offer unusual attractions. No doubt many a suggestion presented itself to be imitated in the arrangement of the home pantry of the future.

We find the bay abundantly supplied with fish, and of excellent flavor, having hauled our seine several times and tested the matter. But all is not play. Our ship is storm-beaten and rusty, wanting paint wherever previously applied, decks to be caulked, sails mended, etc. Indeed, we may now be said to be in our own private dockyard, and our dock-master Kell is hard at it. No recreation does *he* indulge in until the work has at least been cut out in its entirety, and is well on the way to completion. He is ably assisted by the corps of fitters-out in the persons of boatswain Mecaskey, gunner Cuddy, sailmaker Alcott, and carpenter Robinson. These gentlemen have advised with and worked under the direction of our efficient executive from the fitting-out of the *Sumter* to date, and you will find the *Alabama* looking like a bride before she weighs anchor for Cape Town. It is rarely that a ship has such a complete dockyard within her-self, and it explains clearly the ability of Semmes to complete a cruise of two years in all climates, and undergoing more wear and tear than falls to the lot of most men-of-war in twice this time, without once going into a regular dockyard.

Jack is having the least fun now, hauling the seine being about the only congenial occupation for him. Hunting has no charms; the fatigue incident to heavy hunting accou-trements soon brings him "on his beam-ends," and he wan-ders back to his boat the victim of ennui and restlessness, and glad when time arrives to return on board. A sailor, with all the romance of his composition, as a rule fails to appreci-ate the quiet and calm of rural existence, demanding the more exciting presentments of life. There is no lively thor-oughfare here, no casino, and no towboat in the way of a sailor boardinghouse runner to "steer him" to the rum mill, steep him in oblivion, rob him of his floating home, and fi-nally reship him, suddenly turn his paths in a contrary di-rection, and open up new scenes and strange companions. Such are the delights of the sailor's life.

We are doing rapid work on the repairs to the ship, the result in a measure of the apathy of the men as to liberty, and we are nearly ready for sea. Our ship, however, is to make but a short cruise this time, only as far as Cape Town, for coal; and at same time to pay our respects to the governor of the colony, Sir Philip Wodehouse, who has already given us assurance of a hearty welcome so soon as we are ready to accept the hospitality of the Cape. We are to have at this point a great sorrow in our home circle.

A hunting party formed for duck shooting, and composed of engineer Cummings, master Bulloch, and the writer, had passed the day, August 3, 1863, at the head of the bay. Late in the evening, on the return to the ship, Cummings shot himself through the heart in an effort to pull the gun to himself by the muzzle. The hammer of the gun caught the thwart. Without an outcry or groan, but with a look of despair and appeal never to be forgotten, he sank into the bottom of the boat, his body coming together limp as a rag. It was so sudden and unexpected as to stun and appall, and, used as both of us had been to sudden death, tears only relieved and restored our straying senses. Our first impulse was to pull to the beach for assistance from some Hottentot laborers plowing in a field, but were met with raised hands and dilated eyes. Evidently under the impression we had committed the deed, all assistance on their part was emphatically refused. They dropped the plows and ran, leaving us alone, far from the ship, and night coming on.

After a long weary pull, for the wind had left us, we reached the gangway. It was midnight, yet the side of our ship was crowded with heads and the dead silence on board seemed to indicate a premonition of sorrow in our arrival. Reaching the deck, the sad intelligence was conveyed through the officer of the watch to Semmes. The writer was invited to the cabin, and the story of the tragedy retold in all its details. Semmes was deeply affected, trembling with emotion, and brushing away a tear creeping slowly down his weather-beaten cheek, he said, "That will do, sir; good night." Slowly and carefully the body is carried below, the wound examined by Llewellyn, and with a watch by it left for the night, the officers and men with soft step and bated breath retiring to their quarters. And here a pause for the student of human emotions. A soul has suddenly winged its flight to the undiscovered country, and its sudden loss has numbed and paralyzed the senses of his fellows. Now, change the mode and scatter the casket of this same soul piecemeal with the cruel shot or shell, and the dying groans of the companion are smothered in the shout of victory, and not a tear need we spare the dead messmate.

Morning comes, the Confederate flag for the first time at half-mast on our ship, and drooping in the light air as though in sympathy with the surroundings, advises and warns our friends onshore. The news has reached them, and our decks are free of visitors. Jack passes his holystone easily over the deck in the morning clearing, and walks with lowered eye and lightsome step. In single file the full complement of ship's boats, with muffled oars and flags at half-mast, form the funeral cortege, and in a quiet spot, the gift of a sympathizing farmer, we laid our shipmate to rest. Kell read the beautiful funeral service of the Protestant Episcopal Church over the remains. A stone now marks the spot, ordered from Cape Town, and put in place through the attention of the officers of Her Britannic Majesty's squadron on this station.

Our boat is once again in shipshape, and we are not ashamed to compare her with any of the "cracks" of Her Majesty's service. Good-byes have been said, and with the request that our Saldanha friends will keep green the grave of our shipmate, we steam out of the bay and stand south for the Cape. As we are at leisure, the ship at sea and settled to the routine of everyday life, with no vessels of the enemy's merchant fleet likely to require our attention, thoughts will often stray to that faraway home, in the throes of a desperate and unequal struggle. We know that thoughts tending this way are futile, that to do, to act, is practical; yet we cannot dismiss the haunting fear that our brave fellows are but actors in a forlorn hope, a useless struggle; hence cui bono, this knight-errantry of the *Alabama*? But steady; we must strangle these whisperings of the weaker side of our manhood and resolve to strive against all discouragement.

It is now the 5th of August. The *Alabama* nearly a year on her cruise. We are greeted with a surprise today, and an agreeable one. Ahead we make a sail idling along in the light air, and soon we are alongside the *Tuscaloosa*. You must know, reader, the *future* on the *Alabama* is a sealed document to officers and men. No cabinet to our President! Semmes settles everything *in propria persona*, hence the surprise at meeting our young cock-chicken, the Confederate States barque *Tuscaloosa*, in this out-of-the-way place. To Semmes alone it was expected. It had been prearranged, and our skipper was, no doubt, impatient to learn if Low had "struck ile." He had; but only to be cataloged as a grampus. The sum of the cruise being the bonding of the American ship *Santee* with a neutral cargo. This bond is in the category of Confederate notes—simply a curio. After the interchange of experiences, supplying our tender with late news, papers, and light literature, she fills away under orders for Simon's Town, and we on our course for Cape Town. We soon leave her hull-down in the light air. Simon's Town is a safe harbor, hence the *Tuscaloosa* is sent there, for she is needing repairs. Our ship is bound to the Cape Town settlement as the official residence of the governor. The harbor is open and dangerous in heavy weather, yet we have the advantage of steam to work off a lee shore if necessary.

August 5, 1863. One of the most exciting episodes of our cruise occurs today. We had approached within six or seven miles of the town, or rather of the headland, the wind being very light at the time. We made a barque ahead, standing in for the land. She had all the appearance of an American to the average judge on board our ship. Her nationality was soon positively assured by master's-mate Evans; and steam was crowded on to overhaul and capture her before she should reach the charmed marine league. We owe the success of the venture to the light air prevailing, and full steam-power that we happened to have at the time chase was made. We were soon alongside; and, throwing an officer and boat's crew on board, stopped our engine immediately alongside of her. The prize-master made a rapid examination of her papers and having no doubt of the legality of the seizure directed her captain with his papers to our ship, retaining command pending Semmes's action. The barque proves the *Sea Bride* of Boston, from New York to the east coast of Africa, "and a market" or, in other words, on a coast-trading voyage, her cargo consisting of prints, muslins, notions, etc. A typical trading cargo.

The *Alabama* is now at a standstill, the barque hove-to with maintopsail to the mast, while we take the compass bearings of the headlands and lights. We anticipate a controversy over the distance of the barque from the land at the time of capture and are preparing for it. We make the *Sea Bride* six miles from the land, and so record in the logbook with the compass bearings; and Semmes condemns the vessel; Fulham, who has charge of her, receives orders to stand "on and off" the land, waiting for instructions. We cannot, as you know, reader, carry the prize into port.

As may be imagined, the American consul, assisted by the mates and captain of the captured vessel, prepare and present numerous documents and affidavits to the effect that the capture was made inside of the marine league supported, of course, by compass bearings, etc. A long and tedious correspondence grows out of it. A crossfire of formidable documents passes between the governor, Semmes, the American consul, and the skipper of the *Sea Bride*. Statements of lighthouse keepers, telegraph signal men, *id omne genus*, are examined, and the men catechized in person.

It was a muddle as to statements; the significant part of it being, however, that the witnesses on the part of the authorities all agreed with the official statement of Semmes forwarded Governor Sir Philip Wodehouse. The senior British naval commander on the station, at the request of the governor, also made an examination into the subject; and the result was to fully establish that the vessel was from five to six miles from the land at the time of capture, and thus a legal prize and beyond the protection of the British government. The *Sea Bride* hung about outside in charge of a prize-crew, while the *Alabama* came to anchor in the bay. Semmes did not order the *Sea Bride* away, but awaited properly the decision of the English local government. Our position was quite satisfactory. Visits were exchanged between the governor, Admiral Sir Baldwin Walker, and officials generally; although the controversy referred to above was pending. We were not treated as possible culprits; the attention to us was universal.

The scene on the hilltops commanding the sea, the morning of the capture, as viewed from the deck of the *Alabama*, beggars description. As we were informed by the Cape Town newspapers, every vehicle that could be commanded was pressed into service for the ride to the point of vantage, and price was no object to the sightseers. A chance of a lifetime presented itself, and reminded the writer of the appearance of the shores of Hampton Roads the morning of the *Merrimac-Monitor* fight.

It is safe to say Cape Town was almost depopulated, and

the excitement emphasized by the general turnout to visit the ship at her anchors. Every imaginable form and model of boat were represented in the throng around our ship. Boatmen and longshoremen, struggling, vociferating and swearing to get first alongside. Boats of the rowing clubs, their crews in neat and appropriate uniform; yachtmen on their craft; tugs, passenger boats, and even dugouts; anything that could float was brought into requisition. You may imagine our officers and men busily employed. The chief object of the visit—to coal ship—is relegated to the dim future. It is evident our task at present is solely to stand by and be questioned. The English, the foster fathers of the *Alabama*, are naturally proud of their creation, and they appear to be also in sympathy with us and our cause. Our crew are about one-half English man-of-war's men, and have found among the sailors of the English squadron here many old shipmates, and doubtless they have already planned a glorious time together on shore the first liberty day.

So we are entertaining fore and aft, every man of our ship's company being busy; and the wonder is that Kell and the officer of the deck have a hat-brim left, what with the bowing and removal of chapeaux at the gangway. Semmes is not to be envied. Seated in state in his cabin, Bartelli his steward, as master of ceremonies, the crowd surges in and out of the cabin. Now an official, redundant in gold lace, epaulets, and "orders," hands his card to the steward, who, fully impressed with the rank and importance of the visitor, elbows his way to the august presence, presents the card to Semmes, and with an affirmative answer re-elbows the official to the presence of our all-important functionary. Bartelli is a scientist in his way, knows all the grades of grandeeism, and just when to pop the champagne. It is amusing to watch the air of consequence that sits upon the countenance of our captain's steward. A very Chesterfield he, when the occasion calls for it, and he is a born diplomat in disposing of such as in his opinion are not an honor or ornament to the cabin. Bartelli, however, never offends. The ladies, in person or by attorney, in the way of a delicately scented billet-doux accompanying a present of choice fruit or bouquet, are in great force; and it frequently occurred to the writer as he glanced his eyes cabin-hatch-ward, that as least *one* lady in Dixie's far-off land might have felt some jealousy at the enthusiasm of this female inundation of the *Alabama*'s cabin.

Day after day this avalanche of visitors is poured on our deck, until we verily wish we had a printed form of answers to questions pasted around the ship. The weather at this time is delightful. The last of the winter, but balmy and soft, approaching in temperature our spring or autumn; and, as we learn, this colony is the Elysium of consumptives. So far the storms prevalent at this season have not visited us, hence the ship is crowded. Later on we shall have a heavy gale and clear decks. Boats cannot live in the sea kicked up in this anchorage by a blow, if we except the heavier ones for special service. Our officers are the recipients of many kind invitations to parties, balls, and country outings; and as only duties such as keeping port-watch demanded the attention of officers and men, both, by watches, are on shore. Jack and his chum from the English fleet are to be seen arm in arm standing before the wind with light kites out alow and aloft, bound to sailor town, the newfound mate from the *Narcissus* being the pilot.

All Cape Town is agog; and the sailor boardinghouse keeper and the ladies of the "east end" are on the tiptoe of expectation, the latter drawing heavily on their stock of ribbons and furbelows for the evening ball. We visit, by invitation, the celebrated "Constantia" vineyards, a few miles from the town, and are hospitably entertained at dinner and shown over the vineyard. The proprietor is a Hollander, an old settler, and with his family of grown sons and daughters entertains us quite royally. We find them cultivated and refined, their hospitality vying with that of our English hosts. Fruits of various kinds are abundant, particularly grapes, the latter being of exquisite flavor and unusual size, weighing many pounds to the bunch. The Constantia wine is celebrated the world over for its exquisite flavor, being a ladies' wine, sweet and but slightly intoxicating. A present of a cask of this wine was made our commander by our hosts, a most substantial one when one appreciates its market value.

We were forcibly reminded that we were now in the land of the tiger by observing, as ushered into the parlor by the servant, the stuffed form of one in a crouching attitude, in the act of springing, its eyes glaring with fearful realism. It startled us sensibly. The country is richly diversified with mountain and valley, and in the highest state of cultivation, the Boers of the colony being ideal farmers, thrifty and industrious. Verily John Bull knows a good thing when he sees it, and this is a land of milk and honey and diamonds. Our commander is entertained by Admiral Sir Baldwin Walker. The dinner was appointed for the evening, and the captain's coxswain was instructed to have his boat ready for the trip. At the appointed time, the gig was manned, and Freemantle, proud of his boat and mission, shoved off from the side of our ship. The gig reached the pier after dark; and Semmes, calling his coxswain aside, instructed and warned him not to leave for the town, nor to allow any of the boat's crew away from the dock. Upon Semmes's return he was not long in discovering that his heretofore trustworthy coxswain was "three sheets in the wind," and "catching crabs" with the stroke oar. He was ordered to trail his oar, and soon sank to sleep under the seats of the boat. The next morning Freemantle was brought to the mast for punishment and disrated. The next day he asked to see the captain again.

Removing his cap, he asked permission to go onshore, adding that he did not wish to stay but a short time, and if the favor was granted he would not ask liberty again during the cruise. The captain, struck with the earnestness of the man and the request coming so soon on the top of punishment, asked an explanation. "You see, Captain," he answered, "I was doing my duty faithfully, keeping both myself and crew on the dock. You had finished dinner abovestairs, when the admiral's coxswain appeared on the pier and asked me to dine downstairs with him, and try a bottle of the admiral's grog. I several times refused, but he stuck to me like a barnacle. Yielding at last to the tempter, I left the boat, and you know the rest. I can say, however, Captain, for my boat's crew, they did not disobey your orders, only myself. Now, what I want is a few hours' leave, until I can come up with that admiral's coxswain, and give him the d—dest thrashing he ever had." To this the captain replied, with a smile at the oddity of the situation, "Your anger is misplaced. You alone are to blame; the man was simply tendering you hospitality and a compliment. Go forward; you cannot go onshore." I will add that Freemantle's case blew over, and he was reinstated to his former position.

We are cut off from the shore for a day or two by one of the periodical storms; and many officers and men are shorebound, unable, except at great risk, to reach the ship. To all intents and purposes, she had as well, or better, be at sea. None but a class of boats constructed for the purpose can approach her. She is riding to a mountainous sea and fairly dipping her nose under as she plunges in the trough, our chain cables vibrating and groaning like taut fiddle strings. We have both "bowers" ahead, and cables payed out to extreme length. As dangerous an anchorage as our ship ever had. We have a tough time in getting our crew on board, indeed do not succeed fully; but as we are going to the safe and near port of Simon's Town, we can, with the assistance of the police and our own efforts, get hold of Jack later on, we presume.

It is now the 9th of August; and, arrangements completed by our worthy paymaster as to provisions, etc., we weigh anchor and under steam start for a safer and more comfortable anchorage. We have been so busy and excited as verily to forget the numerous hints given us by the officers of the English squadron as to the *Vanderbilt*. This cruiser was really on our track, and close aboard of us several times, most likely within sound of our guns. We have had descriptions of the power, speed, and battery of this ship, and the fate awaiting us upon capture (as put by the officers of the *Vanderbilt* upon her late visit here) such as might bring our hairs to gray and our appetite to nil. But of one thing be assured, Semmes intends keeping the noiseless tenor of his way; and unless the *Vanderbilt* puts in appearance in very substance we shall keep on burning ships wherever found. We have to double the Cape of Good Hope in going to Simon's Town—a bold rock headland, the clouds spread over its summit much like a tablecloth for the genie of storms. We have a pleasure trip of it, however, the air balmy and soft as spring. What a time we should have now if the *Vanderbilt* is hiding on the other side to carry out the program laid down to the officers of the English squadron! We shall have a side-wheel steamer to tackle, at any rate; and in spite of her formidable battery of eleven-inch guns we have a chance of disabling her paddle wheels.

We are not looking out for prizes now, or thinking of them; and, as the unexpected always happens, here we have it. "Sail ho!" right ahead we make a ship, pronounced at once by our expert to be American. We are under steam, so that in an hour we are alongside of her, the wind being very light and she making little or no progress. Upon being boarded she proved to be the *Martha Wenzell* of Boston, from Akyab for Falmouth, England, with rice. She was christened at her launch under a lucky star; for she was, upon taking bearings of the land, found to be within British territory. And our English friends have been too kind to us in the matter of the *Sea Bride* (to say nothing of leaning affectionately otherwise towards us) for us to think of jeopardizing friendship by opening up a new controversy in international law. The *Martha Wenzell*, though five to eight miles from the nearest land, was within the mouth of the bay, hence a question as to the legality of the seizure. The captain of the *Wenzell* was dumbfounded upon learning he would be allowed to proceed on his voyage. A poor compliment, however, this amazement at our according simple justice to him. We fill away and leave him to the enjoyment of the surprise.

We haul inshore, sight the light ship, take a pilot, and anchor near our protégé, the Confederate States barque *Tuscaloosa*. The usual naval etiquette is gone through, a boat from the flagship *Narcissus* visiting us with a lieutenant in charge and with the compliments of the admiral tendering us the hospitalities of the port. Nothing could exceed the attentions and kindness extended us here, and indeed at all British colonies we called at. You may have noticed we make no reference to an interchange of salutes, a custom of all time in the navy. It was omitted in our case; the British government having decided that we were not entitled to a salute under a status of simple belligerent rights, acknowledged by the principal nations of the world. Hence it was omitted, pending the absolute fact of a conquered peace, and entry into the catalog of nations. But naught else was omitted to show respect for a young nation struggling for independence, or for its representatives. Balls, entertainments, and dinner parties are the order of the day and night here; but sandwiched in we manage a little work also, for a ship (like a young lady) is never quite finished.

Our men are again treated to a run on shore, Jack being in his element here, surrounded by chums from the English men-of-war; and then he received in the Cape Town mail sundry epistles of a tender nature from Nancy and black-eyed Susan—gushing epistles such as require his personal acknowledgment; and the mail-coach is driving the liveliest trade it has had for many a month. An impromptu boat race is gotten up between crews of the *Alabama* and the flagship; but honors are easy, both crews and boats being English and about equal as to muscle.

A little trouble was caused us at this point by the American consul, the presence of our new cruiser, the *Tuscaloosa*, in the port undergoing repairs, having stirred up the ire of the American representative. A communication is addressed by him to the governor, calling attention to the status of the *Tuscaloosa* (which was formerly the barque *Conrad*), captured and fitted out by Semmes in June last, and suggesting that it was England's duty to seize and restore her to her former owners. This the governor very properly refused to admit, having no right to inquire into the antecedents of the *Tuscaloosa*. He could simply know the vessel as a Confederate man-of-war, and as such extend her the hospitalities of the port and permission to recruit both ship and crew. The right of commissioning the vessel was within the provisions of international law.

You may be sure Semmes had a case that the twistings and windings of law officers could not muddle. Still, the consul had done but his duty in making all efforts to restore her to her former owners. We shall see later that the matter is not fully settled at this time, the Queen's counsel upon the later return of the *Tuscaloosa* to Cape Town advising the seizure of the vessel, and test of the case; which resulted in the loss of the services of the ship to our cause for the remainder of the war and her final surrender to her original owners. It was decided that, as she was never taken to a home port and condemned by a prize-board, she could not be held by us in a neutral port. The case was, however, re-opened by Semmes, the British Crown *finally* admitting the perfect right of Semmes, as the representative of his government, to commission and use the ship on the ocean, and that the *Tuscaloosa* was entitled to *all* belligerent rights accorded other Confederate cruisers—an absolute triumph for Semmes.

We are ready for sea now, but in a most disabled state. What between the American consul's efforts and those of the boardinghouse sharks, seducing and hiding the men away, and the hospitality of the English man-of-war's men and of black-eyed Susan, we are shorthanded, but must put to sea, matters of vital importance demanding our attention. We get the *Tuscaloosa* off this time and follow her on the next day.

August 15 we leave Simon's Town for a cruise off the pitch of the cape, having the day before dispatched the Tuscaloosa to join the *Sea Bride* at Angra Pequeña. We are now in the perpetual stream of commerce from the East Indies. The *Vanderbilt* should be here. We are having alternate storm and calm, day and day about. In all cases under close reefs. We remain here ten days, nearly stationary, giving our tenders ample time to reach Angra under sail. We board many vessels day and night. Not a Yankee in the vast fleet.

Our nearest approach to collision with the *Vanderbilt* occurred during this short raid. In the first night watch, just before four bells (ten o'clock), the weather thick and night dark, the strike of four bells was heard by our watch-officer, on a vessel close aboard. The night-glasses disclosed a very large steamer, looming high out of the water and lying, like ourselves, in a loafing attitude. It would be a mere accident if she should make us out, our vessel lying so low in the water, and weather favoring. To order that our bell be not struck, put up helm, and report the fact to our captain, were precautions of a flash. By the time "Old Beeswax" had bunched into his pea jacket and reached the deck, even scout Evans, with his selected night-glasses, failed to conjure up her outlines. The *Alabama*'s fate is to be other. You need not doubt, reader, but that we had sighted the *Vanderbilt*.

The *Tuscaloosa* is bound to Angra Pequeña, as also the *Sea Bride*, in command of master's-mate Fulham. Both are to rendezvous at this point; and the *Alabama*, after making a short cruise off the pitch of the Cape, is to meet them. Angra Pequeña is a bay on the African coast and claimed by nobody, that is, no civilized power is exercising jurisdiction over it. It is the land of the Hottentot, who know nothing of international law and care less. We are to be there soon.

The *Alabama* is now battling with the "brave west winds" again, "hove-to" in the great highway of commerce, awaiting her prey. A more dangerous and uncomfortable fortnight the *Alabama* never experienced during her entire cruise. It is blowing incessantly, with spit of rain and snow, for we are now about sixty miles to the southward of the Cape and weather cold. Vessels are flitting past us in the darkness like specters, and woe to us if we should be run down. We are thinking more of this than of the *Vanderbilt*, which vessel is cruising off here likewise. We make and board many sail, but they all prove to be neutrals or transferred Americans—a most unprofitable experience every way, nothing in it to reward extreme exposure, labor, and suffering. The elements are too many guns for us. The seas are tremendous, and gales practically incessant. And, besides, merchant ships of the enemy have the run of several degrees of latitude here, if they choose to make an unusual course to keep out of our way. The reason for our making the attempt to waylay them here is then peculiar, as will be seen anon. Enough, at present, to say it was utterly fruitless. And now, having thoroughly satisfied ourselves of the uselessness of continuing it, we clew up our canvas and steam into Angra Pequeña, where the *Tuscaloosa* and *Sea Bride* are waiting for us. We anchor in the beautiful and roomy bay in the latter part of August, and here close the first year of the cruise of the *Alabama*.

CHAPTER IX

WE MAKE A DEAL; A CHANCE FOR HANDLING PRIZE-MONEY; ADVENTUROUS CUSTOMERS; SALE OF THE *SEA BRIDE*; FISHING; THE *VANDERBILT* AGAIN; SECOND VISIT TO CAPE TOWN

IN THE BAY OF ANGRA PEQUEÑA we find our two ships as expected, and near them an English vessel having on board several merchants from Cape Town. The truth is that our rendezvous here, as well as our late stormy cruise off the Cape, was instigated by an incident of most unexpected and surprising character. In short, Semmes was approached by several merchants who had formed a syndicate with a view to purchasing and disposing of his prizes. That such a thing as realizing on our captures was possible, when they could be taken into no civilized port without being seized and held for the original owners, had not once occurred to us. But the scheme as unfolded looked easy enough of accomplishment, and of course it was most attractive to us. If we could not deliver the property within British waters, there were hereabouts several ports that nobody owned but the Hottentot, who neither knew nor cared for the provisions of international law. And as to the disposal of the goods by the purchasers, here was a whole continent, more densely populated, probably, than either North or South America, to find a market in.

There was disappointment, no doubt, at our putting in an appearance without the expected string of prizes from our late cruise. But the *Sea Bride* and the cargo of the *Tuscaloosa* were substantial assets and well enough for a first venture. As it afterward proved, perhaps our ill luck was the means of saving the speculators from ruin.

> The best-laid plans o' mice an' men
> Gang alt agley.

And that they do so is not always to be accounted a misfortune.

Proposing to keep our trading place a secret between those interested, we had of course turned over the master and crew of the *Sea Bride* to the care of the American consul, though we had taken care to keep the ship at sea. Perhaps for the moment the lust of gain was upon us sufficiently to give us a touch of the feeling that inspired the buccaneers of old. Our customers were certainly dipping into the adventurous, since they proposed to purchase and trade from port to port in a ship that had no nationality, no responsibility, and no protection but what she could give herself. The affair seemed to us romantic, anyway. And the chance of realizing for our crew, as well as ourselves, some of the wealth that figured so nobly on our ledgers, and putting it beyond the chances of war, marvelously sweetened the severities of our service while we thought we had it.

But now, in the cabin of the *Alabama*, as we look down through the skylight from the deck, may be seen a serious and businesslike group. On one side Semmes and the paymaster Galt with the invoices and other papers necessary to an estimate of values. On the other, the gentlemen who were making the venture, with their clerks and their bags of gold.

The subject matter has been discussed and satisfactorily arranged, and now may be seen the opening of the bags of gold and telling them out on the cabin table. For hours, in the quiet of our safe and close retreat, may be heard the clink, clink of British sovereigns as they are verified by our careful paymaster. It was interesting to observe our Jack, one by one, cast a sidelong glance down the cabin skylight and take in the counting of the gold, and with a wink and remark of satisfaction to his shipmate saunter leisurely forward. Jack is taking in the practical demonstration and no doubt mentally endorsing the (at the time taken with a grain of salt) persuasive words of "Old Beeswax" at Terceira some months since, when in a speech of honeyed phrase he was bidding for a crew. No better proof of the judicious methods of discipline outlined by Semmes could be submitted than that under them, though engaged in acts somewhat suggesting the pranks of the buccaneers, our crew were as well held in hand as though serving on an English man-of-war in times of profound peace, and at the same time in a state of perfect contentment.

The entire cargo of the *Sea Bride* has been sold with the vessel. The wool is to be shipped to England and sold on joint account for the benefit of both parties to the contract. Wool, being a product of the Cape Colony, was not included in the purchase for evident reasons. The transfer is completed, and the *Sea Bride*, a wanderer like ourselves, starts out on her trading venture. The idea of her purchasers is to move along the coast from village to village, disposing of the goods in the way of barter, and upon the completion of the cruise to transfer the purchased cargo of ivory, wool, etc., to a regular British vessel, destroying or otherwise removing the identity of the purchased prize. It is a paradoxical position, this of the *Sea Bride*. She has no papers, no nationality; at the same time, she cannot be regarded as a pirate or outlaw, the act of purchase having been consummated with the agent of a duly recognized government. However, the embryo entanglement that might have occupied the attention of an admiralty court was settled in a summary manner by the loss, later on, of the vessel. She was wrecked on the African coast, and became a total loss.

About one-third the market value of the *Sea Bride* and her cargo was realized by us; and, weighing the loss of time and upsetting of the routine of daily man-of-war life, we have not profited greatly by our fairy market. However, the visible handling of gold in exchange for something we had heretofore been offering up as a sacrifice to the ocean gods helped our crew to realize that not only glory is theirs, but substantial prize-money.

We are anchored on the skirt of a barren, bleak backcountry. There is nothing to tempt us ashore; but we have a visit from over the ridge separating the beach from the interior—a small lot of Hottentot, the only inhabitants we have seen. They are poor and emaciated, naked, and look as though half-starved. Timidity and wonder at first hold them spellbound; but gathering assurance from our gestures and invitations they advance, and being pressed by signs make the acquaintance of our rations, devouring the food as though long deprived of any.

We hauled seine, supplying ourselves and newfound acquaintances with delicious fish of unknown species to us, but palatable, and an agreeable addition to our salt horse and rice. I have no doubt our Hottentot friends, if they have the science of language, chatted many a day after over the visit of the strange vessel and her generous behavior. Such a feast must have been an event in their lives. We are put to inconvenience here by the disarrangement of our condensing apparatus, and have to depend upon the three companion vessels for a supply of fresh water for our ship's company. This is a sterile coast, no water, no green thing, not so much as a stunted bush; sand everywhere. However, we are *near* civilization; and our own engineers are fully equal, with necessary material, to the repairing of the condenser. Low being ordered to cruise off the coast of Brazil in the moderate latitudes, and take his chances of picking up the fish that slip through our net in the Strait of Sunda, we see him off and wend our way once more to Simon's Town. The *Tuscaloosa* is to meet us here some months hence upon our return from the Eastern raid.

Again we find ourselves on the highway of commerce off the Cape, our commander no doubt vexed and impatient at his want of luck here, and unwilling to revisit our old friends of the British squadron without being able to report even a bite. But, so it turns out, we see neither the *Vanderbilt* nor any but neutral sails. Our enemy is getting wary, no doubt, doubling the Cape outside the beaten track; but, nearer the truth of the case, he is laid up in the India ports, his occupation gone, and waiting for some John Bull or others with plethoric pocketbooks to come along and make the purchase of a fine clipper ship at fifty cents on the dollar of value. The English flag is just now safer to fly than the Stars and Stripes. Wonderful the work of a single modestly armed cruiser. We remain here without result (save we shall be reported to commerce as guarding the highway of the Cape) until the middle of September, when we fill away for Simon's Town.

The first news we get upon arrival is that the *Vanderbilt*

had coaled ship here, and left two days since for another cruise, so supposed, off the Cape. She is evidently hot in the chase, having vibrated between Cape Town and Simon's Town nearly ever since our departure for Angra Pequeña. There would be some chance either in fight or run for us, but none for Low in the *Tuscaloosa*, so we are gratified to know he is winging his way up to the latitudes of the Brazils. Again are we the victims of the *ghost stories* imparted to us by the officers of the fleet and the citizens of the town. We soon learn all about the battery, power, and speed of our affectionate seeker, and can almost give you a diagram of her gun-deck and other appointments, so faithfully are they pictured to us by our friends. No doubt the officers of the *Vanderbilt* are equally well posted as to our strength of armament, speed, etc., and their mouths are watering to gather us in and suddenly become heroes and admirals.

Should the two vessels sight each other, it is a puzzle to predict the result. The *Vanderbilt* is much the more powerful vessel in every way, but very vulnerable in her paddle wheels, slow to answer to her helm, owing to her great length, and in a seaway unable to handle her heavy battery with safety. On the other hand, the *Alabama* is quick to the touch of her helm, low in the water, and with pivot-guns of sufficient weight of metal and projectile to cripple the enemy in her paddle wheels. We should not have run from her; indeed, from all we could gather, she had the speed of us, and it would have been no option, a case of "in the corner and fight it out." But we are simply indulging in the speculative. We never had the chance to tackle her, and hence shall never know.

We could get no coal here, the market having been exhausted of supply by the *Vanderbilt*—a great coal consumer she. We order a supply by vessel from Cape Town and await its arrival. Now is your time, Captain Baldwin, if the fates are smiling your way. You should have some signal rockets in the hands of the American consul of sufficient force to apprise the *Vanderbilt* of our presence, and withdraw her from her occupation of hide-and-seek off the Cape. Again the rounds of pleasure and dissipation are the order of the day and night. Our crew have soon again forgotten their ship and the object of their cruise. We shall have a difficult time scraping them together. They are the heroes of the hour, and we greatly fear we shall lose many of our most valuable men. We have many influences working against the gathering of them in. The dear girls, with all their assumed Southern proclivities, are, in fact, enemies, intoxicating our heroes with their attractions; the boardinghouse runner has his eye to business, and the American consul is not idle; for the first time perhaps in his official career he has the inward consciousness of feeling his salary well earned. He is plying our simple, befuddled lads with grog and cash, and placing a further sum "where it will do the most good." But it is the unavoidable consequence of port visiting, and we must make the best of it. We can, of course, recruit our complement, but not in quality. The drillmasters will have the old, and to them humdrum, gun exercises to go over with raw men.

The ship is again somewhat in confusion, decks thronged with visitors. We have reestablished the land ferry to Cape Town, and officers and men are journeying back and forth. Occasionally one of our truant men puts in an appearance, having succeeded in running the gauntlet of Susan and the other shoals, and we are too well pleased to hint of "irons" or the "brig." We have, as a cicerone to the officers, a member of the reporters' staff of the Simon's Town newspaper, and as usual just the fellow to fill the bill. Not only can he suggest, or cut out plans for fun and frolic, but he knows how to pilot. We are soon made acquainted with all the snug retreats where that "friend" is to be found, and have pointed out to us, in the park or on the boulevard, the "belle" of the city. But shortly we must put an end to the carnival of fun on the part of the officers and debauch on that of the crew, gather the fragments together, and be off.

One incident of consequence remains to be recorded. Among our visitors were two young gentlemen of the Prussian naval service, on furlough, "traveling abroad." They had recently been shipwrecked on the coast near Cape Town, and having the romantic chord in their souls touched, applied to Semmes for the privilege and honor of serving on our ship. Their worth at once appreciated by our commander, they are tendered warrants as master's-mates, entering upon their duties with the zeal and experience of old hands. Baron Maximilian von Meulnier of Bremen and Julius Schroeder of Hanover are our newly acquired officers. Our captain never had cause to regret these appointments. The young gentlemen fully confirmed his judgment, formed on sight, that they were accomplished gentlemen and sailors.

CHAPTER X

FROM CAPE TOWN TO THE EAST IN-
DIES; OCEAN ROADS AND CURRENTS;
DIVIDING POOR JACK'S EFFECTS; IS-
LAND OF ST. PAUL; DRILLING; MORE
PRIZES; PULO CONDORE; ENJOYING
LIFE; SINGAPORE

OUR DEPARTURE FROM Simon's Town was taken at
night, in the teeth of a gale, and with a heavy sea to pitch into
under steam to get an offing. The truth is, we were willing
just at present to avoid the *Vanderbilt*, which it was only reasonable to suppose must be by this time pretty well informed
of our whereabouts through the good offices of the American
consul, and as likely as not to be waiting for us outside the
bay. We had lost altogether twenty-one of our trained men at
Cape Town, and among them some that we could ill spare.
Their places we could only fill by stealth, the shipping offices
not being open to us and the neutrality laws not permitting

us to ship them openly. We got men enough all the same; but getting them on board had to be done secretly; and then it was not wise to remain in port until the consul could lodge information (doubtless his spies kept him well-enough informed of all our movements in spite of our precautions) with the authorities. They were not, of course, efficient just now; and it was not the part of wisdom to engage a superior adversary in our crippled state. So this night's work was rather anxious and exciting. The gale shrieked through our bare poles and rigging with fierce and vicious opposition; the black rifted clouds overhead spit alternate lightnings and scared moonbeams about our path as they fled shoreward, revealing out of inky gloom ghostly glimpses of the rockbound shore and the tossing sea. Such a night in this latitude must have inspired the weird tradition of the Flying Dutchman; and I do not doubt that Jack was looking out for him and would have felt a most uncanny indisposition to report a sail, even had it been bearing right down upon us. Such aspects of nature impress themselves strongly upon memory and the imagination, though they give no rational cause for dread. The absence of physical danger seems in fact to intensify the shudder of the soul, as if it felt the warning of a wrath impotent for the present, only that it may be saved up to its appointed day of judgment.

But by hard knocks we have conquered our offing, set our sails, and fallen off to a "full and by" where we ride easier. The propeller is hoisted, the fires banked, and we are stretching away to the strong westerly wind that is to "run down our easting" for the Straits of Sunda. Daylight soon breaks now; and with it the last touch of ghostly fancies melts away. Jack lets his eye sweep the horizon as bravely as ever; but there is nothing now in view but sea and sky and the circling birds.

We are steering due east. The map makes our course

The *Alabama* at sea, from a painting by Samuel Walters

THE PIRATE RAPHAEL SEMMES.—[FROM AN ENGLISH PHOTOGRAPH.]

Raphael Semmes as depicted in the Northern press

The author photographed aboard the *Alabama*

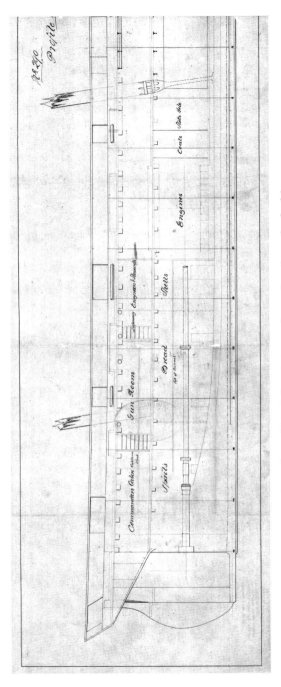

Inboard profile of the *Alabama* from the plans drafted by
John Laird and Sons Company, Birkenhead, England

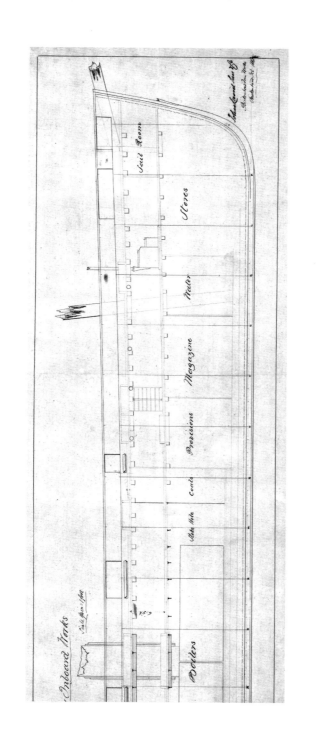

Lieut John McIntosh Kell
Executive Officer

Surgeon
Francis L Gall

Masters Mate
James Evans

Commander
Raphael Semmes

Lieut Marines
Beckett K Howell

Chief Engineer
Miles J Freeman

Masters Mate
Julius Schroeder

Sailmaker
Henry Alcott

Masters Mate
Baron Max Von Mulnier

Lieut Arthur Sinclair

Engineer Matthew O'Brien

Officers of the *Alabama*

Sailing Master Irvine S. Bulloch

Lieut Richard F. Armstrong

Lieut Joseph D. Wilson

Comdrs Secty
W. Breedlove Smith

Engineer
John Pundt

Midⁿ E
Maffitt Andersen

Midⁿ E
Andersen Maffitt

Masters Mate
Geo T. Fulham

Engineer
W. P. Brooks

Gunner Thos C. Cuddy

Midⁿ William H. Sinclair

The *Alabama* with the captured *Tonawanda*

The *Alabama* in a cyclone in the Gulf Stream, October 16, 1862

Raphael Semmes photographed leaning against
the aft pivot gun

The *Alabama* in Table Bay

The *Alabama* in Singapore

The *Kearsage*

The duel between the *Alabama* and the *Kearsage*

The sinking of the *Alabama*

Officers of the *Kearsage* with the "Gun that sank the *Alabama*"

about northeast. And why? Ah, even on the wide seas arises the paradox that the direct way is not always the shortest. We are following the way laid out by Captain Matthew F. Maury, once of the United States Navy, and superintendent of the naval observatory at Washington—now of the navy of the Confederate States. Maury's sailing directions bid us make the little barren isle of St. Paul in the South Indian Ocean before taking our departure for the straits. Thus we shall have the winds and currents in our favor. How natural it is for the landsman to regard the sea as a known and well-traversed plane of waters, all of whose surface secrets, at least, are known to the navigator and the chart! But could he take a bird's-eye view of the oceans, how narrow and thread-like would the traveled roads appear on the vast waste! How completely a ship, or even a large island, might lose itself in the wilderness "out of the track of ships"!

The oceans, like the great body of air above them, are traversed by currents whose cosmic origin is little understood and whose velocity and locality may vary more or less, but which are practically to be depended on in making a voyage. And then, these have their channels of greatest flow, if not of depth, like the terrestrial rivers; and so the "road" is narrowed in most cases to a few miles, and along these narrow roads the commerce of the earth travels in great caravans.

But, narrow as the roads are, one may travel them for days without getting within speaking distance of or even sighting a sail. One or two hundred miles is a mere ribbon of width on the ocean, but it will carry several ships abreast and out of sight of each other. For our purposes it is not enough to be in the road, even in the very middle of it. We must select places where it is very narrow indeed, and by preference some spot where two or three roads cross. We were in such a position off the Brazilian coast; and we are seeking another at the Straits of Sunda.

Our first task after we are fairly at sea is a sad one. It is customary when a sailor dies at sea, to distribute his relics (the contents of his bag or chest) among his messmates, unless he has formally disposed of them himself. The poor fellows we now mourn are not dead, so far as we know; but they have lost the number of their mess, and by this time find themselves cut dead by the friendly consul and his agents, while the boardinghouse shark, well aware that with our departure there will be a cessation of supplies, is arranging to get an advance at once on them for reshipment and refusing further credit on any other basis. Poor Jack! But any way he is lost to us, and there is but one thing to do. Up on deck with his Lares and Penates, and put the new men into their uniforms and traps! And then there is the forfeit of his arrears of pay and his prize-money, which looks like something substantial just now.

There is no drilling, nor, indeed, is there much work of any sort to be done at present. The gale is right behind us and the sea following is absolutely mountainous, with the sweep of three oceans in it. The helmsmen have to watch her sharply, for she has a tendency to swerve as she slides down the steep slopes, and should we broach-to, one of these toppling hills of water would fall on us with about the effect of so many tons of iron. It looks sometimes as if they would come right over the stern—"poop her" in sailor parlance— but the bonny boat is too quick for them, and just tucks them under as they break.

On this run we sight a few sail—neutrals, of course—and when they are going our way they pass us. The reason is we are under very easy sail, having plenty of time, while they are chasing up the market. Only a chase can make us risk our sticks or even strain our sailcloth. Then we are in some danger of running upon icebergs, which at this season drift up this way, and we don't care to scud any faster than the seas compel us to.

The run of nearly five thousand miles with such a gale behind us is quickly made. Early in October we find ourselves in sight of the two small islands, the larger of which is the St. Paul we are in quest of. We might find it to our profit to make something of a stay here, for plenty of vessels will come this way, and it is also a resort of whalers. But the weather is stormy yet, and we are tired of it. The only thing we regret seriously is the chance of catching the fish which abound at the islands. We would enjoy the sport, and not less the change of diet.

We pass through the doldrums and shape our course for Sunda, light airs and variable, no calm belt. We are favored in this. Soon we take the southeast trades, and are rollicking along, all kites out and studding sails lower and aloft. The gallant winds soon dry the decks and raise the drooping spirits. The departments and mess quarters are emptied of wet and soggy material, and lines and hammock nettings, and even the decks, are encumbered with them. The appearence of the spar-deck is that of a secondhand clothing shop. Our recently acquired recruits are busy overhauling their bags and taking an inventory of their stock in trade. These ragamuffins had been pitched over our side in every nondescript style of outfit, dirty and ragged, the natural sequence of "a glorious time ashore." We have now to shape them up and make man-of-war's men of them. We shall be busy without letup, until we make the Sunda Strait, drilling at all the exercises. We are not troubled with coaching them for sailormen, however. They are picked-and-tried veterans in this respect.

Our companions, the birds, have left us. Our old acquaintances, the dolphin and flying fish, reappear, the former playing around the ship and at times darting for the schools of the latter, as, startled from the sea by our motion, they wing their way to leeward. We are again treated to fresh fish, the outcome of grains, hand fishing, and the trolling line. The ship is soon sparkling as a diamond, in fresh paint and polished brasswork, and is verily a nautical school. During the entire passage from St. Paul to Sunda Strait, the various warlike exercises are daily going on for hours together, an hour or two at "great gun" drill, a shorter time to boarding and repelling boarders, small-arm (infantry) squad or division drill with pistol target practice (at bottle slung from the foretopmast-studding-sail boom). It is an active and at times stirring and exciting drill, particularly in the "boarding rushes," where examples of wonderful activity and quickness may be observed; for Jack takes real interest in his exercises and studies, if we except the handling of small firearms. Here no compromise can be effected with Jack. He has a thorough contempt for this sort of a weapon; and you may resign yourself to the stern fact that he will slight and avoid it as far as he dares to the bitter end. He will never allow you to make him a "sogger."

Later on the news that the *Wyoming* is holding the passage of the strait emphasizes the excitement, and the crew feel that something more than playing fighting may take place in a few hours. A stranger suddenly dropped on our decks would at once detect the marked warlike aspect of surroundings. If no duel comes off, at least our lads will have hurried on to a state of thorough efficiency. We have prepared many a fellow for Her Majesty's service, and she will find them well up in gun-drill without a question.

Sunday muster has now been resumed; and as our tars, hat in hand, double the capstan, the eyes of our skipper and executive speak eloquently their approbation of the men's natty appearance. Order now reigns supreme. We are off the strait, the land in sight but distant. October is on the wane. The strange cry (to us latterly) comes from aloft, "Sail ho!" We speak, and communicate by boat, with an English barque just out of the strait. We get by her some later news from the seat of war than our last advices at the Cape supplied; but our interest is principally centered in the news that the United States cruiser *Wyoming* and tender were holding the passage of the strait, leaving but seldom and then only to make the port of Batavia for coal. Our English captain was very communicative, bringing with him as a present a recent chart of the strait, and pointing out on it the usual anchorage ground of the cruiser. The *Wyoming* had adopted the precaution of mooring at night to a buoy off Krakatoa, an island athwart the passage of the strait, the currents being rapid and variable and the seas in this latitude studded with coral reefs, making it dangerous to "box" about them at night.

We are surely in for it now, for we shall not shirk a fight with a cruiser not much our superior in point of weight of metal, and to get through without being sighted seems out of the problem of chances; the passage is so narrow that vessels are easily made out from shore to shore. We have the information of the presence of our enemy verified each day or two by neutrals, one of them reporting being boarded by a boat from her. We are loafing off and on in sight of the land, awaiting the prey. We are safe to carry on the work of destruction until we speak a vessel inward-bound and be reported, when we must look out for number one. So far, no inward-bound vessel has been spoken, and all the boarded ones have proved neutral. Poor sport indeed! What has become of our once-immense China fleet of clippers? Dissolved as the mist before the rising sun! Mortifying and humiliating state of affairs, and vexing to our enemies to have to acknowledge it. The work of an insignificant second-class gunboat, outcast from home, and, save in English ports, without friends. But she sails on undaunted, pursues the even tenor of her way, and you shall see, burning and destroying in the very lair of her foe.

We now get up steam, and furling sail make a morning visit to the stream of vessels coming out of the passage. We find them "at home," receiving our "cards" with every token of hospitality. They impart all important news they are possessed of and fill away. But still we are not happy. We want to burn something. We are like the fireladdies after a long and tedious interregnum, spoiling for a fire. These new-made acquaintances also remind us so often and forcibly of the presence of the *Wyoming*, the formidable appearance of her eleven-inch guns, etc., that we have the crew all excitement, grinding the edges of their cutlasses, reloading rifles and revolvers, and making all manner of hostile preparation. Indeed, the ship looks quite warlike. But we have our reward. "Sail ho!" from aloft. We pay no particular attention to it, having been disappointed so often. But the opinion of our Bunsby alters the case; and soon we steam up with the American barque *Amanda* of Boston, from Manila bound to Queenstown, with the usual cargo of sugar. She is condemned and burned, after being looted of attractive stores.

The ice being now broken, we take it as a new departure and omen of renewed luck, and cheer up. You see, coals are expensive in these latitudes, thirty to forty dollars per ton, and in gold at that; so we have to look about sharply to pay expenses. We light up the heavens with the glare, and no doubt the conflagration is the theme of conversation on many a passing ship, speculation marveling as to the cause. As often as practicable we burned our vessels in the daylight. After boxing around a while longer, and feeling the need of fresh provisions and fruit, we steamed in, bearding the lion in his den, and anchor in the mouth of the strait close to the Sumatra coast. It has been a weary, monotonous, and boisterous voyage of a month and a half. We have cruised off the strait for some days, boarded an immense fleet, and yet found no inward-bound vessel, finally announcing our own arrival.

The fact is, the *Wyoming* happened to be just at this time absent on one of her periodical visits to Batavia for coal. If we had not used extraordinary economy during our run across the Indian Ocean, and from St. Paul to the strait (not even keeping our banked fires as we had always done before), we must have gone to Batavia also, and in that case not only missed the work we were now doing, but almost surely have met the *Wyoming* and a fight.

We draw a relieved breath and sleep the sleep of the weary, with an anchor-watch set. We are at daylight looking on one of the most beautiful pictures of the earth. On one side Sumatra, the other Java; in the center, the smaller island, Krakatoa. To describe the luxuriance of the tropical verdure, the flocks of birds of varied and beautiful plumage, the parrot, cockatoo, bird of paradise, paroquet, winging their flight from island to island over the sea of green sparkling in its gentle undulations, is beyond my feeble pen, and has doubtless been conveyed to your senses long since by the descriptive talents of a preceding voyager. Krakatoa was, as you recollect, submerged some years later by an earthquake, which destroyed vast property and a holocaust of human victims.

Anger Point is on the opposite side of the strait from our anchorage, on the Java coast—a military post of the Dutch, occupied by a small garrison in command of a lieutenant. It is a stopping place for all vessels in- and outward-bound, either for water or provisions. The town is insignificant, with none but natural attractions, the chief being an immense banyan tree. On a former cruise, the writer remembers taking advantage of its cooling shade and estimating with his eye that it would shelter many thousand people. This tree has many trunks; the branches of the parent trunk reaching down and taking root, until by and by a vast pavilion has been formed. This particular tree is many hundred years old.

Our ship is the center of a fleet of native boats of the canoe order, everything about them but the hull the product of the bamboo reed, indispensable to these islanders, hence supplied by generous nature. Of this reed they fashion sails, masts, spars, etc., and in their homes, mats, chairs, vessels, and utensils; indeed, one has to look about to see what is *not* made from it. Fruits of varied kinds indigenous to the tropics, poultry, eggs, and vegetables are in superabundance; and our appetites being of the growing order, we keep the two stewards of the cabin and wardroom messes busy purchasing and preparing. Fore and aft a perpetual barter and trade is in progress with the natives. No rum to be had from them, fortunately, so Jack keeps up a good appetite, and is enjoying himself in a rational way. Reader, if you have never made a voyage such as we have just completed, you cannot appreciate the perfect sense of abandonment that has stolen over us. We are absolutely given over to enjoyment and feasting, and even the land has no attraction for us as to touch. We are satisfied to sniff the spice-laden breezes of the monsoon, and under the awnings puff our Manilas and watch the boatmen and the graceful maneuvers of their boats under paddle or sail. The tailor's bills of these fellows, it may safely be affirmed, should not be permitted to run the length of time of a New York swell, that is, if the cost is proportioned to the elaborateness. It should require no great strain on the pocket-book to liquidate the debt promptly.

We find the dolphin swarming these straits; and when under way and moving through the water rapidly, the trolling line keeps the sportsman busy, the deck frequently covered with the floundering fish, changing with each struggle from one bright color to another in his dying gasps. No liberty can be allowed officers or crew at this point; the

Wyoming's proximity rendering it imprudent, if not hazardous, to allow any portion of our complement to stray even
a short distance from the ship. Still, there is little inducement to visit, beyond bringing this luxuriant verdure within
touch; we are breathing its sweetness at every breath. The
swarm of native boats supply us with every article of luxury
that is native, and much also in the way of English and
French imported sea stores, obtained by these enterprising
traders from Singapore.

In the midst of our *dolce far niente* we are awakened from
dreamland by the report from aloft that a vessel having the
appearance of a man-of-war has taken in all sail, and is
standing for our anchorage. We "cat" the anchor, jump to
stations, steam being in the meantime ordered; and for some
time we think the long-expected fight is about to come off.
About the time we are ready for action, the rainsquall which
had enveloped everything has passed over, and discovers a
merchant vessel clewed down to the squall. It was a false
alarm, after all. And so we have it now off and on for weeks,
until we have worked the salt pretty well out of us.

But presently we steam through the straits, passing the
little garrison of Anger and the myriads of islands studding
the pass into the China Sea. We have seen nothing of the
Wyoming. But just as we are thinking of anchoring for the
night, which we shall always do in these treacherous seas of
shoals and uncertain currents, we make a taut, fine ship
standing towards us—and not a doubt of her nationality.
The chase is short, we being under steam and the wind light.
A blank cartridge brings her to. She proves the ship *Winged
Racer*, a magnificent full clipper from Manila, and bound to
New York. She had the usual sugar cargo. She was condemned; and, much to our surprise, our captain came to anchor off one of the islands, seeming to be in no hurry to fire
her despite the fact that the enemy could not be many miles

off. The truth is, a number of stores were manifested on her, which Semmes did not propose to sacrifice. We passed well into the midnight-watch despoiling her as the spider does that other winged racer, the fat and juicy fly. The captain of the doomed vessel making the request (the sea is smooth in these island waters), permission was granted him to take the full complement of boats of the prize and pull for Batavia. Provisioning the boats for the trip and taking the prisoners of the late prize *Amanda*, he bids us adieu, as happy as circumstances permit, and shoves off. We afterwards learn of his safe arrival under the wings of the American consul. These captains could testify in person to the *Wyoming*, upon their arrival at Batavia, how much her absence for coal had cost them.

What a change from the deck of a superb clipper bound to New York, and the quarters of a jolly boat bound to Batavia! In the meantime, a number of bumboats are alongside from the adjacent shore, driving a lucrative trade with the stewards and forward messes. We have now finished ransacking the prize and preparing the *Winged Racer* for the torch. Trade with the Malays is in full tide of its prosperity, the waters of the straits still bearing to us boats from the inlets loaded with additional attractions intended to deplete our pocketbooks and stock of tobacco.

Suddenly the flames shoot up from the cabin and forecastle of the doomed ship. Our boarding-officer has fired her. The two vessels are lying near each other, only a safe distance intervening. Suddenly, with shouts and exclamations, a stampede as of a routed army takes place among the Malays; and with paddle and sail, as hurriedly as these could accomplish it, the boats are away to the inlets. It would puzzle one to interpret the impression made on these islanders by the sudden fire. The most plausible is that being themselves pirates upon opportunity, as well as traders, they put an evil construction on the act and, fearing their turn might come next, concluded to get out of the way. They knew how it was themselves. Luckily we had secured plenty of provisions and fruits in advance.

Steaming for the Gaspar Strait, we overhaul scores of vessels, but not of the nationality we search for. We are twenty-four hours in coming up to Gaspar. This is the second-most used exit from the North China ports. We should probably have met with no further luck in the other direction; as we had already lit up the full distance with the flames of two vessels, and the trading boats left behind would have advertised us far and near as they travel the length of the strait in the fierce competition for foreign-vessel trade. Do not think, reader, we are rushing off to dodge the *Wyoming*. We are following up the natural logic of chances and hunting our own game, leaving it to her to catch hers. Our harvest in these lower narrow systems of outlet will be of short duration, and we must gather it while we may. Captures are getting too infrequent to justify us in a protracted loaf at any one point. We shall accomplish more in the utter consternation and demoralization spread among the China fleet than in the actual destruction of ship. Two months from our advent, the remainder of the proud clipper fleet of the American marine was laid up at anchor in the Eastern ports, awaiting foreign purchase.

We are near the Gaspar Strait and are rewarded by one of the most valuable captures of our cruise. "Sail ho!" We have a stiff breeze at the time; and as the sail had already been pronounced by Evans American beyond all doubt, we must be cautious. The vessel is a splendid clipper, close-hauled, standing southward, a homeward-bound ship. You must know, reader, that the *Alabama* is not the fleet-footed greyhound she once was. Old "Time" and the elements have worn the copper from her bottom and curled it in rolls on her bends. Her boilers are eaten into by incrustations of salt, so that it is positively dangerous to carry but very moderate steam. Hence, we shall have from this time out to pocket our pride of ship and make up for her sloth and dullness by maneuver, strategy, and stealth.

We are under sail and steam, and keep off warily a point or two to intercept her. We are showing United States colors and trust she will take us for her own cruiser, the *Wyoming*, known to them to be just here, and about the class of vessel, rig, etc., as ourselves. She smells a mouse, however; at least, she proposes to be on the safe side, and rather shoulder the ignominy of being thought timid and unsociable to her countrymen than take any chances. She is rather too valuable a ship to light up the way of the strait for foreign bottoms to steer by. As we keep away, she throws to the breeze her studding sails, and the chase has begun. No occasion now for deception; that point is passed. We must get her in our clutches by sheer steaming and sailing qualities. We haul down, therefore, the Stars and Stripes, and float at our peak in its place the white flag of the Confederacy, recently adopted by our Congress and not unlike St. George's Cross of the English. A blank cartridge is given, but she does not respond to it. She intends to struggle for liberty. We are more excited now on board of our ship than often before in our experience. As a rule, the chasing of a sail is a matter-of-fact, everyday occurrence; and both officers and men follow their duties or amusements without comment or thought of the chase.

But not so now. Our rail and hammock nettings are crowded, even the watch below curious to see the "Derby" of the Gaspar Strait. The sail is evidently gaining on us. The *Alabama* has at last met her conqueror in speed, and her day of humiliation seems about to be on her. Steam is forced to the danger point, and still the chase is leaving us—slowly it is true, but still leaving us. We conceive the idea the ship is out of trim too much by the head and shift our battery aft, and even call to the rescue our "livestock," congregating the officers and crew clear aft. This was a judicious thought, for we now at least hold our own. Still, this does not satisfy the longings of our discontented souls. We are anxious, no denying it, and somewhat demoralized. It has resolved itself to this: If the breeze does not die out, night will overtake us, and the enemy dodge us in the darkness or a squall. We are doing our level best, steam and sail with a smashing breeze, and gaining on the plucky and gallant fellow absolutely nil. We are within rifle range of her, about four miles; we hesitate to sheer our ship for the shot, losing so much distance by it; but it seems neck or nothing, and the projectile is finally sent after her, striking the water and throwing the spray over her quarterdeck. Gallant shot for Armstrong! Still she keeps on, evidently having made up her mind to be sunk rather than captured and burned.

The determination of the brave skipper rather causes the mercury of our hopes and ambitions to drop; and nothing seems left but the chance shots of our one-hundred-pounder shell disabling her to land victory on our side. Suddenly we discover we are gaining on the racer. The wind is going down with the sun, and the elements have conquered the race for us rather than the speed of our bonny boat. We are approaching her rapidly. All hope is then abandoned on the part of the victim; she luffs to the wind, and with maintopsail to the mast lays quietly awaiting her doom. The boarding officer returns with captain and papers, but we can anticipate. The earnest efforts at escape had already told the tale. She is the American clipper ship *Contest*, from Yokahama to New York, with an assorted cargo of Japanese curios, teas, silks, etc. As predicted, the cargo was not covered, and both are condemned to the torch. We are at anchor in the midst of the archipelago, smooth sea, and now light breeze, and (an unusual thing) the prize is visited by our officers in numbers. We had never captured so beautiful a vessel. She was a revelation of symmetry, a very racehorse. A sacrilege, almost a desecration, to destroy so perfect a specimen of man's handiwork. We could but pat the gallant skipper on the back for his display of pluck and nerve. His owners should reward him handsomely for it. After despoiling the prize of stores, etc., the torch is applied; and by the time we are under way, the flames are licking in hungry mood the spars and sails of the doomed ship, lighting up the landscape and waters with a lurid glare. Strange sight!

The captain is leaning against the rail, looking on in silence. His brow is unruffled and face calm. We will not inquire into his thoughts. He has merited our respect by his pluck, and we know how he must feel to lose such a ship. But he admits no personal grudges. We found the skipper of the *Contest* a frank, clever fellow. He told us his late command was unexcelled in speed.

An incident of the chase may here be apropos. O'Brien was on watch in the engine room, and working his fires for all they were worth, when the inquiry comes from our skipper to know if we can't have more steam. The answer comes, "The teakettle will stand no more; if we attempt it we shall scatter the pieces for the chase to pick up."

We are eating the "white bread" of our romantic cruise just now, sailing over calm seas, being wafted idly through archipelagoes, supplied almost daily with the dainties of the tropics by the adventurous Malay boatman, with nothing to mar the perfect sense of ease and security but the dangerous navigation. Those seas are constantly adding to their shoals through the activity of earthquakes and the busy coral insect. We are combining business with pleasure. We usually anchor at nightfall, nothing lost by it, as the stream of sails have to pass us. We have also, since entering these close seas, fitted out our launch, a fine stout boat, and with a heavily armed crew and howitzer patrol the surrounding waters in watches, and thus take every precaution against anybody's slipping past our net.

We are steering now for the Carimata Strait to the eastward of us, another channel of egress for the China fleet, making of course many sails, but slow luck again. We are in the northeast monsoon, but not strong yet. We pass through this strait after an unusually quick passage against the prevailing wind and anchor off the Island of Souriton, and remain here several days, the position offering every chance of intercepting the homeward-bound fleet. We board the British ship *Avalanche* from Singapore, homeward-bound. For a consideration the captain of this vessel agrees to take our prisoners to the nearest point convenient for him where an American consul can be communicated with. So with bag and hammocks our friends of the *Contest* are transferred— pleasant parting on both sides. This English skipper reports American commerce as approaching zero, and it is our only consolation for the news we get through him of the gradual tightening of the folds of the anaconda around our beloved land. Reader! we will not attempt the translation of our feelings for your sympathy—too imperfect the thoughts and tongue to convey them. But the reflection over what we have already done is, in a poor, weak way, consoling—a barren refuge for the sick and anxious heart. Do you wonder that the would-be generous impulses of our soul, yearning to stretch out to our brother in his deep affliction, should be smothered in their very birth and fade away at the approach of the solemn funeral march of the wrongs imposed on *us*? And thus are our feelings swayed hither and thither as we cull the war news from each batch of newspapers obtained.

Meeting with no success here, we weigh anchor and are

off for the coast of Borneo, the land of the baboon, who, some people would have us believe, is near relation. However, we do not stop to pay our respects to him, not being on pleasure bound. A stop of a few days on this coast, and we stretch over to the coast of Cochin China. We now have variable weather, calms, rainsqualls, and the wind all around the compass. We are anchored for several days, the currents sweeping by us sometimes as rapid as four or five knots, making it most difficult to get the lead to the bottom for soundings. We frequently anchor in twenty fathoms or more. You can scarcely appreciate the danger of navigation in this uncertain archipelago. Observations of the sun are useless, the uncertain currents throwing your calculation of compass-course to the winds. It can safely be asserted that more splendid ships have laid their bones on the reefs and shoals of the lower China seas than in all the remainder of the world beside.

Our commander has our full sympathy, but how he manages to keep up under the loss of sleep is amazing. He must have a rugged constitution and iron nerves to pull through it as he does. At all hours of the day and night he may be seen bent over his chart in the cabin or on deck conning the soundings. A heavy responsibility, for the lives of all are in his hands, to say nothing of the inestimable value of the charge he is piloting through this labyrinth. Perish our pride and sweetheart rather by the shot and shell of the enemy than ignominiously by the treacherous shoal. As in a previous cruise of the writer in these seas, we observed the water covered with snakes of a yellow hue striped with black and lazily basking in the sun, moving but slowly on the water. They are harmless, our men dipping them up in buckets at night in the quiet. If at anchor they will crawl up the anchor chain, through the hawse-hole to the deck. Immense fields of seaweed cover the seas, floating in a solid mass, with

breaks in them looking like rivers made by the strong current, which are the abode of shellfish of varied kinds, some
of the crabs being large enough for table use. What a multitude of God's creation find food, rest, habitation, and safety
here! "They that go down to the sea in ships, and occupy
their business in great waters, these men see the works of the
Lord and his wonders in the deep."

We are taking the change of the monsoon, hence the dis-
turbance of nature, squalls, rain, etc. We are meeting none
but neutral sails, and may at any moment have that dread of
the navigator of this archipelago, the fearful typhoon, down
on us. It is the season for it, coming with the change of the
wind. These monsoons prevail for six months each way, the
northeast and southeast, giving the traveler of the Eastern
seas two shakeups in the latter fall and spring months.
We have had one experience already off the Newfoundland
Banks, in an open ocean with plenty of sea room, and have
no taste for its duplicate; but here it is a gray horse of another
color. We are cribbed, cabined, and confined to heave-to in it
and drift with the current on a shoal or island, or anchor in a
rushing, surging current and drag anchor to the aforesaid
shoal or island. It is no overdrawn picture. Again, we should
have these apparently well-disposed Malay bumboat men,
alias pirates, to contend with should disaster overtake us.

It may be the fear of the dangerous season has deterred
our friend the *Wyoming* from seeking us, for she beyond
doubt has heard from us daily through the immense fleet
overhauled and boarded by our ship. A longer sojourn in
these seas has probably taught her the imminence of the
danger at this time of change of monsoon, and caused her
captain to await a more favorable time upon our return on
the backtrack home to interview us. I do not think our
watch-officers ever experienced before or since the anxiety of
the past week or so. We have been in tight places before and

worked out all right; but here we have no sea room, and if anything takes a sailor's nerve it is this. Our watches are now no holiday or half-doze on the horse-block; and Jack is not bundled up under the weather bulwarks, but wide awake, the lead constantly going, soundings noted, and chart examined to determine to a dot the position of the ship.

It is now the latter part of November. Luck has again departed—no prize. Cui bono, this battling with fickle currents, and almost scraping over the shoals? Restless life, ours! We must have constant bustle and excitement to smother our rising thoughts of the far-off land we love so well. Our captain begins to show the wear and tear of weary months of watching, thinking, and anxiety. It is true, we of the watch and boarding party must be on hand always and stand up to the calls at all times and hours. We get the weather with no backout, answer the notice of the quartermaster at dead of night that a sail is to be boarded, frequently board a vessel in wet clothes, and remain in charge of her until time has made them dry and warm again; yet we are young and full of warm blood, and pull through all right. Different the position of our commander. True, he can go below at desire, be at all times comfortable as to dress, and has no watch to keep; but these privileges are more than offset by the irregular sleep and hours, grave responsibilities, and disadvantage of more than twice our age on his shoulders. We are as tough as hickory, the truth of the assertion borne out by the fact we are never on the sick list, pulling through with slight ailments always.

We skirt the coast of Cochin China without so much as making a single capture, and shape our course for the small Island of Condore, reaching and anchoring outside of it for the night. A welcome rest. We are under the lee of the land, snug and cozy, and can draw a breath of relief. We have come here for some slight repairs to the ship, not to be attempted but in a still harbor. Quiet and deathlike sleep refreshes both officers and men, only an anchor-watch being kept. Our skipper must have enjoyed it particularly after his recent battle with perplexities. Island (Pulo) Condore is a French settlement of recent acquisition, and at the time of our visit in charge of a French naval officer as governor, with headquarters on shore in the small Malay village, his protection only a small nondescript vessel carrying one insignificant carronade, but which politeness compels us to designate a French man-of-war. The crew are a mere handful of sailors. Onshore we have the garrison on an equally small scale. We had thought ourselves rather insignificant in this wide world of powerful fleets, but we felt the impulse of strut strong in us.

Here is a chance for conquest seldom met with. We can carry the fleet and garrison by storm without the loss of a man. But we surely have no need of the island, beautiful as it is, except as a temporary abode for work on our ship, and relaxation for our officers and crew; and, indeed, cannot, with our republican ideas of colonization, see what Johnny Crapaud wants with it, there being no market we know of for apes and vampire bats except in a moderate way. Condore is a bold specimen of the work of the coral insect, jutting up perpendicularly from the sea, and with its dense tropical verdure and relief of huts and white coral houses, almost hid from view by the luxuriant vegetation most pleasing to the eye and senses. What a vast period of time is required to finish the work of the busy little insect and clothe the surface with soil thick and rich enough to support so much luxuriant vegetable life! Well may we pause in wonder at unfathomable nature and as to the why and wherefore of it. We are anchored in a landlocked bay of comfortable anchorage, and French ownership and occupancy back of us as protection. But in the absence of a French naval force sufficient to add might to right in enforcing the laws of neutrality, we com-

bine discretion and valor, putting a "spring" on our chain cables, so as to command the narrow passage to the bay should
our enemy put in an appearance and attempt an overt act of
hostility. Our French naval officer and governor is as usual
the demonstrative exponent of native courtesy and attention,
welcoming us to his empire with all the inherent grace of his
race. Quite a young man, too, about two and twenty, and a
fine specimen of a man and sailor.

We are told to make ourselves at home and stay as long as
agreeable. We have a present from him—a small bullock sent
to the ship, with the addition of vegetables and fruit. Save
the absence of congenial companions, our worthy new-made
friend should be perfectly contented on this paradise of an
island. Luxuries of the table in superabundance, and most of
them to be had for the simple gathering; a grateful monsoon
tempering the atmosphere, blowing first from the northeast,
and then the southeast, the year-round, with slight pauses of
wind in the change; epidemics unknown; and nothing to dis-
turb the even beating of the pulse, the natives even partak-
ing of the character of these calm, unruffled surroundings.
Bloodless conquests these, too, as a rule. Without discussing
the abstract question of the right of appropriation by the
Western powers, one thing has been made clear; the world is
better for it. Gradually these labyrinths of islands have been
almost relieved of the presence of native pirates, and it has
been accomplished more by the moral effect of the presence
of Europeans than by the force of naval arms.

Our indefatigable executive is in his element now, putting
things to rights. This sometimes means stirring up things
into quite a muddle at first; the decks lumbered with the
tools and material of the four heads of department, the boatswain, carpenter, sailmaker, and gunner each overlooking his
gang and securing from time to time orders or suggestions
from the superior. The paint pot and slush bucket are also in

requisition, and our garish uniforms in danger from the tar bucket; so, as we are ready for a visit to the governor on-shore, let's be off.

Port is the Elysium of the watch-officer; the first luff has the prime polish of the ship to attend to; the keeping it up the after-duty of the watch-officers. We are having *our* good time now. With permission to go onshore, we step into the cutter and land at the head of the bay, near the garrison grounds and close to the official residence. The boat's crew are a picture for the artist, dressed in their summer uniform of white linen duck and straw hats; the boat, with a fresh coat of paint, snowy cushions, and scarlet trimmings, testify-ing to Jack's pride in his visiting coach. No use of cautionary orders not to leave the boat; go where you please is the un-derstood arrangement. No rum here! Coconut milk in abun-dance. We have no fear of it; and, besides, Jack's stomach doesn't take to it over-kindly. We have, as usual, brought some arms with us. We visit the governor and have the free-dom of the island extended us; and after a pleasant inter-change of civilities, during which questions multiply on questions as to our expectations, hopes, etc., of the result of the war, our gesticulating Frenchman, with his hot southern blood, grows excited and belligerent, and is really jealous of the opportunities before us and denied him! He has visions of "decorations."

It may naturally be supposed that much of our conver-sation with Monsieur Bizot took the turn of our Civil War and the chances of final success, and, incidentally, our in-dividual prospects under the hoped-for termination. The Frenchman was amazed to learn that no reward was ours in the way of promotion out of the regular plod, with perhaps the exception in our commander's case; and nothing in the way of "orders" or crosses of merit to be looked for even in that. And that our selection for the work now being done was considered by our government and also by our brother officers a substantial reward in advance, passing expression, and the part we were filling the envy of our compeers. Our Frenchman could not, with his imperial notions and long-ings, either understand or approve this. His whole education taught the inestimable value of "orders" and substantial recognition in the way of promotion, and I doubt not the French commander would not have been an enthusiast if suddenly placed in our shoes. He evidently was a lukewarm if at all a republican sympathizer. I have often thought since of our many conversations, and wondered what his feelings would have been had he lived to see the "bone and sinew" of his own land raise up a republic for him to live under. He was sui generis—a monarchist.

We make a visit to the garrison and indulge in a trial of the comparative merits of the French and English rifle, proving at each distance of target the superiority of the En-field arm, much to the discomfort and chagrin of our French marine. We find on the island an abundance of wild animal life securely hid away in the dense woods and undergrowth, and have some anxiety for our men as well as ourselves as we roam, rifles and guns in hand, around the foot of the steep perpendicular and up its sides where practicable. The under-growth is dense masses of tree and brier interlocking in the struggle for supremacy, many of the vines of a poisonous character; and the surface of the ground the habitation of the scorpion, centipede, and many species of venomous serpents.

We watch the gambols of the ape and monkey with un-flagging enjoyment, their antics calling forth shouts of laughter. Verily, for ways that are odd and tricks that are cute, commend us to our far-removed (?) brother. For hours they will sport from tree to tree, forming in marching line, and making an almost endless chain by locking tail to tail and swinging as a pendulum, making a bridge of bodies from

tree to tree. If one only could speak "monkey" now, what lots
of fun! Our French governor here might practice some of
their gesticulations and poses for future use in assisting language, and introduce into the salons of Paris some new con-
tortions of the face and limbs. Chatter, chatter till sunset;
when an adjournment is made to the sand beach for what?
A mystery to all but themselves. So far as we can judge, it
seems to be a meeting for the interchange of civilities and
gossip simply, or swapping of views of the ups and downs of
monkey domestic life. These reunions are made, as we observe from the anchorage, each early morning and evening;
and the hours would suggest that their meetings are not of a
political character.

We were guilty of an act of wanton cruelty, and, by the
way, did not repeat it. Someone from the deck shot a female
ape on the beach, wounding her grievously. Her cries were
heartrending; and the sorrow of her young deprived of their
natural protector seemed fully to equal that of a human
being. Nor did the distress confine itself to the immediately
interested, but extended to the whole colony; it evidently
being regarded as a general national calamity. The assassina-
tion, or whatever name else they assigned for the "damna-
tion" taking off the head of the family, had evidently been
the topic of serious discussion and moanful resolutions; for
in the next early morn the whole monkey and ape population of the island, apparently, assembled on the beach, and
after an evident ceremony and digging of a grave, laid the
departed to rest amid cries and groans almost human. Upon
mentioning the incident at the garrison, we learned it was
the undeviating custom of the animal. And here again Dar-
win's theory of evolution presents itself, and the experience
gathered by our observation offers explanation if not excuse
for the idiosyncrasies of the theorist.

But we will return to the forest and exploration. As before

stated, serpents of venomous character are numerous, and our party has come upon a nest of them. One of our men, Michael Mars, a very daredevil, is amusing himself by seizing the snakes by the tail, and by a dexterous and swift jerk as of a whiplash breaking the neck of the reptile; utterly indifferent to, and apparently ignorant of, the imminent danger, and against the warning and protest of the officer in charge. We come upon something in the way of animal life ensconced on a limb of a tree, high from the ground. We recognize animal life by the almost imperceptible movement, and the sight of hair on it. Its large size calls for a halt and consultation. We are anxious to bring it down with rifle or gun, but first wish if possible to ascertain *what* we are to bring down. Momentous question; not convenient or desirable to land a wild beast at our feet wounded and furious. Hence the pause. We had often, since our arrival in these regions, heard of tigers, lions, etc.; yet so far had no personal acquaintance with them and no knowledge of their eccentricities. We are in a quandary. Ridiculous scene for fellows who had faced the battle and the breeze. But don't let this lower us in your estimation, reader; we are simply out of our element. Not frightened! Not a bit! Who says so? Here we go! Fire! and tumbling out of the tree comes to the ground with a thud an immense vampire bat, wounded and eyes inflamed with rage, hissing like a serpent and showing its sharp fangs. We now know our game and bag a number of them; some specimens as much as six feet from tip to tip of wing. We amuse ourselves shooting parrots, cockatoos, and other birds of gay plumage; but nothing in the way of game, either animal or bird species, that is edible.

By mutual understanding no further warfare was undertaken against the ape or monkey tribes. It seemed too closely allied to murder. A most remarkable habit to be noted was the sudden cessation in the gambols and antics of these troops of apes and monkeys. In the full tide of their play, as though by the signal of a leader or a concerted prearrangement, the wild hurly-burly would suddenly cease, and they would gather in a body. For a moment or two there would be chattering and gesticulating, as if in mass-meeting, and then a lapse into silence. Then the meeting seemed to dissolve as if by magic, the whole tribe disappearing and reassembling in a distant part of the woods.

Our life here soon becomes decidedly pleasant. We have little to do but amuse ourselves when off duty; and what with the boating, fishing, swimming, and hunting, we are not hard put to it for the how. With the advantage of a fine seine, we are able, at very little cost in labor, to take all the fish we want, and also to supply our friends onshore; and we receive in turn plenty of beef, poultry, vegetables, and delicious fruits. It is a land of luxury and profusion; and we rather wonder that our particular friend John Bull, with his penchant for good real estate, has not put in some sort of claim on this archipelago. Here at Arcas and at Saldanha Bay, we have enjoyed real vacations. At ports of the civilized world we are oppressed with social duties and good clothes, to say nothing about the trouble of looking after Jack. Your common sailor soon tires of such a life, though. He should, it would seem, be a true child of nature, since civilization has been so unkind to him; but he is nothing of the sort. Pipe, grog, and black-eyed Susan are his paradise, and for the rest, give him the open sea, a topsail breeze, and regular watches. He soon tires of going ashore where there is no dance house; and will only leave the ship to oblige some of the younger officers or to join a fishing or swimming party.

We remain altogether two weeks at the Island of Condore. I doubt if Monsieur Bizot would have objected had we decided to fritter away with him the remaining time of the war. He either did not know or did not care for the neutrality laws so much as for the freemasonry of sailor-craft. Quite likely he excused his laxity in the matter by the reflection that he was ill-prepared to enforce, in a military way, regulations which we might deem inconvenient—by way of salve to his conscience, I mean; for there can be no doubt of his personal goodwill or his courage.

But let it not be supposed that we had no object in anchoring in the snug harbor of Condore except to get a rest and change of diet. The copper on the ship's bottom, as has been mentioned, was getting into a deplorable condition; and besides its hindering our speed under sail or steam, it was leaving our planking and timbers at the mercy of the teredos, which swarm the tropic seas and soon destroy the woodwork of the stoutest ships. Our ingenious first luff had contrived a hydraulic caisson to be let over the side and held by pressure to the bottom—a "suction" affair, in which repairers could work at ease underwater. The carpenter, Robinson, made a success of it; and the work was done excellently, giving us once more a smooth hull. Once more in shipshape, officers and men refreshed and ready for work, we take leave of our friends onshore, weigh anchor, and steam seaward. Securing an offing, we let steam go down and hoisting our screw proceed towards Singapore in the Straits of Malacca; we are purposely under moderate sail, with fine weather, an occasional sail sighted and overhauled, and, as usual now, *neutral*. The squalls that come up in these seas are often severe; and the condensation they cause in the saturated air is extremely dense, often refusing to refract even the faintest ray of the solar beams that fall so brightly above it. But the squalls that actually touch the sea are not numerous, and the experienced sailor does not much mind mere blackness in the upper air.

The peculiarity of "bullheads" has not appealed to one of our officers, the lieutenant of marines, Mr. Howell. He has the distinction of being the only marine on board, as we have never enlisted men in that capacity. But he is a relative of Mrs. Jefferson Davis and rather in Semmes's confidence; and, except that he isn't even the "making" of a sailor, a good fellow enough. He has a horror of squalls and a rooted conviction that the officer of the deck is disposed to be careless or reckless about them. The terrifying appearance of those we see here utterly unnerves him.

On one occasion the monotony of existence was considerably relieved by a little scene on the quarterdeck, of which Howell was the hero. In order to fully appreciate it, one must realize the dignity and exclusiveness that belongs to the commander, and the gravity of any situation which would require him to interfere with the officer of the deck. It so happened that while we were in the "variables," one of these "vortical condensations," of unusual blackness, attracted Mr. Howell's attention. There is a light air, just filling the royals. He waits a while to see what the deck-officer will do; but finally, as that gentleman seems quite oblivious of danger, he approaches him.

"Mr. Wilson, that's an ugly-looking squall to windward!" Wilson nods towards it thoughtfully, and then goes on tapping the rail with his trumpet to the cadence of some far-off music, in which he seems quite absorbed.

"Don't you think you'd better get in your light sail?" the "sogger" persists, after waiting impatiently a moment or two for action.

The officer stretches himself with a lazy yawn. "Oh, I guess there's time enough. That's a long way off yet."

Howell waits a while. At last he is sure the squall is almost upon us and can endure the suspense no longer. He approaches the horse-block for a last appeal.

"Mr. Wilson, you'll certainly have the sticks out of the ship if you wait any longer!"

"No, I reckon not," Wilson answers calmly. "Pretty heavy

squall, I'll admit, Mr. Howell. But I'll jerk in the light sails and be ready to clew down topsails before it reaches us—never fear."

Howell is, however, of a different mind, and determined that the *Alabama* shall not be capsized or dismasted by the foolhardiness of a sailorman who is too jealous of his dignity to be advised. So he ventures on his intimacy with Semmes and hurries down with a report. "Old Beeswax" is in some way persuaded to come on deck, when he instantly takes in the situation. But he does not smile, only remarks,

"Well, Mr. Wilson, you have a black cloud to windward. I don't think there's anything in it, but it's quite as well not to trust a squall. Take in your light canvas, and look to your topsail halyards."

This delivered, he returns below, leaving Howell to enjoy his triumph. But when the ship is denuded, and the cloud passes over without so much as a breath of wind in it, he begins to notice the smile going round and realize he has given Wilson serious offense by his interference, and hastily seeks his stateroom and the consolation of his guitar. It was some time before he permitted his constitutional dread of dark clouds to prompt him to appeal again to Semmes. The words the captain had used, and his quiet manner in directing the officer of the deck, conveyed, on reflection, no compliment either to his sagacity or sense of responsibility. It was a peculiarity of Semmes that he could reprove an impertinence effectually without seeming to be aware of it at all. And in some cases he was generous enough to look over errors rather than compromise the dignity of his officers.

It is now the middle of December, and we have crossed the Gulf of Siam with a fresh monsoon and without a capture or incident of note, except the small excitement now and then of a dolphin hauled on board by some lucky fisherman. We ran in and anchored in deep water off the Island of Aor, at the mouth of the Malacca Strait. We were soon surrounded with the trading boats of the natives; and a lively trade, principally with pipes and tobacco, was established for the usual products of this latitude. The persons of the men here, and women too, are protected from the gaze by a simple clout, the weather requiring no clothing the year-round, and no impulse of nature or education suggesting it. It has struck us at all the points visited in these seas that curiosity as to who or what we are does not seem to bother these islanders at all. No questions as to antecedents, or where bound, or what doing. They are born traders and attach more value to tobacco, muslin, cloth, and gimcracks than English silver. In their peregrinations over the ship we had no occasion to watch them, having found them honest towards us; and yet, in a way, they are the veriest thieves and vagabonds alive, looting shipwrecked vessels and not stopping at the taking of life if opposed. Perhaps *petty* thieving is beneath their dignity. They may want a whole ship. Nor have they the incentive of want; for such a thing as real hard labor is not known among them, the climate supplying every necessity without money and without price.

In the meantime, what has become of the *Wyoming?* We have cruised and bowed around everywhere, have been reported at Batavia and Anger Point, as here, there, and everywhere, and yet we have had no news of her since leaving the lower strait. We are now bound to Singapore. Perhaps we may clash there. But we begin to think Othello's occupation is gone. We saunter and loaf from cape to cape, headland to strait, yet interview none but neutrals. We visited the shore here. Pulo Aor is but a repetition of the islands of this group; the natives, a jolly, rollicking, take-the-world-easy set, go fishing when they fancy that diet and to the fruit trees when the stomach suggests it. They have some idea of music, but it seems to require the most inharmonic discords to gratify it. Or perhaps it runs entirely to rhythm, which they are unwilling to dilute with harmony. They use it to dance by at any rate. In this recreation the women alone seem to do the leg business; the men choose places of vantage at the corners of the huts and seat themselves. The women who do not dance are not allowed to sit, and they are useful at the castanets while their lords whack the tom-toms. The dancers keep excellent time, and the dance is quite graceful—something on the minuet order. The crew, oddly enough, do not care to go ashore, though the place is a veritable Garden of Eden, with plenty of Adam and Eve in it. The people here are quite exempt from the "curse" of labor and the evolutions of the fig leaf, and have nothing to do but enjoy life and trade the bounties of nature for such of the fruits of others' toil as they may fancy.

Next morning we weigh anchor and start under sail and steam for Singapore. The weather has become thick and rainy; and the navigation of these waters, as the reader has already been told, requires our best consideration. In the end we have to come to anchor, and wait for the air to clear up. But soon a Malay pilot comes to the rescue. These fellows are safe to trust, and Semmes drops the responsibility upon them with a sigh of relief and we steam along briskly into the harbor.

Singapore is a British possession and the stopping place of the Peninsula Oriental Co.'s steamers. It occupies the southern coast of the island of Malacca for several miles, spread out along the waterfront. At the time of this visit of the *Alabama*, it contained a population of about one hundred and twenty thousand, of as mixed a character as that of the renowned fortress of Gibraltar. Of these, about half were Chinese, and in their control lay the mass of the commerce that poured into this central depot from all parts of the Far East. But there were also Japanese, Siamese, Sumatrans,

Hindus, New Zealanders, Persians, Bornese, and besides, the representatives of every Eastern and Western race under the sun. Of course John Bull, the Lord Paramount, is there; but even he is overshadowed in all matters except that of political rule and protection by the industrious and wily Chinaman. It is only in situations where his influence is dominant, and the protection of justly administered laws is secured to him, that one can note how great a commercial talent John Chinaman has. With all disadvantages he will distance other competitors, and nothing but the lack of moral vigor and capacity for noble aspiration prevents him from taking a high rank among the peoples of the earth. »In the mechanical and industrial arts his ability to execute is well known. But the inspirational and inventive faculty seems to have died out.

The first news that greeted us on our arrival was that we had been playing fast and loose with the *Wyoming*. She had followed or anticipated us wherever we had been, but somehow managed to miss the golden moment. We are beginning to realize that this sort of thing happens too often to be deemed accidcnt or "good luck." There is a special providence in it; and its chief medium is the reticent, thoughtful man who directs our times and places and quietly demonstrates that the Southern Confederacy has naval genius enough to defy the best counsels of her foe, if not the overwhelming superiority of his resources. It can be said with simple truth that the officers and crew of the *Alabama* to a man (and I certainly do not except Semmes) would have liked well enough to try issues with this pursuer. But the real triumph was not to meet, or even to destroy her, but to elude and defy her. When the *Alabama* was of no more use as a scourge to her enemy's commerce it would be time enough to risk her bones. The commander was not the sort of man to be tempted from his deliberate purpose by passion, ambition, or any other weakness, noble or ignoble. Looking back at it all now, one can hardly escape from the conviction that a man who could do what Semmes did, and do it so faithfully and successfully, must have possessed the very greatest qualities, not only of a naval officer, but also for any dignity of public life or of affairs. There is nothing in the final sacrifice of the *Alabama* to offset this conclusion. Her work was done, and the cause for which she toiled was then lost. She had returned from her work to report it completed; and it was most fitting—and even Semmes could have planned nothing more fitting—that she should now meet, with the wounds and infirmities of her long triumph upon her, the fate which warriors of all ages have accounted most glorious. *Dulce est pro patria mori.*

CHAPTER XI

ENGLISH HOSPITALITY; IDLE AMER-
ICAN SHIPPING IN PORT; A FIGHT
WITH YANKEE SKIPPERS; A CAB RACE;
A GENEROUS OFFER; U.S. GUNBOAT
WYOMING; A SUSPICIOUS CASE; SEMMES
AS BOARDING-OFFICER; CHRISTMAS
IN THE MALACCA STRAITS; A BOAT
FLEET

WE EXCHANGE COURTESIES with the governor of the
island, an English officer and colonel of the garrison. His official home is on the outskirts of the city, hid away in a very
jungle of tropical verdure. Our experience of English hospitality is at once renewed. No objection is made to our coaling
and provisioning; and we are bidden to make ourselves at
home and stay as long as suits our convenience. Of private
hospitality and courtesy we are also made the immediate recipients, and to a degree that taxes our fullest capacity of ac-

ceptance. Our correspondence alone would give plenty of employment to a qualified private secretary, if we could find one. Just at first, our officers are at liberty to enter into the whirlpool of social dissipation, the ship duties being reduced by our considerate first luff to the minimum consistent with good order and discipline. The crew are also allowed liberty; but with the reasonable fear on our part that the result must be the shortening of our own. We have had experience of these visits to English colonial ports and have little doubt that our full staff will shortly be needed to search the byways of sailor town and save the fragments of Jack. We are moored to the docks of the Peninsular Oriental Company, from which we have had to purchase our coal; there is none to be had elsewhere. The company does not deal in coals; and we were under great obligation to them for the sale of what was so indispensable to us, especially as the price was very moderate.

Moored to the dock as we are, the ship becomes at once the scene of bustle and disorder; a perfect pandemonium of sound and babel of tongues; our ship overrun with people of all climes, chattering and gesticulating as so many apes. The officers' quarters have to be guarded by our men to exclude the rabble and announce the important caller. Our decks are begrimed with coal dust; the song of the Malay coal passers mingling with the cries of the fruit vendor. Truly the *Alabama* has been boarded and carried by overwhelming numbers and without resistance.

Our crew are having a good port rest, no coaling or other work to do. One would think the days of patient labor spent at Pulo Condore a waste of time and raw material, and that Kell would be disheartened and disgusted with the sight of his idol in such sad plight; but we must take the bitter with the sweet; holystones and paint will correct the most of it as soon as we get to sea, and our worthies over their headaches. Excursions to the town are the order of the day, the ship

being a long distance from the city proper, and the ubiquitous cabman called into requisition. It is doubtful if ever
such a harvest of fares poured into the coffers of these Jehus;
the distance from the city to our ship being great and the
sun's rays too scorching for a walk. It may be safely asserted
that the stock of New York in cabs could have found service
during our short stay.

It was the privilege of the writer and messmates to form
the acquaintance of Mr. Beaver, of the firm of Cumming,
Beaver & Co., London and Singapore merchants, and become indebted to him for many attentions and delicate evidences of sympathy and friendship. Nothing was left undone
for our amusement and comfort that could suggest itself.
Our ship's affairs were in his able hands; and through him
the labors of our industrious paymaster were reduced to the
minimum, and all the intricacies of bargain and trade
smoothed out. To the officers on pleasure bound he was adviser and guide; and when the labors of the day were over
with him, and the round of pleasure and sightseeing with us,
his home was the haven where our rest and refreshment
awaited us. Indeed, we could not very well have dispensed
with his care, and have achieved a tithe of the enjoyment he
managed to secure for us. The same completeness of hospitality at his London home was later extended to the writer.
Of generous and whole-souled English hospitality, we never
met with a more notable example; and the officers of the *Alabama* did not lack for the kindness of Englishmen.

We roam from ship to town, and return each time on
some new pleasure bound. The principal hotel of the place
is, of course, landlorded by an Englishman; and here we find
all the accompaniments of a hotel on the European plan—
billiards, ten-pin alley, and, to our astonishment, the "simon
pure" American "bar," with its world of mixed drinks, including the insinuating concoction with "grass" in it. We met

at this hotel café the representatives of the great American clipper fleet, caged up in this harbor, passing away the time waiting for some Britisher with plethoric pocketbook to suggest a trade and a change of flag for his ship, or for the *Wyoming* to come along and bury the bones of the "piratical corsair" in the waters of the Malacca Strait and free them.

We found here, upon our arrival, twenty-two American clippers rotting at their anchors—birds escaped from the flushed and frightened covey, taken to refuge in the British swamp; and we expected, upon entering the billiard parlor of the hotel, an unwelcome reception. Our party of some four or five from the ship were enjoying the pleasure of the game and the aforesaid concoction with "grass" in it, when we were, to our surprise, approached by a group of American skippers; and upon an acquaintance of their own seeking, our party are invited to partake of their hospitality. The invitation seemed extended in an open, manly way; and, sailor-like, we grasped the extended hands of our once-countrymen and were ready for the fashions.

Prudent it would have been to beware the Greeks and those bearing presents; for a toast proposed by our newly ac-quired acquaintances bore on its face an affront that called the hot blood into play; and soon the quiet coffee room was the scene of an uproar equaling that of a Donnybrook fair (minus shillelaghs). Our opponents were seriously worsted; so much so that prudence suggested our seeking the ship at once, a question of appeal to municipal law looming up. We were none too soon. The cab race between the police and our Jehu equaled that of John Gilpin against time. Our heroes of the laid-up fleet had not counted on the hidden muscular force of our stalwart engineer officers. The affair, which was a clear case of *in vino veritas*, blew over, and became the sub-ject of merriment and joke; not, however, without a mild de-mand of the police on our commander for our persons. It was evidently a perfunctory appeal; and, besides, our flag protected us with its weak but lawful folds.

You may be sure our American colony here is stirred to the depths, even the ladies and missionaries of the Northern church taking a hand. These latter became men of war and breathed out threatenings and wrath, and with the American consul were plotting schemes and plans for our destruction; based, however, on the chance of communicating with their champion, the all-important *Wyoming*, as they could not hold the small boy till the large one came back home. The thing to do was to apprise her of our presence and to allure us to stay. And to these ends all the arts of strategy were called into play. We are twitted through the English press at this point as being afraid of the American cruiser; charged with being bold and industrious in burning defenseless merchant ships, but wary and crafty as a fox in skulking from the presence of a man-of-war of equal power.

These efforts of harmless "stinkpot" throwing were like pouring water on a duck's back to Semmes. He had positive orders from his government to avoid an engagement with the enemy's vessels of whatever size or strength. The inherent dash and bravery of the man dared to disobey an order that was explicit and founded upon wisdom, but not until his own judgment approved the time. He could see through these newspaper intermeddlers; and if he felt their insinuations, it was doubtless rather for his officers and men than on his own account. He could afford to await the justification of the event.

We have to acknowledge the receipt of an acceptable and handsome present at this port, consisting of one thousand Manila cigars for each of our officers; and, as we number somewhat like the locusts of Egypt, the reader will appreciate the scale upon which our generous friend dispensed his gifts. On the order of Shakespeare's Timon of Athens, we refrain to do violence to his feelings by the mention of his name. He will be grieved to learn that most of them were offered up a sacrifice to Neptune. They went down in the ship off Cherbourg. We had many enthusiastic sympathizers at Singapore, one of them testifying his sincerity in a most practical way. A gunboat built in England, and, if the writer's memory serves him, for the Taeping government (then in rebellion against the Chinese emperor), for some reason not now remembered, was for sale; and our friend offered to purchase her for Semmes and await the convenience of the Confederate government for his reimbursement. The offer was, of course, refused with profuse thanks. Still, the circumstance conveys the estimation in which our ship and cause were held, and could but bind the bands of friendship with hoops of steel.

We should not tire of this hospitable city by a stay be it ever so long, or fail to find profit and amusement in its streets and wonderful bazaars. In the latter we recognize the same shrewd, crafty, but cool and polished Chinese merchant, noted some years before by the writer at Canton. They are unexcelled in thrift or any of the requirements of an accomplished merchant or tradesman. Their stocks are a revelation, and eclipse the shops of our own country vastly. The wealth of some of these traders equals that of our money kings of this time, and at the date of which we write far exceeded it. Indeed, the situation was of this character. The Chinese merchant was the receiver of the riches of the archipelago, the English merchant the purchaser and distributer to the Western consumer; the heterogeneous remainder of the merchant and shopkeeping population merely existing on the crumbs of the wealthier tables.

We were attracted by the violent ringing of a bell on the street, and at the same time a perceptibly quicker step of the throng, and were amused to learn that ice cream was ready to be served at the saloons. Ice being of the high order of luxuries, you must rush for your refreshing dish with all speed or you will be left. It is not to be doubted that in this age of ice machines our present inhabitant of the East would be as much amused as we at the time at the odd advertisement.

We pay another visit to the hotel, the scene of our late unpleasantness. We find here a number of our new-made friends of the army and navy, and the time is passed in joke and conversation; the latter facetiously inquiring as to our appetites pending the arrival of the *Wyoming*. We learn from them that the majority of the American merchant fleet at anchor off the city had laid up here since our arrival and report at Sunda Strait. It suggested itself to them to ask why the United States cruiser did not convoy this immense fleet to sea, not seeming at first to take in the fact that they might be jumping out of the frying pan into the fire; and again, if they reached home in safety, the expenses must go on as usual, and there would be nothing for them to do. They took in the situation finally, but could not but be struck with the fact that all this panic was the result of the existence of one insignificant vessel. Well may the value of even *one* formidable cruiser of the present day force itself on the powers that be. What a havoc she would make against the commerce of such a nation as England or the German Empire! If we may take the career of our ship as a criterion, the number and power of the pursuers do not seem to be a factor towards success. The difficulty of overhauling seems the puzzle. A ship at sea is like a needle in a haystack. We just learned that the *Wyoming* had been at Rhio, a Dutch possession, and coaled ship. She must have been hunting us all the time under steam; so that we have in our late hunting expedition after the China fleet crossed each other's tracks several times.

We must turn our attention somewhat to the crew. Moored to the coal dock and crowded with visitors and tradesmen from early morn to late eve, our fellows have every opportunity for the smuggling of grog on board. Indeed, Corporal Rawse, had he the eyes of Janus, could not keep liquor out of the ship. A most villainous distillation, too, it is. This Chinese "samshee," a production from rice, for rapid and effectual work would cause "Jersey lightning" to blush. The number of "snakes" in it would make a head of hair for Medusa. Our vagabonds are in every stage of drunk, from kitten playfulness to fighting trim, and are to be found scattered from the dock along the broadway into the city. No occasion for money to keep up the sport (so called); for our Jacks are the pets of the people, and money doesn't count in it. Here you will see an old sea dog, making "half boards" to windward, coming up to the wind, and shivering his canvas, then steadying and filling away again. Another making better weather and standing before it. Our friends the cabmen are busy, too, with the blackguards, voyaging them from point to point. Our officers are hard at it, boarding and capturing the runaways; the principal difficulty in the way being the so-called attentions and hospitality of the townspeople, who are making heroes of our worthies, hiding them away without thought of the seriousness of the fun to us, and supplying the liquid refreshments ad libitum. Our worst fears as to the loss of our crew here are not realized. We finally secure the most of them, and altogether through the efforts of our own young officers, without the assistance of the police force. Sailors are more easily managed and led by their own officers than through the force of municipal law. The remembrance of severe training on board in obedience seems never to desert Jack; and at the command of his superior will usually, drunk to excess though he be, fall into line and return to his ship.

We are ready for sea now, and show our appreciation of the kindness and attention of Her Majesty's public servants by smuggling off enough men to supply the places of those we have had enticed away. We are willing to lay the blame of their loss on the broad shoulders of the American consul, and if he is innocent we are sorry for it; but we must have some excuse for smuggling off these subjects of the Queen. Why not put it on the consul? What hypocritical mortals we be! Always an excuse with us for dereliction of duty, or injustice done individual or state.

The report comes today that the *Wyoming* is off the eastern entrance of the Malacca Strait, "hove-to" and watching for us. Be it as it may, she has lost her chance. We shall not go to sea by the western exit, and must therefore leave her to mourn lost opportunities. We suppose a further and last attempt will be made to overhaul us at the west end of the island, should our departure be known soon enough. Our slow movement through the archipelago of the China Sea has been noted by this time, and its repetition through the Malacca Strait no doubt discounted. We have lost at this port five seamen and one messenger boy, and ship in their places, as soon as we clear the port, four others. These men stowed themselves away on board and were supposed to be on the blind side of Master-at-Arms Rawse. James King II of this batch was a splendid specimen of an Irishman and lost his life in the fight off Cherbourg. Being fatally wounded and taken to the *Kearsarge*, he died on board and was buried from her. We shall have more to say of him later on.

It was the 24th of December, 1863, when we left Singapore. We are ready now for the long pull back to the North Atlantic. Kell has his "bad boys" safe back home. Gait has filled the coal bunkers and storerooms through the potency of the money safe; and with the Malay pilot on board and steam up, we cast off from the dock; and amid the cheers of

the vast multitude on the shores and the waving of handkerchiefs from the ladies, we wind and twist through the immense fleet of American clippers at anchor, and soon leave
sight and sense of this cosmopolitan city in the past.

We had cleared the coal docks early in the morning; and just
about twelve o'clock, dinner hour, the cry comes from the lookout aloft, "Sail ho!" It being dinner hour and the men at their
messes, the cry made no excitement, as we were sighting and
exchanging colors with vessels constantly, the mass of them
showing in rig and hull the truth of their bunting thrown out
for our inspection. We soon came up with the sail and hove her
to with a blank cartridge, her build positively showing her
American origin. She displayed, however, the English ensign
at her peak; and master's-mate Fulham was sent on board of
her. He soon returned and reported the vessel as the English
ship *Martaban*, of Maulmain, India, for Singapore with rice;
and that her papers were all in due form, register, and clearance
signed and properly attested by the customhouse officers; but
that the surroundings did not fully satisfy him, the crew being
the greater part Americans and both of the mates long, slab-
sided specimens of the down-east sailor. Further to excite his
suspicions, Fulham explained to our captain that the reason he
had not brought the skipper on board was that he threw himself on his rights as an English subject and refused to come on
board our ship and bring his papers. Fulham was a bright fellow, an Englishman, used to the appearances of an English
ship; and in this taunt, clipperbuilt vessel, with her flaring bow
and sky-scraping skysail masts, with the addition of a rawboned skipper talking through his nose, and the further ad-
junct of two mates of the same model and rig, could not
reconcile the *tout ensemble*. There was nothing to do but to let
her pass on to her port only a few hours' sail off, or our captain
must board her. "The mountain won't come to Mohammed;
Mohammed must go to the mountain."

The gig is manned; and for the first and last time of our cruise Semmes assumes the part of a boarding-officer. Often since has the writer thought that had this boarding event taken place off the banks of Newfoundland in the winter season, our worthy commander could more fully appreciate the danger and discomfort of the trip. The weather was beautiful, however, just now, and the sea smooth. From all accounts, there was a stormy scene on board the *Martaban*. Her suspicious makeup militated against the ship; still, there was no serious flaw in her papers, and it became a momentous question. We had just left John Bull; and he had been a good fellow to us and had as much right to buy an American vessel as anyone else, and having paid for her and holding his receipt for the purchase money, to hoist his flag and drive his bargains under it at will. The puzzle to Semmes was why, *if transferred*, did the vessel still retain an American skipper and mates?

Our captain, however, took the "bull by the horns," and assuming the risk, turn out as it might, informed the skipper he should burn his vessel. Under strong protest the ship was prepared for the torch. Removing the crew and chronometer, Fulham fires the prize. The last hope abandoned, our captain, by a little gentle handling and cross-questioning, draws from the skipper the plain, unvarnished tale. The vessel just destroyed was the *Texan Star* of Maine, but under bogus name and papers. So we were not to be blown out of water by John Bull for the rash act of destroying one of his ships and making prisoners of English subjects. Strange to say, Bulloch (now our sailing-master and in charge of the captured flags and chronometers) has an English ensign, instead of an American, to tag and turn over to the signal quartermaster's care to represent a capture.

Fulham afterwards remarked he was never in such a dilemma before. He did not wish to hurt the skipper's feelings, representing, as he did, a flag towards which, as an Englishman, his sympathies decidedly and naturally tended. Yet there were so many earmarks of Yankee ownership to be argued away he could not make up his mind to let her go before fully communicating to Semmes his doubts and suspicions. It was against reason to associate *that* flag with the twang of the rawboned down-east skipper and his mates; for surely its folds were utterly distasteful to them. The sequel was, of course, most gratifying to our vigilant boarding-master.

After the firing of the prize, her skipper, finding we were not disposed to criticize his questionable methods, became quite resigned and sociable; the easing of his mind to Semmes satisfying his conscience, no doubt. With the crime attached to the forgery of ship's papers, we had nothing to do. It was a matter absolutely between himself and the British government. We never found her proper flag; so Bulloch had to represent her capture by an alien ensign, and Semmes by forged papers.

We run in and anchor at nightfall off the little village of Malacca. We had burned the *Texan Star* on Christmas Eve, and tomorrow we shall pass our second Christmas (1863) in the Malacca Straits. Our last was spent at the Areas Islands, Gulf of Mexico. What changes have come to the panorama of our lives in the short year! And, meantime, thousands of new-made graves of our heroes are turfed now by the departed summer, the wounds of the sod healed, leaving those of the widow, parent, and child still open and bleeding. Ah, if this year of toil and success could have brought us evidence of triumph for our cause on home soil! But that was not written in our horoscope. All this watching, hardship, anxiety, and hope, withered leaves to be!

In the morning permission is had from the English commandant to land the prisoners; and the character of our vessel soon being noised about, the officers of the garrison and their families pay us a visit. The same scenes as at Singamore are reenacted—on a very small scale, but with the same hearty English warmth. Remaining long enough to land our prisoners and give the colony time to inspect our ship, we bid adieu to both; and with hearty exchanges of "Merry Christmas" and "Happy New Year," steam away, leaving them to the joys of the season, a boon beyond our reach. We pass our day, each rather gloomily wrapped in his own thoughts. What a Christmas to our beloved land—this day of peace and goodwill among men! We had opportunity to replenish our supply of fruit and vegetables, but no run on-shore, excepting the boat's crew; hence have no pleasant rec-ollections of the little colony. We pass a number of foreign sails during the day, and at eight bells (supper hour) give the only public reminder of the day by "splicing the main brace"; and though all hands have had a heavy pull at the Chinese ardent the past few days, still a "tot" of pure "Jamaica" may come in play, as "the hair of the dog is good for the bite."

We are moving along under steam; and just after dinner make from the masthead, dead ahead, two ships at anchor in the strait, waiting a fair wind. They have all the appearance of Americans in their spars; though we have no opportunity of judging from the cut of their sails, they being clewed up and furled. But Evans pronounces them the right sort to our wishes. A short steam, and we are alongside of them. We show our bright white flag with the cross and stars—a strange flag to these skippers, as well as to the rest of our re-cent visitors; for we had only made and bent it since reach-ing the East and learning of the change. There is no occasion for subterfuges; so we are answered at once by the Stars and Stripes from both of them. On boarding, they proved to be the *Sonora*, of Newburyport, and the *Highlander*, of Boston, bound in ballast from Singapore to Akyab, where they were to load rice for England. Delayed by calms and head winds in the straits, they had fallen into our clutches. They were both splendid clipper ships of large tonnage. After overhauling them for articles we required from their stores, the torch was applied as usual.

We have today another example of the average American sailor's cheery and buoyant spirit under adversity. The captains of the destroyed ships, learning the uncertainty of where they might be landed, whether in Australia or Yokahama, if prisoners with us—for we shall deliver them over to the first foreigner willing to have them—expressed the wish to be allowed their boats and make the trip to Singapore, distant about four hundred miles. Being near the equator, with a minimum chance of rough weather, Semmes consented. Fitting out their boats with sails and oars, we provisioned them to bridge over any possible long voyage. Bidding us good-bye, and with a hearty handshake, they shoved off in the light air under oars. As the boats strung out in line, the crews opened with a familiar sea song. The refrain borne over the still waters, intermingled with the dip of the oars dying away gradually in the distance, emphasized the romance of the situation. We could but admire their never-say-fail pluck, and you may be sure our sailor sympathies were with them. Add the scene—the burning ships near us, the roar of the fierce flames licking the masts and loose sails—and you have a subject for the painter. We move on under steam, passing the lightship, into the Indian Ocean.

CHAPTER XII

WESTWARD HO!; SUMMING UP RE-
SULTS; SUNNY SEAS; ROUTINE WORK;
PICTURES OF SHIP LIFE; A BARMECIDE
FEAST; BAY OF BENGAL; CEYLON; MAL-
ABAR COAST; A SEA OF FIRE; ELECTRIC
SQUALLS

W̲E HAD ENTERED THE SUNDA Straits the first day of
November, and reenter the Indian Ocean December 25,
1863. We have to sum up as the result of the hunt six vessels
of the enemy destroyed, and all first-class and valuable
prizes. We have escaped the dangers of the intricate navigation of the lower China Sea. Above all, we have had proof of
the indirect damage we have done our enemy, not only in the
American fleet idling away the time at Singapore, but in the
assurance that others are laid up at all the ports of the East
from Japan to Shanghai, and the other four free ports of
China, and in the English, Spanish, and Dutch colonies of

the lower archipelago. We have swept morally as with a net the whole Eastern seas. It will be some time before the game peeps out of the covers, even after our departure is known; and then the fear of capture nearer home will at least keep them out of the home-carrying trade. We shall be reported at Singapore by our two captured skippers as bound west. But who will ensure their bones now under the flag of the United States?

We now coast along the western side of the island of Sumatra before letting go for our stretch over to India. We overhaul in the next week many vessels, but all neutrals. Indeed, it is getting so now that but little interest is taken in the hail from the masthead; and Evans has put away his glasses, formerly worn as constantly as the Western pioneer wears his six-shooter. Even the hint from aloft that the stranger is American has ceased to excite the pulse, so often has it proved a snare and a delusion. Transfers are so common of late in the vessels overhauled that the excitement of the chase has passed away forever; and if one proves a prize finally, the fact develops so gradually that its announcement from the cabin of our ship has no effect upon our emotions.

We have settled down once more to the ordinary routine of ship duties, and are engaged in putting our cruiser in man-of-war trim; all departments under the mechanical and nautical heads at work at the various jobs; and the first lieutenant perambulating the spar-deck, up and down, ordering here and suggesting there. Boatswain Mecaskey may be heard piping the belay of some work completed to his satisfaction. The plane or adze of carpenter Robinson is smoothing or trimming a timber; gunner Cuddy and mates, pots in hand, are polishing up the battery; sailmaker Alcott is mending a rent in an awning; Jack, seated on deck, a midshipman looking on admiringly, is pointing a main brace; a topman swung around the mainmast on a triangle is slushing down the mast. On the yardarms and rigging, topmen here and there, under the supervision of boatswain Mecaskey, are securing chaffing gear on the yards and rigging. The signal quartermaster is airing with proud consequence his mass of flags, the trophies of our captures, and no doubt as proud of them as the Indian of his scalps or the hunter of his antlers. An old quartermaster off watch will be doing some embroidery work for one of the messenger boys he has taken under his wing. Forward, out of the way of the working gangs, groups are deeply engaged in the intricacies of checkers, or passing their opinions of this or that move on the board. Jack is an expert at this game. You had better not tackle him except to improve your own experience.

On the quarterdeck you may observe a midshipman or two engaged under sailing-master Bulloch, taking a sight with his sextant for longitude, or marking time by the chronometer for him. On the quarterdeck is the leader of us all, Commander Semmes—the man we have followed now for many weary months. Where he has directed, we have gone confidently. He has carried us so far without a disaster, and we would trust him to the utmost and follow still. He is pacing the deck, his brow contracted, pulling, as is his wont, at his gray mustache. Back and forth he strides, not a word to anyone. He is in deep communion with his own thoughts. What can be so occupying him that he is oblivious to surroundings? Perhaps hatching some deep scheme for future punishment of his enemy. Maybe his thoughts are reverting to our dear land in the last throes of a sinking cause; for he is only human like ourselves, and under a haughty bearing carries a touch of sympathy for sorrow and love for home. He may be in a daydream now, bringing dear ones close to himself in fancy. Be his thoughts what they may, the silent man before you will never seek your sympathy for himself.

That man of loneliness and mystery,
Scarce seen to smile, and seldom heard to sigh,
Whose name appals the fiercest of his crew,
And tints each swarthy cheek with sallower hue,
Still sways their souls with that commanding art
That dazzles, leads, yet chills the vulgar heart.

What should it be that thus their faith can bind?
The power of Thought—the magic of the Mind?
Linked with success, assumed and kept with skill
That moulds another's weakness to its will;
Wields with their hands, but still to these unknown
Makes even their mightiest deeds appear his own:
Such hath it been—shall be—beneath the sun
The many men must labor for the one.
'Tis Nature's doom; but let the wretch who toils
Accuse not, hate not, him who wears the spoils.
Oh! if he knew the weight of splendid chains,
How light the balance of his humbler pains!

And here you have, reader, a rough sketch of many such deck scenes for the next few weeks, as we wend our way to the Indian continent.

Semmes was happily situated in his officers; all of them with the exception of the executive and chief engineer being young men in their twenties, of fine physique and robust constitutions; many of them descendants of old naval families, intelligent, and with the marked difference in rank and age between the leader and themselves could but naturally look up to him for guidance and with full confidence. They had most of them been under fire before, many of them frequently. And as it was not long after inaugurating the cruise that Semmes discovered their ability in practical seamanship, he was much relieved in mind and body and enabled to take regular rest at night, feeling full assurance that the deck was ably manned, and did not hesitate to say so frequently. Indeed, in chase and maneuvering around prizes, he seldom offered a suggestion after passing the word as to his wishes. In practical navigation Semmes undoubtedly had no equal on the cruiser, having had many years' experience on the Coast Survey. In knowledge of international law, there was no one on the vessel at all competent besides himself. Indeed, we should not be far amiss in stating that he had no equal in this line in either navy. He had made an especial study of it. It stood him well on many occasions, nor did he ever come out of a controversy in this connection second-best. Had the watch-officers under Semmes not fully answered to his expectations and hopes as seamen and relieved him thus of much care, his career would doubtless have been shortened; for as it was, the three years of active service in the *Sumter* and *Alabama* left him quite a physical wreck, as he freely admitted.

And here (to stray a bit from the subject matter in hand) is food for reflection in the matter of the slow promotion in the navy of our country at this day. Long before an officer has reached a responsible position, he has passed the age to stand the hard knocks and irregular life experienced by the working officers of the *Alabama*. There seems but one way out of this dilemma—a more generous retired list.

We have rigged a bottle from the foretopmast-studding-yardarm, and have the divisions under marine officer Howell practicing pistol drill. Jack always will be an awkward fellow with small arms. And as soon as the weapon is handed him to illustrate the lesson, Howell had better get out of the way, for the lad is more apt to "pink" a marine officer than the suspended bottle. It is an amusing but dangerous pastime, watching Jack's revolver practice. So with infantry drill. Our worthy drillmaster has a squad, a gun division of men, putting them through the manual of arms. Now if you, reader, have been in the army and imagine you can "coach" the job, Howell will cheerfully hand these to-be-made soldiers over to you; and if your exhaustion at the end of the attempt does not surpass that of a rapid day's march, well, you shall drill them hereafter. Attempt to "dress" the squad, and a "Virginny fence" is a mathematically straight line alongside Jack's alignment; and as to marching and countermarching—after he has "weighed anchor" with them and "filled away," you can find them meandering the spar-deck like a grazing flock of sheep—some on the quarterdeck and others on the topgallant-forecastle. Falstaff's ragamuffins answer to Howell's pets. No! Jack is at home behind a big gun, there is some "heft" to that, but he looks upon a rifle as a toy and has only contempt for it. Throw him, however, on the deck of an enemy, and he will, in his own awkward but vigorous way, handle his cutlass and bayonet with good effect. Dear old shipmate Howell, now sleeping quietly in his own sunny South, how the recollection of fun poked at you after your return from the deck, exhausted and upset in temper, pricks the memory now! If ever man was dubbed patriot for serving his country faithfully and patiently, you deserved the name after a morning of squad drill!

We are running along the Sumatra coast, weather fine, and all who are off duty can enjoy the scene. Fish are abundant in these waters, and the trolling line is furnishing us with a dolphin now and then. We will visit the wardroom mess this fine morning. Kell and Galt are engaged in the intricacies of a game of chess, heads down and elbows on the table; Galt has his opponent in a tight place and is patiently awaiting his next move. Parkinson, the steward, is busy in the pantry near by, exercising his culinary brain and puzzled to invent some new dish from his limited stock of luxuries. Kell makes his happiest move on the board, followed instantly by his opponent, and with a laugh of triumph, "checkmate!" With a frown and an air of defeat, Kell turns to the steward: "What have you for dinner today, Steward?" The cornered chef, realizing the state of the first luff's temper, "hems and haws," and slowly jerks out the information that the standard dish of "salt horse" and rice will adorn the dinner table. Our hero is a Georgian and can manage his share of "swampseed," but does not pine for it every day. As though a happy thought had struck him, Kell turns to Galt, and says facetiously, "Let's dine at Verrey's today." "Agreed," responds the latter. They had had some experience at this temple of gastronomy, and were willing to take the chances again, as against Parkinson's bill of fare. "Take up the *carte*," says Kell; "You order the dinner, Galt."—"What do you say to green turtle for soup?"—"Admirable!"—"How about turbot, next?"—"To the Queen's taste!"—"And now; well?"— "Roast beef rare and pheasant and"—"Well, what is it, messenger boy?"—"Please, sir," touching his front lock, hat in hand, "the master-at-arms has a couple of men at the mast, sir; been fighting, sir." The dinner at Verrey's is ordered to be kept hot, and Kell mounts the companion ladder to take a hand in the row.

We leave Galt to retrospective dreams of the dinner and visit old Joe Wilson in his stateroom. Joe has vamoosed from the "country" to have a quiet retired "air" on his guitar all to himself, and is assaying a love song, no doubt suggested by thoughts of his inamorata awaiting in faraway Florida his return with glory and prize-money. Joe is not like his mockingbirds at home, first-class as a songster, but he fingers his guitar well. "Come in, old fellow, I want to play an accompaniment for you!" And soon the book, draughts, chess, and the learned argument are dropped, and Joe's privacy is utterly wrecked. First one and then another of the glee club take a turn at a song; and, the wardroom members of the club exhausted, the guitar is taken to the steerage and the music continued, and thus we while away the hours of leisure.

We also may visit the steerage, and taking a campstool observe our midshipman youth. Here is one deeply engaged in the mysteries of "pointing" a bit of rope as exercise in the line of his profession. He is wrapped up so deeply in the intricacies of the task as to be lost to all around him. Suddenly he rises and, reaching the deck, interviews the boatswain or one of his mates; and having been led out of the puzzle by explanation or help, returns to the steerage and his task. Here also you find one of Bulloch's pupils deeply engaged, working out a sight recently taken to determine the longitude; and to watch his serious face, you would suppose the captain or the sailing-master is awaiting it to prick off the position of the ship on the chart. But they are not anxious, having already performed this task. Another youngster has his ditty bag out and is perspiring over a rude attempt to darn a pair of dilapidated socks or sew on a button. All are busy here, and at something useful. It is too light for pranks yet—they want the dim of the lantern for this—and argument is a peg too high for our middy; he leaves this to the erudite occupant of the wardroom. He has been taught practically that "sea lawyers" cannot vegetate luxuriously in a steerage. They are very quiet, industrious chaps just now, but you had better not trust them with a fair opportunity for mischief; they are as full of undeveloped deviltry as your college sophomore and rather more reckless of dignities. Their only absolute immorality, however, is prigging grog out of Higgs's tub.

We may pay a visit also to engineer O'Brien. We are on a round of cruising, enjoying the tramp as the Yankee old maid does the rounds of a village. "Well, good morning, Matt, how is the old 'teakettle' getting along?" (You must know the boilers of the ship are in a most dilapidated state)—"Well, we are nursing them, but it can't be long before they will be about like so much coral, the salt water has honeycombed them so."—"I hope you'll get us to the English Channel anyhow before the blowup comes off. By the way, Matt, can't you let a fellow have a gallon of fresh water if he sends the boy for it? You know it's hard lines this hot weather on allowance."—"Yes, but don't let the chief know it." We thank him and depart. You must know one gallon is the daily allowance for all purposes and comes hard in the tropics.

Let's go forward and listen to Jack spin a yarn or two. Here they are, dinner over, but not the exhilaration of the stiff "tot" of grog; and the fellows are loquacious over their pipes. A story has been started. "Well, you see, when I was in the *Narcissus* frigate in the South Sea Islands, our admiral was paying a visit of return to the American commodore. I was 'bow' in his gig's crew, and the coxswain in the stern sheets, sitting on the rail steering. There was a large 'man-eater' keeping with the boat, the nasty brute gliding along and showing his fin. Don't you know, I thought something ugly was going to happen."—"Of course," chimed in the audience, now excited and anticipating. "Well, the first thing you knew, Bill Bowling lost his balance from the stern sheets, and overboard he went. The admiral lost his coxswain, for all we saw was a dart by of the shark and a streak of blood on the water. Well, the admiral kept on and paid the visit; and the next day, don't you think, here comes Bill Bowling's head alongside, wrapped up in an old newspaper, with the compliments of the Yankee commodore. You see, the men on the Constellation frigate had been fishing some time for this very same man-eater and had caught him from the 'bridle-port'; and when they cut him open, there was poor Tom's head in the belly."—"Humph!" from some doubter in the audience. "Fact, I assure you."—"Well, one thing more, shipmate, did poor Tom wink his eye?" And a shout of laughter goes up. The yarn-spinner knocks the ashes from his pipe, and saunters aft at the pipe of the boatswain, "all hands," promising a yarn at supper to knock "seven bells" out of this one.

We have thus reached the year 1864, and it looks as though our occupation is gone. We board vessels occasionally, but no luck. We are stretching across the Bay of Bengal to round the Island of Ceylon. We overhaul and board a British ship more for pastime and the hope of late newspapers than to examine her papers. She is too English to suggest the hope of a bonfire. Fulham has a good time on her, "rigging" the passengers who were Mohammedans from Singapore, bound to the port of Jiddah, thence to the shrine of Mecca. A most remarkable idea had gotten abroad among them, and we had heard of it first at Singapore, that we carried in our hold, chained, an assortment of huge giants to let loose on the Yankees; and they wanted to know how "Their Royal Highnesses" fared. Fulham reported upon his return that he had found true believers among them as to the monsters, and that he had stuffed them to the full. We can believe it, for Fulham is fully competent to get off a stunner.

We double the Island of Ceylon without so much as the smell of a capture, and it is the middle of January. We are moving along the coast of Malabar, dejected as the weary hound sneaking back home from his lone private and unsuccessful rabbit hunt, when "Sail, ho!" No particular move on the part of anyone until the scout has mounted the rigging, and from the crosstrees pronounces the sail American. This does not now excite much either, for it does not by a deal certify a prize, so many of them having been transferred. We come up with her without the necessity of a blank cartridge. She proves the *Emma Jane*, of Bath, Maine, from Bombay to Amherst in ballast. See what they have come to. Wandering the earth in search of a cargo. We have no occasion for a court of condemnation, she having no cargo. We lay near her, removing such naval and other stores and provisions as in need of and adding to our stock of flags and chronometers, remove her crew and passengers, and apply the torch. It is the first time we have lit up the Indian Ocean.

Coasting along, we anchor off the small town of Anjenga. Communicating with the Portuguese official, permission is obtained to land the prisoners, the native boatmen steering them through the surf. This is an open roadstead. Our prisoners are provisioned, the governor offering to forward them to the nearest port where British shipping could be found and reship them to the care of some consul. The natives flock about us in their canoes, and we have, on a smaller scale, the counterpart of our late China Sea scenes. We are now busy in the work of swapping our sovereigns for a heterogeneous mass of luxuries of the table. We have been on ship's rations but three weeks; still, we could put up with this change and wish it to last indefinitely. The natives here are dark chocolate in color, finely formed, active and lithe figures, straight hair, and absence of Ethiopian features. Expert in handling their canoes in the surf, they would put you through the breakers, either in their or your own boats, and give you but a mere sprinkle of the salt water. Some of our officers visit the shore and inspect the town, but not much is to be seen. Though an English possession, but few English reside here. Being a town of no commerce, it offers few inducements to our trading-friend John Bull, and is kept alive by the Hindu-Portuguese inhabitants.

So soon as it is known that the smart clipper-looking crusier in the offing is the *Alabama*, the decks are crowded with seminude natives of all ages and both sexes. They have heard of us and our exploits in the China Sea, even in this out-of-the-way town; and though we cannot make matters as clear to them as to our Singapore visitors, having no interpreter, they seem charmed with the graceful boat. Bartelli does not seem to attach the importance to his visitors here as at Cape Town and Singapore; and, though he has as a caller upon our captain the governor's son and his aide, we do not hear the pop of champagne in the cabin nor does the young official emerge from the cabin with one of Semmes's manilas in his mouth. Our captain's steward is an aristocrat, no doubt. A governor's son coming on board without a visiting card has evidently failed to make a good impression on our punctilious steward. Who knows but he may be an Italian noble, exiled from the ancestral soil?—poor Bartelli! He was a gentle, faithful servant. The writer can see him now, performing his tonsorial labors in the wardroom; for he was ship's barber to the whole wardroom mess, and took such pride and pleasure in brushing and platting Kell's luxurious beard!

But we are ready for sea, and get under way in the afternoon, the Ghaut mountains towering up in the distance and casting their shadow over the landscape to the very beach. Our surfmen salaam us a good evening as we get off; and we stand through the archipelago, paralleling the Malabar coast, and then stretch over for the Arabian Sea. We are in the embrace of the northeast monsoon, blowing a fresh but not strong breeze; and for two weeks not a brace is touched, and scarce an order given by the officer of the deck. So quiet is it at night, you might suppose the *Alabama* a phantom ship. We are moving along under full-sail royals and studding sails alow and aloft, the watch on deck curled up under the weather bulwarks asleep, and nothing to break the silence but the sound aft of the eddying sea in the screw well. The weather is balmy, every star scintillating in the heaven, and thin clouds drawn out in long, narrow ribbons of gossamer. A paradise indeed is old ocean for a sailor now. Our evenings are truly delightful; and after supper Jack gathers in groups, and the yarn spinner, given a point of vantage and where our skipper can *accidentally* overhear the yarn, begins.

"I'll tell you what it is, shipmates, the way 'Old Beeswax' always picks out Sunday for his big licks goes to show he's got his weather eye on that blamed, blarsted Friday. Don't you see he put this here craft of ours in commission on Sunday. It may be chance he captures our first prize on Sunday; but he picks up the California steamer on Sunday by regular appointment, as it were, with Captain Jones; and then he sneaks up off the Texas coast and gathers in the *Hatteras* on his favorite day. Did you twig him run the blockade of the *San Jacinto* at Martinique on his pet day? So likewise from the *Vanderbilt* at Cape Town; and bless your soul, my hearties, we should have tackled the *Wyoming* sure and no mistake if the old man hadn't sheered off from Friday and closed in with the Sunda strait on his saint-day. 'Old Bim' don't keep them little saints and angels lit up all the time with them wax candles in the cabin for nothing. They's got their little arrangement together. Don't you see Bartelli firing up upon 'em all the time? Them's the signals! Yes, give me a skipper that ain't flying in the face of Providence all the time by tending to business on Friday. I'll give you a little experience in the *Formidable* frigate. I disremember the year, but it was on a Friday. Our admiral would leave the roadstead 'cause we had a fair wind. Just think of it! You may be sure there was growling and swearing fore and aft fit to lift both bowers from their holding ground. But no use; the admiral allowed it was all d—d humbug and wasn't going to listen to any old woman's nonsense. Well, we got an offing by the skin of the maintopsail, when the wind chops round in our teeth and blows 'great guns.' We were close-reefing the topsails when the foot rope on the maintopsail yard to leeward parts, and overboard goes half the maintop men."
"Did you pick 'em up?" almost gasps one of the listeners. "Pick 'em up? Bless your soul, we didn't even lower a boat! A Mother Cary's chicken could hardly live in such a sea. No,

the poor fellows went to Davy Jones! Our admiral began to
look blue, but he was just gettin' the *little* end of it. The
frigate was bound to the slave coast to look out for slavers.
We had hardly got out of this lee-shore scrape when the
crew was completely upset, all thought of duty gone on liberty. It seems when hammocks was piped down and the
watch below turned in, the dead men's hammocks was
swung to their number hooks on the berth-deck every night,
but they wasn't unlashed. The master-at-arms swore the
hammocks was in the nettings; but when you come to look
they weren't; only in the morning back in the nettings you'd
find 'em. The devil knows how!

"We knew something was coming. Sure enough, one
dark, squally night (we had nasty weather all the way to the
coast) the cathead lookout sung out 'Breakers ahead,' 'Hard
down your helm'; and quicker than you could get your grog
stopped the frigate struck. You ought to see the crew look at
the admiral as he crawled on deck with his eyes started and
hair standing on end. The frigate had run foul of a whale
asleep on the water. It was all we could do to keep her free
with the pumps till we made the French coast for a dock.
When we got to port the devil was to pay. The cholera was
raging, and the officers and crew was taken down and died
like rats in a fumigated ship. Our old admiral 'kicked the
bucket' among the first. There we thought the matter ended;
and so it did, so far as the frigate went. But there was one of
our ships here going home; so they put the old admiral up in
a puncheon of rum and shipped him home to Plymouth;
and, don't you know, when they got him to Plymouth there
was very little of him left, for the men had tapped him and
drawn off the rum, leaving very little admiral to bury. So you
see the bad luck payed out like a maintop-bowling; no end
to it. No, messmates! Catch me sailing on Friday! Shiver my
timbers if you do! I'd jump overboard and swim ashore

first."—"Say, Messmate, was there anything out of the way in the taste of that rum?"—"Don't know much about that. Wa'n't invited to sample it. Was on the royal yard when this grog was 'served out.' But you look out, and don't sail on a Friday!"

Our glee club is in the full tide of song; and even Semmes unbends from his dignity and, with his campstool on the bridge and manila lit, smokes away the hours and listens to the plantation songs interspersed with the more sentimental, and winding up with "Dixie" and "Bonny Blue Flag" just before the sound of eight bells. We have secured, in our recent batch of recruits, a fiddler, and the scratch of the violin is heard again; and Jack has mastered some new steps and flings, picked up from the dear girls at Cape Town and Singapore. Never such a run before on the *Alabama*. The new pieces are fresh on this stage, for we have theatricals as well; and weather now permitting, the forecastle is packed from bridge to hawseholes, and the merry laugh goes round. How often ignorance is bliss! This grand breeze is wafting the *Alabama* to her fate, and many of the gallant, lighthearted fellows will never see dear home again. But do not reveal the future to them or stop the joyous pastime.

We met on this passage a curious phenomenon. I was keeping the first watch one night and noticed about half past eight an appearance of milky whiteness in the sea ahead, as though in shoal water, accompanied by a brilliant phosphorescence. Although the chart indicated no shoal or land within hundreds of miles of us, still volcanic upheavals can occur in a day. The sight was so startling and sudden as to cause us to stand by for a grate on the rocks. The captain was called immediately, and the ship hove-to. Sounding with the deep-sea lead and getting no bottom at a great depth, our fears were allayed, and we filled away. A bucket of the water drawn showed innumerable bright particles sparkling and moving through it; but being kept for examination by daylight, it presented no unusual appearance. There was an unnatural light over the sea as far as the eye could reach, and to tell the truth it thoroughly alarmed everyone. We thought the *Alabama* was to lay her bones in the Indian Ocean. We were several hours passing through it, showing it to be at least twenty-five or thirty miles in extent. The cause of this remarkable display of marine fireworks we could not determine, and even Semmes's experience was for once at fault.[1]

We are in the latter part of January experiencing variable winds, and expect soon to be in the "doldrums" of the equator. The quiet of the ship is suddenly disturbed by an incident which evokes another instance of the signal courage and address of the man Mars. We are close-hauled on a wind, under sail alone, the screw being, as usual, triced up. The wind is blowing a good "topgallant breeze," with a clear sky and rather a frisky sea. One of the crew who had been on the sick list for a long time, now convalescent, was ordered by the surgeon to be carried on deck for sun and fresh air. While lying on the topgallant-forecastle, by some means not positively known, the man went overboard to leeward. At once the cry was given, "Man overboard!" Wilson, the officer of the deck, gave the order, "Hard down your helm! Cut away the life buoy! Man the weatherbraces! Light up the head sheets! Brace aback! Lower away the lee lifeboat!" The vessel was at a standstill in a twinkling, with the struggling invalid some distance astern battling with feeble strength for life. Mars took in the situation instantly. Seizing a grating, he rushed to the lee gangway, and throwing it overboard ahead of him mounted the rail. All this was done, and he was

---

1. A similar phenomenon sometimes occurs in the Gulf of Mexico. It is probably of rare occurrence.

in the water swimming with the grating ahead before the vessel had been hove-to.

Meanwhile the first lieutenant reached the deck, and observing the intent of Mars, ordered him not to go to the rescue of his comrade in such rough water; the boat could pick the man up, and one of the crew was enough to lose if any. But his order was not heeded; humanity had asserted itself, and all thought of the gravity of disobedience of orders was thrown by Mars to the winds. Only replying, "Keep cool, Mr. Kell, I will save the poor fellow," he swam rapidly to the now nearly exhausted sailor. He reached him, and shoving the grating under him awaited the approach of the lifeboat, which was not long in taking them both in, the invalid being more dead than alive. A wild yell broke from the throats of the gallant tars. The yards were braced up, the head sheets hauled aft, boat hoisted to the davits and secured, and the vessel was once more on her course.

As soon as order was restored, Semmes had officers and crew mustered on the quarterdeck, and, mounting the horse-block in a speech of ten minutes delivered a flattering tribute to the superb gallantry of the man. He called upon the rest of the officers and crew to endeavor to emulate his example in all hours of danger and trial. The speech was an endorsement any man might be proud to receive from his commander. At the conclusion of the remarks, the order was given the boatswain and mates to pipe down. As the crew were strolling forward, Mars, with a hitch of the trousers so common with Jack tars, remarked, "The captain has made a bloody fuss over nothing." During the entire time occupied by Semmes in addressing officers and crew, Mars stood hat in hand, head down, and blushing like a schoolgirl at the well-earned compliments showered upon him. Michael Mars was an Irishman and had served time in the British navy. It must be confessed that, if his courage seemed at times foolhardy, it was justified by an unusual adroitness in handling himself.

We are so evidently heading up now for the Mozambique Channel that we know without telling that Cape Town is to be revisited, and that we shall have a chance to delight the ears of our acquaintances there presently with the story of our adventures in the Indian Ocean and the China Sea. Also, maybe, to explain to courteous Governor Wodehouse how we happened to run away with sundry British subjects and to make the earliest possible restitution of the same; meantime, humbly praying His Excellency to give us his potent aid toward the recovery of some of our own lads, which our hasty departure in stress of weather compelled us to leave behind. We also desire to tender our respects to Captain Baldwin of the *Vanderbilt*, should he still be burning coals around the Cape, and to obtain some news of what has been going on at home. We have heard nothing for months. Yet this latter desire is not unmingled with dread. It is becoming only too plain to us that the resources of our foes are practically boundless, and that we are to be left unaided to cope with them. At last advices, Lee was still breasting the avalanche with his "Stonewall" brigade. But how long could such a contest last with seaports sealed, homes devastated, and the enemy, with an immensely greater population, abundant means, and the whole earth to draw from, pressing upon us from every side? But it was not ours to utter, even to each other, the doubts we felt. We kept them in our hearts and talked cheerfully.

We entered the Mozambique Channel and stood for the Island of Comoro on the African coast. As soon as it was sighted, we clewed up all sail and put the ship under steam. Being near now to Johnny Bull's coal pile, we feel we can afford this luxury; and as we have run out of the trade winds into doldrums—an alternation of calms and light, shifty airs that leave us too much at the mercy of the currents—we could hardly make the port we are bound for without it.

Johanna, the chief harbor of the group to which Comoro belongs, is our destination. No pilot is required here, as the shore is bold and rocky, with deep water to the very base of the cliffs. We run in and anchor right off the town. These islands, strange to say, are not claimed by either "John Bull" or "Johnny Crapaud." It may be a case of crouching each on a side of the carcass, and awaiting developments. Both have a craze for the acquisition of good building sites, and for settling families on them.

The Comoro group rises perpendicularly out of the sea and is of volcanic origin. The present ruler is an Arab and self-styled "Sultan Abdallah," which cognomen is about as frequently found in the vocabulary of Mohammedan proper names as "Smith" in Christian lands. And we should judge the "sultan" to be as commonplace an individual as our ubiquitous Smith aforenamed. Upon sending an officer onshore to announce our arrival and desire to confer with him upon sundry subjects, he sent off to the ship his grand cockalorum, or vizier, with the request that we excuse him, as he was superintending the erection of a *sugar-mill;* but his representative would attend to our wants, and we were quite welcome to the comforts and hospitality of the port. Adding, with an eye to business, that his factotum would be pleased to bargain with us for fresh provisions, etc. Shade of an emperor; and what a fall is here, my countrymen! But why should fellows roaming the ocean for the purpose of aiding in establishing, if possible, another republic, and disseminating democratic ideas and institutions, criticize our brother sultan found engaged in the laudable handling of his saw and jack plane? Surely a more admirable ambition and useful occupation this than sitting around on a throne and ordering bowstrings for unlucky subjects. So we wish his august majesty success in his humble and useful occupation, and trust he may turn out a first-class article of sugar. No doubt he shows his plain common sense in plodding on with his work, rather than removing the sweat of toil visiting the *Alabama* and swapping senseless compliments not meant and not swallowed. Beyond a doubt he is proving a good practical ruler at present and, with his sensible methods, bids fair to become a better.

Our paymaster, Galt, has no difficulty in arranging with the prime minister for a supply of meats, vegetables, and fruits; and we will do the colored gentleman the justice to say that his prices were moderate and supplies excellent. If he is as satisfactory an adviser to his sultan as caterer to us, he will long hold his cabinet seat. "May he live long and prosper!" The inhabitants here are a mixed race of Hindus, Africans, and Arabs, but all Mohammedans in faith. They are cordial, polite, and hospitable, and quite intelligent and well posted in the history of the Occident. Their high priests and teachers are especially well informed. Many American whale ships, as also English men-of-war and merchant vessels, stop here for rest and refreshment. The islands are naturally healthy, the temperature sultry in the valleys, but moderate as you ascend. English is spoken by very many of the people, intercourse with the outside world being pretty constant. The *Alabama* was well known to them by report, and they told us our visit had been looked for months before. American shipping, until recently, was almost always to be found in the harbor. We had evidently cut into the trade of these islanders considerably by our former presence in their neighborhood.

Our surgeon, Llewellyn, is constantly called upon during our stay, not only for attendance, but medicines; and the sick bay is daily the rendezvous of all classes of the people seeking advice and physic. We were informed that disease had been introduced into the islands by the American whaling fleet, and its spread had been general. At the time of our visit it could be designated a national calamity.

The walk through the town we find quite interesting, the booths and bazaars attractive in Eastern bric-a-brac generally, Turkish pipes, tobacco, etc. A party of us from the wardroom entered a café for the purpose of enjoying a cup of Mocha coffee, in the making of which these Mohammedans excel; it being their hourly beverage, taking the place of spirits or wines, which their religion prohibits. We found the proprietor on his knees at his devotions; and waiting some time for him to arise, we were observed by outsiders and advised to go farther for the refreshment, as our friend had just commenced his prayers and would probably be some considerable time engaged. We learned that it is not uncommon for them to spend several hours at a time in prayer. Altogether, we can but admit them a thoroughly sincere people in their religion and practices, and in the total-abstinence feature they certainly present us an object lesson. We had not the pleasure of seeing the sultan during our week's stay; not that his august presence was denied us through the sacredness of his person, but rather that his occupation suggested a mechanic's apron and the accompaniment of dirt and grease.

Several of us ascended the precipitous side of the mountain, following the well-worn path winding to the summit. The view from the elevation is varied and extremely beautiful, embracing ocean and landscape, the latter a paradise of tropical verdure. Birds of the parrot species abound, chiefly of the gray variety, and wild peacock are also plentiful. Following the path, a mountain stream of clear, cold water paralleling it, about halfway up the mountain we find a cascade falling over the rocks about twenty feet, forming a deep pool several yards in diameter. The suggestion of a bath was natural, the temperature of the water being about right. We

have the evidence before us that we are not the first Europeans to enjoy the luxury of this mountain tub, for on the
rocks we read "H.B.M.S. Medusa, Jan. 12, 1837," in large
letters in white paint, artistically lettered, showing it to have
been most probably the handiwork of the frigate's painter. It
seemed to guarantee the safety of the pool; and so we found
it, swimming up under the cascade to be buried under, and
coming to the surface some distance below. We enjoyed the
sport for some time. We should have painted the name of
our ship on the rocks, as at first agreed among our party, but
difficulties intervened to prevent. It would have been an interesting landmark now, had we done so.

Our crew do not take advantage of the liberty permit
here to any great extent, and would not at all but for the
fine coast-bathing. No rum to be had here and no dance
house; nothing but the bazaars and cafés to attract; and
though Jack is fond of a cup of fragrant coffee, *that* is soon
settled. Our natives are anxious to witness a bonfire, and
the selfish fellows actually hope that an "unfortunate" will
come along. So here is some more human nature of the
baser sort, willing and anxious to see the fellow going down
the hill receive an additional kick. We find an English
whaling vessel here, rara avis anywhere, Americans and
Portuguese almost monopolizing this trade. Whales are
plenty off the Madagascar coast in the season; and we are
in hopes of a prize appearing off the harbor, but are
doomed to disappointment.

We take in a plentiful stock of fresh provisions, vegetables, and fruit, including a number of the double-hump cat-
tle of this region—a supply for many days and an attraction
to our ship's butcher, whose hand is getting out in the line of
his trade. We must have proved the best customer to the sultan in many a day. The old fellow evidently has an eye to
business, for our paymaster swaps our sovereigns for the sup-

plies all the time, no presents greeting our view and no ceremonies requiring to be provided for.

We weigh anchor and stand to the southward, bound now to Cape Town. The weather is delightful in temperature but variable as to style, squally, with little or no wind, torrents of rain, and tremendous electrical discharges. An old quartermaster who had visited these parts years ago in an English man-of-war had warned me previously what to expect in this neighborhood, and I recollected something of my own experience on a return voyage from Japan some years before. "Horsburg's sailing-directions" (undoubted authority) makes mention of the marked character of the squalls of this locality. We caught some of it off the south end of Madagascar. It was in the first watch of the night, about half past eight. The sky had been promising for some time a rainsquall, and it did not tarry long once the lightning lit up the horizon. The quartermaster sidling up to me remarked, "Well, sir, we are going to have it." The flashes approached very rapidly, accompanied by torrents of rain such as must have visited old man Noah, but with little wind. The lightning ran down the three conductors to the masts in constant streams, entering the water with a hissing sound and jumping from gun to gun, and even to the engine below. The crash was like the explosion of a heavy mine blast or battery of artillery; and between the flashes the night was as black as Erebus. The ship had been ordered under low sail as a precautionary measure. But the heavy dark clouds evolved no breeze. Nearly blinded by the flashings, there was nothing to do but recline on the horse-block and take the deluge of rain with mouth shut to keep from being drowned. The captain, putting his head out of the companion hatchway and looking around for a few moments, remarked, "Well, sir, you do not seem to be getting any wind out of it, though, on the whole, I do not envy you your watch"; and retired to his law books again.

As a flash of lightning lit up the deck, Midshipman Maffitt of the watch was noted close beside the writer. His post was on the forecastle; and to the query, "What can I do for you, Mr. Maffitt?" "Nothing," is the reply; then for some time we gaze at each other inquiringly, as the flashes allow. "Well, sir," he at last said, "I came aft because it is so lonesome." The reason was appreciated *fully;* but his place was forward. So with an "I'm sorry, sir, and would like to have your company, but it *won't do;* you had better go forward," we parted. It must be confessed I would have preferred to pass the remainder of the watch near somebody to divide the scare with myself. No damage resulted to the ship, beyond injury to one of the conductors. I have heard it stated that no steamer has ever received serious damage from lightning, but cannot vouch for the accuracy of the statement. You have never, reader, seen lightning at its worst unless in these straits; and its frolics are of a character to provoke dodging, though of course it is of no use, as the danger is over ere you have dodged. This remarkable carnival of the lightning lasted nearly the whole watch; and its cessation did not anger Wilson, who relieved me at midnight.

Dolphin are in large schools around us now constantly, and the young officers and men have grand sport fishing for them with grains and line; the most attractive bait being an artificial fish of pewter, or a white cotton rag. So soon as you skip your hook over the water, a rush for it takes place, and you fasten on to a fine fellow from three to four feet long. We have been in the company of this fish more or less for several months—ever since leaving St. Paul in the South Indian Ocean—but shall leave them now in a few days. An interesting sight on a pleasant afternoon it is to observe the boys of the ship, as also the younger officers, taking exercise in the rigging, springing like squirrels up the lower rattlings to the lofty tops and over the futtock shrouds to the crosstrees, and crossing by the fore- and aft stays to another spar, and so on down to the deck again. These young fellows are lithe and supple. You would not know them to be the same that eighteen months ago, innocently and in good faith, mounted to the maintop to pick gooseberries for Semmes's dinner; and again evaded the catlike watchfulness of Steward Bartelli, entering the cabin while the captain is engaged in taking a "sight" on deck, to get a pull on the "binnacle downhaul"; the aforesaid rope requiring immediate hauling taut and leading to and belaying under the captain's bunk. Yet these are the identical boys, no longer "green," and you may be sure would deny the soft impeachment should you be indiscreet enough to hint at the aforesaid orders received and seriously obeyed some months since.

It is the first week of March, and we have sounded on the Agulhas bank; the longitude and the dark green color of the water indicating our position. We make a cruise off here of two weeks; but as before results are nil. Nor do we find the *Vanderbilt*, though this may be because Evans *doesn't want* to find her. Don't tell him so. He will tell you angrily that he don't care a d—n for the *Vanderbilt*, and that Baldwin is not looking for us with a very powerful telescope. Strange luck that we have never captured a vessel off the pitch of the Cape, though it is one of the great highways of commerce!

We have made now a six months' cruise from the time we left Cape Town; and though we have only destroyed a few vessels during this time, they have been valuable ones, and the indirect damage cannot be estimated. It will ever remain an unknown quantity.

It has not been mentioned, I believe, that Jack is something of a theologian; but you will find him no insignificant opponent in religious discussions. While he has full faith in heaven, he has none in hell—that is, in an eternal one. His belief is rather in a halfway house, called "Fiddlers-green," where you pass the lonely time as best you can, awaiting a better state and doing penance in the meantime by dancing to very poor music. You cannot shake the faith of an old sea dog in the positive existence of the aforesaid territory. Jack has full faith in God's mercy, and freely confesses his need of it. The earthly types of this abode of shades are found off Cape Horn and the Cape of Good Hope, with their rough seas, baffling winds, and chill storms.

We are anxious now for the skipper to give up the futile boxing off the stormy Cape and let us to our old friends at the town. We shall burn no ships here. They are scarcer than hen's teeth; and the "equinoctial" is at hand and daily looked for; and we prefer to ride it out at anchor, even though in the open roadstead we are bound to.

CHAPTER XIII

CAPE TOWN AGAIN; OLD FRIENDS;
THE NEWSPAPER MAN; BAD NEWS;
RE-ENTERING THE ATLANTIC; THE
ROCKINGHAM; THE *TYCOON*; OUR LAST
BONFIRE; WE ARRIVE AT CHERBOURG

W E ENTER THE ROADSTEAD OF Cape Town, and almost immediately are riding to the heavy gale with a long
range of chain cable. Our ship has been signaled from the
lookout station; but, with the exception of the heavy storm
boats carrying extra anchors and chains for hire to vessels drag-
ging their anchors, we can have no means of communication
with the shore. One had as well, excepting the strict watch to
be kept, be at sea; the swell causing the ship to dip her nose
under at each dive and throwing the spray clear aft, making
wet and uncomfortable decks and confining all hands to close
quarters. Our cruiser does not at this moment present an appearance answering to Kell's notions of shipshape. Still we re-

ceive through the storm boats provisions, newspapers, etc., for all hands; and await the breaking up of the equinoctial. We have communicated with the governor and received permission to coal ship, without a reference to the late dodging of the neutrality laws; and our prediction that it would escape notice in the darkness is verified. We hear nothing further from it. On the next day the gale ceases, and the ship once more is crowded with our friends of all stations and degrees.

It was most gratifying to note the genuine pleasure manifested by these friends of the Cape Colony in being allowed once more to grasp us by the hand, and to learn how constantly they had watched the advices of us while we were in the East. We were the recipients on all hands of congratulations on our escape from the perils of archipelago cruising, and from the cruisers of the enemy. Our own Southern people could not have shown more heartfelt sympathy.

Our local reporter of the Cape Town *Argus* is also on deck, and as live a specimen of an impudent and cheeky reporter as an English colony could be expected to furnish. He has you by the buttonhole before you know it; and next will have applied a modicum of his patent glue to the seat of your trousers, and fastening you to a campstool, without a thought of ceremony or apology, proceed to pump out the experiences of your life. You may as well keep still and banish thoughts of "tiffin," for your reporter is neither hungry nor tired; he may be a little thirsty, and if so will gently inform you. But he doesn't know what he wants, and you will have to designate it. So open your mental budget. This fellow intends to let the Cape Town good folks know tomorrow morning what you have been doing since your departure. In return he will "paint the town red" in your company if you incline that way, and will also leave all the headache with you to bring on board ship. He has no personal use for a swelled superstructure.

We have little time at our disposal on this visit, our captain seeming in a bit of a hurry; still, we have a run onshore and see again the delightful vineyards but little removed from the town, and have the pleasure of looking upon and sampling the luscious grapes and figs now in their full perfection. Steward Bartelli is in his full glory, bowing and scraping to gold lace and epaulets, passing in visiting cards, and, by the way, scrutinizing them with the air of a state master of ceremonies. Our sailor boys are not having the good time of yore, at least not as yet; Jack is at present begrimed with coal dust and otherwise uncomfortable. Poor soul! He is yet ignorant that we shall have but three days here; that our discreet captain is purposely keeping this all-important fact safely locked in his own bosom. Our fellows are to have no liberty again from the *Alabama.* Jack toils hard in blissful ignorance that he will never put in an appearance at the snug little home cleped "The Song of the Siren," and that black-eyed Susan will wait in vain the visit requested in a message through Tom Kedge-Anchor, the bumboatman. No, my boys! And in the next port you are to face an altogether different music. No more winding through the mazes of the dance, but a square stand-up fight! A duel to the death, that will lay many a one of you low.

I have omitted to mention that we steamed into port here side and side with the American steamer *Kuang Tung* (Canton) from New York, bound to China, and stopping here, like ourselves, for coal. She is a gunboat, intended for the Teiping rebels, and has narrowly escaped capture, being just within marine league as we make her out. Rather a coincidence—our coming so near duplicating the capture of the *Sea Bride* off this harbor a few months since. The skipper of the *Kuang Tung* may consider himself a lucky fellow, and the circumstances a good omen of future success in the Flowery Kingdom upsetting the Imperial government. On the subject of the *Sea Bride* we may mention that our strongbox was liberally filled with sovereigns at this visit, the proceeds of the wool sale in England, part cargo of the *Tuscaloosa*, transferred at Angra Pequeña some months since. The *Alabama* is now a wealthy as well as a bold buccaneer.

We have late newspapers from all parts of the world, and read of the utter demoralization of American commerce. Indeed, in this connection, our eyes had beheld the desolation of Israel in Egypt. During our absence in the East, the *Tuscaloosa*, our tender, has returned to Cape Town for repairs, having experienced heavy weather off the Brazilian coast, and has been seized by order of the English home government as unlawfully fitted out. The English government has no more right to inquire into her antecedents than into the antecedents of the *Alabama* herself, indeed, *less* authority. It was so plain a case, as argued by Semmes in a correspondence with Admiral Sir Baldwin Walker, that the *Tuscaloosa* was released subsequently. She was, however, of no use to us further; Low, her commander, with Sinclair, his first officer, and the crew, having taken passage on a mail steamer for England, after having failed to convince the home or local governments of the illegality of the seizure. The *Tuscaloosa* was finally turned over to her original owners at the close of the war. Still, our point was carried with flying colors, the English interpreters of international law finding in Semmes a worthier opponent in legal lore than in Low. John Bull is a square fellow—does not hesitate to act quickly and firmly when he thinks himself right, and is equally candid and fair in acknowledging his error when proved to be wrong. "May he live long and prosper," to spread liberty and enlightenment over the face of the globe!

We detect in the news received through the late newspapers from the seat of war that our country is in the last throes of dissolution, her sacrifices and sufferings all for naught. Little left but to gaze on the wreck and moisten the turf of the dead heroes with bitter but unavailing tears. We feel as though the destruction of life and property should cease at once, as now a mere wantonness, or at least for the sake of the widow and fatherless. We, situated as we are so far from the clash and excitement, are better able to judge of the situation than those who live in it. We are comparatively cool and can take in the panorama of passing events, not blinded by the desperation of a forlorn hope.

The good folk of Cape Town and vicinity hold a place in their hearts for us, and as the time approaches to speak the good-bye, we shrink from the word. The phantom fails to unveil the future, or point to the *Alabama* where her home now is to be or what her destiny.

> The harbor's past, the breezes blow,
> 'Tis long, ere we come back, I know.

Coals on board, anchor weighed, we are off for the North Atlantic. It is now the latter part of March. We first stand for the historic Island of St. Helena, in the regular track of vessels bound to England or the United States. We shall not meet sails on this ocean path; all will be going our way. Our only hope is in their overhauling us, and we carry short canvas in consequence. But the cruise, or rather voyage, to St. Helena is void of incident and excitement. Nothing to break the monotony but ship duties, and an air of impatience and unrest pervades us fore and aft. We know too well the last act of the drama is being played, and that a painful uncertainty broods over our future.

We sight St. Helena and linger a few days in the vicinity in hopes of a capture from the vast fleet rushing by us for home and a market, but are unsuccessful. Europe is doing the carrying trade of the world by sea. One month from the

Cape we have almost forgotten our calling. Not a prize burned, and standing along in the busy highway of commerce with plenty of company.

It is the 22d of April, 1864, in the track now of vessels from the Pacific. The lookout reports a sail, American rig, and standing our way. We make sail after her, and soon have our expectations raised to the highest pitch of hope by observing her "keeping off" and rigging out her studding sails and light kites. It is night when we make the sail, but she has made us out and evidently is aware we are a man-of-war steamer. She is a dull sailer; but as a stern chase is always a long one, it is an all-night job and daylight before we have her under our rifle gun. We had really not cared to come up with her before day, it being more convenient to board and examine then. A blank cartridge is all sufficient, and she luffs to the breeze, maintopsail aback. The weather is light and handy for the work. She is the American ship *Rockingham* from Callao, bound for Cork and orders, guano-loaded. She was condemned by our prize-court of one member; and officers and crew being removed and such articles of provisions as needed, we made a target of the prize. The breeze was light and sea smooth, and at point-blank and elevated range the gun divisions amused themselves blithely. Considerable damage was done the target in the hull, the cabin particularly being torn up and and knocked into splinters. The practice over, the prize was consigned to the torch and we filled away. It is curious to compare the fine execution in this target practice and the woeful failure in the *Kearsarge* engagement which closely followed it.

We are approaching the track of vessels, both outward- and homeward-bound, and have passed a week without a hint of an enemy's vessel, though neutrals, as usual, pass constantly. The weather is delightful; and as the interdict of secrecy has for the first time in our cruise been removed, and all hands are cognizant of our destination, the crew are in the highest state of pleasurable excitement—never so willing and accommodating. Ring through the trumpet an order, and Jack jumps with alacrity. "Work ship" incessantly the whole watch, you hear no growl from him. He knows the ship is bound HOME; and in a few weeks mother, wife, and sweetheart will be dandling on his knee, and the tale of his adventures on the boat of his choice and under the flag of his adoption will be "always telling, never told."

We are now approaching the equator once more; and just a week since our last capture we make a sail standing towards us on opposite tack, the wind light and sea smooth. It is a capture accompanied with no excitement or incident, a reflection of the state of our feelings. We feel like the surroundings—listless, our toils objectless. The struggle over, the contest settled, of what avail the destruction of this gallant ship? She approaches slowly; we have only to heave-to, hoist our colors to the peak, and order her, per trumpet, to heave-to. She flutters up to the light air like a frightened dove, and upon being boarded proves the clipper ship *Tycoon*, from New York to San Francisco, with a large and valuable assorted cargo. She has no claim of neutral cargo and is condemned. Removing a goodly portion of her wares needed by us, officers, crew, and passengers are transferred and the ship consigned to the torch—the last bonfire we are ever to witness on the ocean, and the last act of retaliation on the part of the *Alabama* for the invasion of the South.

We cross the equatorial line in the usual style, an accompaniment of shifting light airs and calms, with the welcome addition of torrents of rain almost hourly in visitation. We are off the Brazilian coast now and are thinking of the *Florida* and *Georgia* left by us about one year ago, and hoping to fall in with them once more. How different the state of our feelings now than at the time we parted from them!

Our hopes and aspirations at that time were at high-water mark, and our pride in our ship at its height. Then all was encouraging at home with the army, and we were actually anxious that an enemy's cruiser should look in on our squadron of the Brazil station and be gobbled up.

We get papers from neutrals constantly, but not much news to cheer us, quite the contrary. It is the latter part of May, and for the next month there is literally nothing to record. We are only boarding neutrals all the while. Nothing but blue sky above, the blue dreary waste of waters below, and the *Alabama* booming along to reach her final destiny. On the 10th of June, 1864, we make the land at the entrance of the English Channel. We take a pilot, and the next day enter the harbor of Cherbourg, France, and call our cruise ended.

CHAPTER XIV

IN THE HARBOR OF CHERBOURG; FRENCH
HOSPITALITY; ARRIVAL OF THE *KEARSARGE*;
THE CHALLENGE; SCRUPULOUS NEUTRAL-
ITY; PREPARATIONS FOR THE FIGHT; MR.
LANCASTER'S YACHT; COMMANDER SEM-
MES'S PREVISION

WE HAVE CRUISED FROM THE day of commission,
August 24, 1862, to June 11, 1864, and during this time have
visited two-thirds of the globe, experiencing all vicissitudes
of climate and hardships attending constant cruising. We
have had from first to last two hundred and thirteen officers
and men on our payroll, and have lost *not one* by disease and
but one by accidental death. We have transferred of the original crew twelve men (to the *Tuscaloosa*), and go into the last
fight with fifty-nine of the original crew, having only fourteen who swore allegiance to the young Republic, on August
24, 1862, absent on the day of trial. Of these few absentees,

some were condemned by medical survey and sent home to England to be cared for, some were victims to the wiles of our enemies, and two more dismissed the service by court-martial. A record to be proud of, but only such a one as history commonly attaches to the British sailor.

Immediately after arrival an officer was sent with a communication to the port admiral, asking permission to land our prisoners of the *Rockingham* and *Tycoon*, our last two captures, which was promptly granted. Permission was also asked for docking privileges at the only available yard, which belonged to the government. Some delay was experienced before the answer to this request was given; the Emperor, whose permission must first be obtained, being absent from Paris at the watering place of Biarritz. Pending the matter, several days elapsed. In the meantime, the captain of the *Kearsarge*, hearing of our arrival, steamed from Flushing and entered the harbor on the 14th, just three days after we did. Without anchoring, he sent a boat onshore and then steamed to sea again just outside the breakwater. It seems the principal object of the visit was to ask permission to receive on board the *Kearsarge* prisoners recently landed by ourselves. This would seem, indeed, the sole object of the visit; for it was generally understood, both among the officers of the French squadron and the citizens of Cherbourg, and it was noised abroad by the newspaper press, that the *Alabama* was going in dock for thorough repairs. It was also generally known that it had been decided to give both the officers and men of the *Alabama* several months' leave of absence. Winslow could hardly have contemplated cutting us out from under the Emperor's wing as the *Florida* was cut out at Bahia; he could not have contemplated waiting outside the harbor for us until our repairs were made; whether he knew Semmes so well as to be assured of a challenge if he put in an appearance has never transpired. The challenge alone is a matter of history.

Semmes lost no time, however, after the appearance of the *Kearsarge*, in obtaining from Commodore Samuel Barron, the superior officer in charge of naval matters abroad, permission to offer her battle. Then through the United States consul he forwarded to Captain Winslow a communication to the effect that if he would wait until he could get his coal aboard he would go out and fight him. I have often been asked why Semmes should decide to fight in his disabled condition a ship so much his superior as to number of crew, armament, and speed; with the full knowledge, also, that the midship section of the *Kearsarge* was protected by bights of chain cables hung over her sides. That is manifestly a question I cannot undertake to answer. But apart from the unquestioned gallantry of the man, the insinuations he had been forced to listen to regarding his avoidance of armed ships of his foe, and the construction of insult which might be placed on the movements of the *Kearsarge*, he knew he had as gallant and perfectly trained a band supporting him as commander ever had the good fortune to lead. He had two guns capable of quickly sinking any wooden gunboat of the period. He had no suspicion that his powder was damaged,[1] and had

---

1. When the target practice on the *Rockingham* took place two months previously, there was no suspicion of deterioration in our powder. But the condition of it at the time of the action with the *Kearsarge* does not admit of doubt. It was observed by the officers of the French fleet that our powder smoke showed dark, while that of the *Kearsarge* was clear and white. The same thing was also noted by the captain and by the owner of the *Deerhound*. Lieutenant Wilson's later observations when a prisoner on the *Kearsarge*, the writer's testimony, and that of many deeply interested and disappointed witnesses on our decks during the progress of the action may be said to prove the fact. Wilson reported the *Kearsarge* as showing wounds enough in the wake of her engine to sink any vessel if punctuation had been obtained; and he firmly believed that damaged powder lost us the fight. A section of the original *Kearsarge* with the shell imbedded in it is now preserved at Washington.

no reason to think the *Kearsarge* would avoid, or even that she could avoid, his coming to close quarters. Had the one-hundred-pound percussion shell, lodged so early in the action in the stern of the *Kearsarge*, exploded, who doubts that it must have proved her deathblow?

Winslow was not allowed to take off the paroled prisoners. But the action of the French authorities was no more peculiar toward Winslow than toward us. When it became known that Semmes had resolved to give battle, several Confederate officers then in France were eager to participate. Midshipman William H. Sinclair, now acting lieutenant (detached, it will be remembered, to the *Tuscaloosa*), had come to Cherbourg to meet us. He was on leave of absence, domiciled at Paris, and had been awaiting our arrival to rejoin us. But he was not allowed by the French admiral, acting for his government, to participate in the fight. It was a grievous disappointment to this young and dashing officer. Among others similarly restrained should be mentioned Lieutenant John Grimball and William C. Whittle, who both served later on the *Shenandoah*. We may well doubt the justice of this ruling. These gentlemen were regular commissioned officers of the Confederate States Navy and could hardly be objected to as recruits obtained on neutral territory. We were in no position to cross swords with France on the matter, however; and, besides, we had all the officers we really needed. No objection was made to the visit of Commander George Terry Sinclair, a Confederate naval agent abroad, who came on board and conferred with Semmes as to the plan of action and regarding the comparative merits of shot and shell in particular cases. Sinclair was an ordnance officer of acknowledged ability. Then, our two master's-mates, Baron Maximilian Von Meulnier and Julius Schroeder, were able to escape the ruling. They had started home on leave and had got as far as Paris, when, learning that the fight was to come off, they returned at once and were permitted by the authorities to come on board. They did most gallant and effective service in the action. The reason of the decision in their case I have never learned.

It being a settled thing that the fight is to take place, preparations are made for it accordingly. Boatswain Mecaskey has his gang busy stoppering standing rigging, sending down light spars, and disposing of all top-hamper. Gunner Cuddy is overhauling the battery and arranging the shot and shell rooms for rapid serving of guns, and coals are ordered for our bunkers. We had settled down to the presumption that rest had at last been reached. But no rest *now* for the weary. Kell, who doubtless had looked upon his arduous duties as virtually closed, was a busier man than ever, and with perhaps the gravest responsibility ever thrust upon his shoulders. He will have no pleasant run up to Paris, as arranged, and maybe never. We are to enter the arena on Sunday, the 19th. Our officers, other than the special ones engaged in the preparation of the ship for action, are determined to make the most of the days and hours at their disposal with shipmates and brother officers arrived from Paris. A round of pleasures is inaugurated, and the cafés patronized with an enthusiasm only known to the habitually hungry. We had been on the eternal "salt horse" for nearly three months, and, as Joe Wilson put it, needed to be fattened for the slaughter.

We were thrown in a great measure on our own wits and resources for recreation. The French officials were studiously polite, but distant and reserved; doubtless the reflection of the attitude of the government and on the line of instructions. However, the port admiral manifested a fellow-feeling and interest in the lone, expatriated exponent of the Confederacy by informing Semmes, a day or so before the fight, that an officer detailed to visit the *Kearsarge* in the offing had reported the fact of the chain armor arranged on the ship, and strongly advised Semmes not to engage her, for that nothing but unlooked-for good luck could throw the scales our way. Considerate; but Semmes evidently only saw the enemy and had determined to chance the uncertainties of warfare, hoping to throw the lucky dice. The news that the *Alabama* is to fight on Sunday, the 19th of June, 1864, is now the common property of Europe, indeed of all lands, the information being wired to every available point; and the *to-be*-lookers-on are concentrating at Cherbourg from all points of the continent, particularly from Paris. The duel to the death between these representatives of the two struggling powers will perhaps be witnessed by as vast a concourse of people as ever assembled to view a similar scene, not excepting the famous Hampton Roads battle between the *Merrimac* (Virginia) and the Federal fleet.

The hotels and every other available lodging are engaged, and still they come. The yacht *Deerhound* of the Royal Yacht Squadron, E. P. Jones, captain, and John Lancaster, owner, had anchored in the harbor in the meantime. She had made the port to take on board Mr. Lancaster and his family, who had left the yacht elsewhere, and were expected on the 18th. Captain Jones and party asked permission to come on board us; but, for the first time in our cruise, we had reluctantly to refuse, being overwhelmed with duties and coaling ship for the fight. Little did we imagine at the time that these brave fellows we were treating with scant courtesy were to be the means of saving the lives of so many of our officers and crew. In fact, during our stay, our ship, from the nature of the case, had but little intercourse with the shipping of the harbor.

Mr. Lancaster, wife, and four children, with their niece and nurse, arrived on the evening of the 18th and went on board the yacht. Our first meeting with them was after the engagement. We may state that Providence at this stage of the tragedy provided for the ill-starred *Alabama*. On the morning of the fight a consultation was held on board the yacht as to whether they should go out and witness the fight; and the "vote" would have been even but that the youngest child, Catherine Lancaster, nine years of age, held the balance of power and voted "aye." Thus was this little child the instrument of saving many lives. A pleasant retrospect to her in after years, no doubt.

Our wardroom in the meantime is the center of considerable fun and frolic in spite of the grim work ahead. Semmes has sent a bearer of verbal dispatches in the person of our worthy captain's secretary to say the treasure chest is to be sent onshore; and like a wise and prudent guide and counselor, advises us to place in it any valuables possessed, and also that such of us as are fortunate enough to own any property should make our wills. Joe Wilson says this latter gratuitous advice is well calculated to increase our appetites and of little use to him, as all he has of value is his guitar, and that won't go in the iron safe, and besides, he wants it to keep his spirits up. Howell jumps to an idea and wants to borrow it at once as a bracer. Indeed, there is many a joke passing around the mess-table, all having direct reference to the present state of the nerves, and banter is the order of the meal hours. Poor little Dave, our colored wardroom boy (referred to before in these pages), is jokingly catechized as to the state of his courage. The little fellow seems perfectly contented, evidently having every confidence in the ability of those he is serving to bring him through all right, and shows his ivories at each banter. Faithful Dave! Your goal is about reached. "Well done, good and faithful servant." Like Llewellyn, steward Bartelli, and some others, poor little Dave could have saved his life by the mere mention that he was unable to swim. Howell could not swim; and it being generally known, Semmes ordered him to take an oar in the boat conveying the wounded to the *Kearsarge* in charge of Lieutenant Wilson. It is true the boat was much crowded, so much so that Lieutenant Armstrong and Midshipman Anderson declined to go in her, though both were severely wounded. Still, in such an emergency and with a calm sea, the boat could have been loaded "gunwales to" with safety.

The harbor is graced with a powerful French fleet, among the number being the line-of-battle-ship *Napoleon*, and one of the modern ironclads, the *Couronne*; the latter being something new to us, one of the first results of the Hampton Roads action. This vessel is to accompany us beyond the marine league and then see that in the excitement of battle we do not stray within the charmed lines. She certainly obeyed orders to the letter; for escorting us to the verge of French territory she stopped and was soon hull half-down; and had we depended on her assistance we had certainly all perished. We do not state this disparagingly, but simply as a fact. She was no doubt following out literally the doctrine of neutrality as laid down to her commander by the port admiral. We are rather impressed with our isolation here, it is so different from our experience in English ports and especially the warm, homelike hospitality of our friends left at Cape Town a few months since.

We have passed a number of hours during our stay perfecting our crew in boarding exercise, in which they were already quite proficient, and have them now, we think, fully up to the mark. Saturday evening finds us coaled and in fine inspection order. Kell has inspected the ship after his arduous week's labors and reported her to Semmes quite ready in all departments for tomorrow's work. Our men have conducted themselves with perfect propriety, and no breaches of the regulations have occurred. They are fully aware of the importance of clear heads and steady nerves. Our comrades of the navy who had come from Paris, to assist if allowed, have spoken their good-byes and earnest wishes for our success, and the vessel is cleared of all shore people. We are left to our own thoughts. All hands turn in early for a sound, refreshing sleep, so as to be on deck in the best of shape on the morrow.

CHAPTER XV

THE ENGAGEMENT

SUNDAY MORNING, June 19, 1864, preparations for the fight are made early in the day. At breakfast the officers are advised of the last communication with the shore and to make their arrangements accordingly. Soon after breakfast the yacht *Deerhound*, which we had observed to be getting up steam, moved out of the port, passing quite near us. The party on her were watching us with glasses, though no demonstration occurred, even from the ladies. At this time it was unknown to us that the departure was for the purpose of taking up a position of vantage to observe the engagement. We had no communication with the yacht or her people, and did not know but that her owner was continuing his pleasure cruise. She passed from sight, and the French ironclad frigate *Couronne* weighed anchor and stood out of the harbor. We could readily surmise that *her* purpose was to police the Channel at the three-mile limit and overlook the fight. She never moved from the league distance during the entire period of the engagement, nor did she offer any assistance at the termination. The neutrality of the *Couronne* was of the positive, unmistakable kind. It would have occupied a court but a short time to consider and pass upon it.

Between ten and eleven o'clock we got under way and stood out of the harbor, passing the French liner *Napoleon* quite near. We were surprised and gratified as she manned the rigging and gave us three rousing cheers, her band at the same time playing a Confederate national air. It must have been an enthusiasm of local birth, a sort of private turnout of their own. It was much appreciated by us, and no doubt stirred our brave lads to the center.

Sailors are generous fellows and always take sides, when allowed, with the little fellow underneath. The scene from the deck of the *Alabama* is one never to be effaced from memory. We are passing out of the harbor through the dense shipping, the bulwarks of all of them crowded with heads watching our exit, and the shores and mole a moving mass of humanity. The day is perfect, scarcely a breath of air stirring and with but a light cloud here and there in the sky. We soon clear the mole and shape our course for the offing, to testify by blows and blood the sincerity of our faith in the justice of our cause, and to win, if possible, a crowning triumph for our brave commander.

Our ship as she steams offshore for her antagonist, hull down in the distance and waiting for us, presents a brave appearance. The decks and brasswork shine in the bright morning sunlight from recent holystoning and polishing. The crew are all in muster uniform, as though just awaiting Sunday inspection. They are ordered to lie down at their quarters for rest while we approach the enemy. A beautiful sight—the divisions stripped to the waist, and with bare arms and breasts looking the athletes they are. The decks have been sanded down, tubs of water placed along the spar-deck, and all is ready for the fray. The pipe of the boatswain and mates at length summons all hands aft; and Semmes, mounting a gun-carriage, delivers a stirring address:

"Officers and Seamen of the *Alabama*: You have at length another opportunity of meeting the enemy—the first that has been presented to you since you sank the *Hatteras*. In the meantime, you have been all over the world; and it is not too much to say that you have destroyed, and driven for protection under neutral flags, one-half of the enemy's commerce, which at the beginning of the war covered every sea. This is an achievement of which you may well be proud; and a grateful country will not be unmindful of it. The name of your ship has become a household word wherever civilization extends. Shall that name be tarnished by defeat? The thing is impossible. Remember that you are in the English Channel—the theater of so much of the naval glory of our race—and that the eyes of all Europe are at this moment upon you. The flag that floats over you is that of a young republic who bids defiance to her enemies whenever and wherever found. Show the world that you know how to uphold it. Go to your quarters."

Again at quarters, and resting "at will." It is the hour of prayer in old England; and many a petition is now going up to the God of battle and of mercy for these brave fellows, many of them now about to embrace their watery winding sheets. We are soon up with the cavalcade and leave the *Couronne*, the yacht still steaming seaward and evidently bent upon witnessing the engagement. She is about two miles distant at the time we open the ball. The *Kearsarge* suddenly turns her head inshore and steams towards us, both ships being at this time about seven or eight miles from the shore. When at about one mile distant from us, she seems from her sheer-off with helm to have chosen this distance for her attack. We had not yet perceived that the *Kearsarge* had the speed of us. We open the engagement with our entire starboard battery, the writer's thirty-two-pounder of the port side having been shifted to the spare port, giving us six guns in broadside; and the shift caused the ship to list to starboard about two feet, by the way, quite an advantage, exposing so much less surface to the enemy, but somewhat retarding our speed. The *Kearsarge* had pivoted to starboard also; and both ships with helms aport fought out the engagement, circling around a common center, and gradually approaching each other. The enemy replied soon after our opening; but at the distance her pivot shell guns were at a disadvantage, not having the long range of our pivot-guns, and hence requiring judgment in guessing the distance and determining the proper elevation. Our pivots could easily reach by ricochet, indeed by point-blank firing, so at this stage of the action, and with a smooth sea, we had the advantage.

The battle is now on in earnest, and after about fifteen minutes' fighting we lodge a hundred-pound percussion-shell in her quarter near her screw; but it fails to explode, though causing some temporary excitement and anxiety on board the enemy, most likely by the concussion of the blow. We find her soon after seeking closer quarters (which she is fully able to do, having discovered her superiority in speed), finding it judicious to close so that her eleven-inch pivots could do full duty at point-blank range. We now ourselves noted the advantage in speed possessed by our enemy; and Semmes felt her pulse, as to whether *very* close quarters would be agreeable, by sheering towards her to close the distance; but she had evidently reached the point wished for to fight out the remainder of the action, and demonstrated it by sheering off and resuming a parallel to us. Semmes would have chosen to bring about yardarm quarters, fouling, and boarding, relying upon the superior physique of his crew to overbalance the superiority of numbers; but this was frustrated, though several times attempted, the desire on our part being quite apparent. We had therefore to accept the situation and make the best of it we could, to this end directing our fire to the midship section of the enemy and alternating our battery with solid shot and shell, the former to pierce, if possible, the cable chain armor, the latter for general execution.

Up to the time of shortening the first distance assumed, our ship received no damage of any account, and the enemy none that we could discover, the shot in the quarter working no serious harm to the *Kearsarge*. At the distance we were now fighting (point-blank range), the effects of the eleven-inch guns were severely felt, and the little hurt done the enemy clearly proved the unserviceableness of our powder, observed at the commencement of the action.

The boarding tactics of Semmes having been frustrated, and we unable to pierce the enemy's hull with our fire, nothing can place victory with us but some unforeseen and lucky turn. At this period of the action our spanker-gaff is shot away, bringing our colors to the deck; but apparently this is not observed by the *Kearsarge*, as her fire does not halt at all. We can see the splinters flying off from the armor covering of the enemy; but no penetration occurs, the shot or shell rebounding from her side. Our colors are immediately hoisted to the mizzenmasthead. The enemy having now the range, and being able with her superior speed to hold it at ease, has us well in hand, and the fire from her is deliberate and hot. Our bulwarks are soon shot away in sections; and the after pivot-gun is disabled on its port side, losing, in killed and wounded, all but the compresser-man. The quarterdeck thirty-two-pounder of this division is now secured, and the crew sent to man the pivot-gun.

The spar-deck is by this time being rapidly torn up by shell bursting on the between-decks, interfering with working our battery; and the compartments below have all been knocked into one. The *Alabama* is making water fast, showing severe punishment; but still the report comes from the engine room that the ship is being kept free to the safety point. She also has now become dull in response to her helm, and the sail-trimmers are ordered out to loose the headsails to pay her head off. We are making a desperate but forlorn resistance, which is soon culminated by the deathblow. An eleven-inch shell enters us at the waterline, in the wake of the writer's gun, and passing on explodes in the engine room, in its passage throwing a volume of water on board, hiding for a moment the guns of this division. Our ship trembles from stem to stern from the blow. Semmes at once sends for the engineer on watch, who reports the fires out and water beyond the control of the pumps. We had previously been aware our ship was whipped, and fore- and aft sail was set in endeavor to reach the French coast; the enemy then moved in shore of us but did not attempt to close any nearer, simply steaming to secure the shoreside and await events.

It being now apparent that the *Alabama* could not float longer, the colors are hauled down, and the pipe given, "All hands save yourselves." Our waist-boats had been shot to pieces, leaving us but two quarter-boats, and one of them much damaged. The wounded are dispatched in one of them to the enemy in charge of an officer, and this done we await developments. The *Kearsarge* evidently failed to discover at once our surrender, for she continued her fire after our colors were struck. Perhaps from the difficulty of noting the absence of a flag with so much white in it in the powder smoke. But, be the reason what it may, a naval officer, a gentleman by birth and education, would certainly not be guilty of firing on a surrendered foe; hence we may dismiss the matter as an undoubted accident.

The *Kearsarge* is at this time about three hundred yards from us, screw still and vessel motionless, awaiting our boat with the wounded. The yacht is steaming full power towards us both. In the meantime the two vessels are slowly parting, the *Alabama* drifting with her fore- and aft sails set to the light air. The inaction of the *Kearsarge* from the time of the surrender until the last man was picked up by the boats of the two vessels will ever remain a mystery to all who were present, and with whom the writer has since conversed. The fact is, the *Kearsarge* was increasing her distance slowly and surely all the time. Whether the drift of our ship under the sail that was set was accomplishing this alone I am not prepared to say. But both Captain Jones and Mr. Lancaster noted it and were under the impression that the fact entitled the yacht to the greater credit in saving life. There really seemed to be more method and judgment displayed by the crews from the yacht than those from the *Kearsarge*. Captain Jones and Mr. Lancaster both expressed themselves in their communications to the press that in their opinions but few of the *Alabama*'s men would have been saved but for their presence, so little enterprise was shown by our enemy in looking out for us in the water.

The *Deerhound* approaches the *Kearsarge* and is requested by Captain Winslow to assist in saving life; and then, scarcely coming to a full stop, turns to us, at the same time lowering all her boats, the *Kearsarge* doing the same. The officers and crew of our ship are now leaving at will, discipline and rule being temporarily at an end. The ship is settling to her spar-deck, and her wounded spars are staggering in the "steps," held only by the rigging. The decks present a woeful appearance, torn up in innumerable holes and air bubbles rising and bursting, producing a sound as though the boat was in agony. Just before she settled, it was a desolate sight for the three or four men left on her deck.

Engineer O'Brien and self were standing by the forward pivot port, a man from his department near as his companion for the coming swim, a man from my gun division to act in the same capacity with me; namely, mutual aid and assistance. We comprised all remaining on board of the late buoyant and self-confident band. The ship had settled by the stern, almost submerging it, and bringing the forward part of the hull, consequently, out of water. We were all stripped for the swim and watching with catlike intensity the rise of air bubbles from the hatches, indicating that the ship would yet float. From the wake of the *Alabama*, and far astern, a long, distinct line of wreckage could be seen winding with the tide like a snake, with here and there a human head appearing among it. The boats were actively at work, saving first those who were without such assistance.

It has frequently been asked me, and in a recent conversation with engineer O'Brien I found the question had been put to him often, "Why did you remain so long on board?" We both seem to have been actuated by the same motive and impulse, first to avoid the confusion and struggle going on in the efforts to reach the wreckage, but the paramount feeling with me was inability to grasp the fact that the *Alabama* was gone! Our home! Around which clustered memories as dear and cherished as attended that first childhood one, and the faculties utterly refused to have the stubborn fact thus ruthlessly thrust upon them. They are rude wrenches these, that scatter shipmate from shipmate in a twinkling, some to death, as in our case, and bury out of sight forever the ship which had come to be the material embodiment of a cause dear almost as life. A happier ship-hold it would be difficult to realize or picture, a sympathetic heart encountered at each turn of mess room or quarterdeck, and this for two long years. O'Brien broke into the revery or daydream by unceremoniously pushing the writer overboard and following in his wake. It need scarcely be added that the bath cooled effectually the heated and disturbed brain, and turned the thoughts of all four of us to the practical question of the moment—how expert a swimmer are you?

The *Alabama*'s final plunge was a remarkable freak, and witnessed by O'Brien and self about one hundred yards off. She shot up out of the water bow first and descended on the same line, carrying away with her plunge two of her masts and making a whirlpool of considerable size and strength.

The *Kearsarge* mounted two eleven-inch Dahlgren shell guns, four thirty-two pounders, and one rifled twenty-eight-pounder. The *Alabama* mounted more guns; but the difference in the bore of the pivot-guns of the two ships gave the *Kearsarge* much more weight of metal at a broadside and made the disparity very great. The complement of the *Kearsarge* was one hundred and sixty-five all told, officers and men. The action lasted one hour and a half.

A great deal has been said as to the merits of the fight; and no little feeling has been displayed on both sides, each championing its own and seeking to evolve from the result so much of credit and praise as the circumstances permit. With the floods of light thrown on the event from time to time by the actors on both sides, assisted by the testimony of reliable and impartial outside lookers-on, the reader should without a fear of erring be able to judge for himself the amount of credit to be apportioned to each of the combatants, and also to satisfy himself whether or not Semmes is under all the circumstances to be censured for offering battle, and if blamed at all to what extent and in what particulars. Winslow, for protecting his ship with chain-armor, should, in the humble judgment of the writer, submitted with diffidence, be accounted as simply using proper prudence in the direct line of duty. He had not given, accepted, or declined a challenge. But it was his duty to fight if he could and to win. Semmes knew all about it and could have adopted the same scheme. It was not his election to do so. Winslow took every means at his disposal to destroy a vessel which had been a scourge to United States commerce, and most likely banished from his thoughts all sentiment of chivalry as out of place.

The writer has already suggested from his own standpoint the motives for seeking the fight which may have moved Semmes; but after all they are mere speculations, simply the sum-up of his own thoughts. No one will know just why he fought, and the reader has as good a right at a guess as anyone. Semmes took the chances with the odds against him and lost all but honor. He could have stayed in port, refitted, and been in good trim to meet any boat of the *Kearsarge* class. But we can look farther and see that in this case no fight with her would have been probable. The chances are, by the time the *Alabama* was ready for sea, a fleet of American cruisers would have been off Cherbourg to blockade her. So looking at it, surely it was best to take the bull by the horns and fight while there was some sort of a chance. Semmes fought his ship with all the skill possible under the circumstances, and displayed throughout the coolness and nerve you would look for from a man who had guided the *Alabama* to such marked success. The career of the ship under him is perhaps the most conspicuous object lesson of judicious management and forethought in the annals of any navy, and the fact of defeat should weigh not at all against his judgment when we consider the fickle chances of battle.

The courage of the man needs no telling; but the incident of his wounding and the manner in which he bore it may be of interest to the reader. He was on the horse-block at the time, and where he remained during the battle; and upon finding his right arm totally disabled by a fragment of shell, he simply called the quartermaster, and having him bind and sling the wounded arm, kept his position and directed the steering and fighting of his ship up to the surrender. Kell was a devoted friend to him from the moment of his (Semmes) personal misfortune, sticking close by him, entering the water with him, and having the satisfaction of getting with him, safe from all harm, on the deck of the *Deerhound*. In the state of Semmes's health at this time, considering his age and the wearing cruise he had just wound up, it was fortunate for him that such a strong, athletic fellow as Kell kept near him all the while; and who knows how much Semmes may owe to Kell for that companionship?

The writer had the deck just before getting under way, prior to being relieved, as customary, by the first lieutenant. The commander came up from his breakfast, saluted the deck, and received the usual touch of the hat in return; then he said, "If the bright, beautiful day is shining for our bene-fit, we should be happy at the omen"; and remarked how well the deck appeared, and that the crew (casting his eye for-ward) seemed "to enter into the spirit of the fight with bright faces." Finally, he put the direct question, "How do you think it will turn out today, Mr. Sinclair?" I was surprised that he should care to have my opinion, or that of anyone else; for he rarely addressed any of us off duty and never asked advice or opinion of his subordinates on weighty matters, at least not to my knowledge. My reply was necessarily vague: "I cannot answer the question, sir, but can assure you the crew will do their full duty and follow you to the death"—"Yes," he an-swered, "that is true." And leaving me, he resumed his usual pacing of the quarterdeck. Most gratifying to Semmes must have been the sympathy and attention of the gallant, gener-ous souls on the yacht, and no doubt it contributed much to ease his sufferings of body and mind.

In England he was warmly received on all sides; and a number of his naval admirers united in a testimonial, which assumed the form of a handsome regulation gold-mounted sword, presented, it was stated, "To replace the one so gallantly worn, defended, and lost."

APPENDIX

SOME INCIDENTS OF THE FIGHT

WHEN THE ORDER WAS PASSED to lower the colors, and the pipe "All hands save yourselves" was given by boatswain Mecaskey and mates, there was at once a rush of men from the gun divisions to protest against surrender. The excitement was great, the men failing to realize that their ship was whipped beyond a shadow of doubt and able to float but little longer. They demanded to have the honor of sinking with the colors at the peak (or rather at the mizzenmast-head, for the spanker-gaff had long since been shot away). But a few positive words from Semmes and Kell quieted them. The *Kearsarge* was by this time on our quarter, in position for a raking fire, and we were altogether helpless. It was time to stop the useless slaughter, though the lowering of our colors was not apparently seen on the *Kearsarge* for a time, since she did not at once cease firing. No one was hurt on board of us after the act of surrender.

The sad fate of assistant-surgeon Llewellyn has else-where been recorded. Late in the fight the writer went below to get a bottle of brandy to sustain Wright of his di-vision, who had been seriously wounded, and came upon Llewellyn standing deep in water, attending to the injured. "Why, Pills!" I cried. "You had better get yourself and wounded out of this, or you'll soon be drowned!" His reply was, "I must wait for orders, you know." But just then a gang of men came below, and he was enabled to get his injured men off the operating table and to the deck. The wounded were immediately placed in the boat for transfer to the *Kearsarge*. Why Llewellyn did not accompany them it is impossible to say. It is quite likely he did not know the custom in such cases, and he may have waited for orders. The boat with the wounded, under the command of Lieutenant Wilson, ma-rine-officer Howell, and master's-mate Fulham each taking an oar, was at once cleared from the side. It soon becoming known that Llewellyn could not swim, a couple of empty shell-boxes were procured and secured on his person, one under each arm, to serve as an improvised life preserver. He took the water with this arrangement, and when last seen from the ship was making good weather of it, the sea being as calm as a dish. I learned later, on the yacht, that Llewellyn's death was brought about by the shifting of the floats upon his person, which seems most probable. Had he taken a moment's thought for himself and let it be known that he could not swim earlier, he might easily have been saved. But he was the last man to think of himself in a time of general danger.

Lieutenant of marines Howell was known to be no swim-mer and was allowed to take an oar in the boat with the wounded. After the transfer, his dress, or rather undress, not being recognized, and Wilson having gone up the side of the *Kearsarge* and formally surrendered, he was requested by

Captain Winslow to return with the rest of the boat's crew to the wreckage and do all he could to save life. It is hardly necessary to say that the request was cheerfully obeyed, or that the boat took all the men it saved to the *Deerhound*.

During this time I made a second visit between decks. The scene was one of complete wreck. The shot and shell of the enemy had knocked all the compartments into one; and a flush view could be had fore and aft, the water waist-deep and air bubbles rising and breaking with a mournful gurgle at the surface. It was a picture to be dwelt upon in memory, but not too long in the reality. I returned hastily to the spar-deck. By this time most of the officers and men had left for the water. The battery was disarranged, some guns run out and secured, some not. The spars were wounded woefully, some of them toppling and others only held by the wire rigging. The smokestack was full of holes, the decks torn up by the bursting of shell and lumbered with the wreckage of woodwork and rigging and empty shell-boxes. Some sail was set; and the vessel slowly forged ahead, leaving a line of wreckage astern, with the heads of swimmers bobbing up and down among it. Toward this the boats from the yacht were rapidly pulling. The *Kearsarge* lay a few hundred yards on our starboard quarter, with her boats apparently free from the davits and pivot-gun ports not yet closed, nor her guns secured.

I went forward, and with a sailor of my division commenced to strip for the swim, the deep settling of the ship warning us that she was about to go. I was ready first and sat with my legs dangling in the water, which was now almost flush with the spar-deck, trying to secure a handkerchief containing a lot of English sovereigns about my neck while I waited for my companion. At this moment O'Brien suddenly appeared in our rear, and with a hasty "What are you loafing round here for? Don't you see the ship is settling for a plunge? Over you go!" suited the action to the word and shoved us both into the sea. He immediately followed us and struck out sharply for the boats. But O'Brien's hurry cost me my gold, for it was torn from my neck with the plunge and went down to enrich the bottom of the Channel. However, we had got away none too soon; for we had hardly cleared her when her bow made a wild leap into the air, and she plunged down on an inclined plane to her grave beneath the waves. As she leaped upward there was a crash, her main topmast going by the board, and the fore gave way in turn as she took her downward slide. The suction where we were was terribly strong, carrying us all down to a very uncomfortable depth. So deep, indeed, that with my eyes open in perfectly clear water, I found myself in the darkness of midnight. But our struggles soon popped us to the surface, which was by this time quite a luxury; and we kept there very contentedly, swimming in an easy, take-your-time style until picked up. Being rescued, we were deposited, like caught fish, under the thwarts. But my sailor companion soon discovered that it was a boat from the *Kearsarge* which had done us this favor; and promptly consulting, we arranged to give it the slip, which was successfully accomplished in the confusion, taking again to the sea. The next time we were picked up, it was by a boat from the *Deerhound.*

It was an incident of note in the fight that nearly all the killed were allotted to Joe Wilson's division. I can recollect of but one in Armstrong's, and in my division we had only one man wounded; and yet the bulk of the enemy's fire was concentrated at the midships of the *Alabama*, and the death wound was given at the third division, in the wake of the engine hatch.

Nothing could exceed the cool and thorough attention to details of our first lieutenant on this eventful day. From point to point of the spar-deck in his rapid movement he was directing here, or advising there; now seeing to the transfer of shot, shell, or cartridge; giving his orders to this and that man or officer, as though on dress muster; occasionally in earnest conversation with Semmes, who occupied the horse-block, glasses in hand, and leaning on the hammock-rail; at times watching earnestly the enemy and then casting his eye about our ship, as though keeping a careful reckoning of the damage given and received. Nothing seemed to escape his active mind or eye, his commanding figure at all times towering over the heads of those around. How it must have touched him to see the wreck of our gallant boat, of which he was so proud and which had been for two years his heart's chiefest care! One must be in actual touch with such a life as ours to feel the inspiration.

In the latter part of the engagement, Semmes, from the vantage ground of the horse-block, had observed that the *Alabama* was not answering to her helm promptly, and sent for engineer O'Brien to ascertain the condition of the water in the lower hold. O'Brien reported it as almost flush with the furnace fires and rapidly rising, also that the ship could not possibly float much longer. He was ordered to return to duty. Reaching the engine room, engineer Pundt interviewed him; and upon learning that the ship's condition was known to Semmes and the only reply to this statement was, "Return to your duty!" exclaimed excitedly, "Well, I suppose 'Old Beeswax' has made up his mind to drown us like a lot of rats! Here, Matt! Take off my boots"; and suiting the action to the word, each assisted the other in removing the wet and soggy boots. But Semmes had made up his mind, from the report of his engineer, to give the order, "All hands save yourselves!" The furnace fires were soon after flooded, and all hands on duty below ordered to the spar-deck. Nor was the order given any too soon.

Said engineer O'Brien, after the landing of the rescued

party at Southampton, "I think for spartan coolness and nerve these two German messmates of ours (Meulnier and Schroeder) surpass anything in my observation and reading. I was on duty close to them, a few yards only separating us. They had command of the shot-and-shell passing division and were stationed at the shell-room hatch, tending the "whip-tackle." A shell entered and brought up a few yards from them. It must have been a five-second fuse, from the distance of the *Kearsarge* from us at this stage of the action, for it exploded almost immediately. I protected myself as well as I could from the fragments. So soon as the smoke and dust cleared away, I looked, intending to go to their assistance, expecting to find them wounded or perhaps dead; when, to my amazement, there they stood hauling on the tackle as though attending an exercise drill. They were the calmest men I ever saw, the most phlegmatic lot it was ever my privilege to fight alongside of."

A most remarkable case of desperate wounding and after-tenacity of life was noted by the writer in the latter part of the fight. It was imperative to get the ship's head off if possible, the vessel not answering to her helm as quickly as desired and the danger imminent. The *Kearsarge* would soon be in a position to rake us; and though the wind was light, and the maneuver not likely to be of much practical benefit, a sail-trimmer and forecastle-man, John Roberts, was ordered out by Kell to loose the jib. He had executed the order and was returning when he was struck by a solid shot or shell, which completely disemboweled him. Roberts in this desperate plight clung to the jib-boom, and working along the foot rope reached the topgallant-forecastle, thence climbed down the ladder to the spar-deck, and with shrieks of agony and his hands over his head, beating the air convulsively, reached the port gangway, where he fell and expired. He was a man of commanding stature, five or six and twenty years of age, of unusual physical strength, an able sea-man, and as well behaved at all times as would be expected of an officer. An Englishman by birth, and a typical English man-of-war's man.

It was a touching scene, the transfer of our wounded men as prisoners to the *Kearsarge*, in our only boat left seaworthy at the davits. Among them was James King II, an Irishman and a man of powerful frame. He had been made quite a "butt" by all our crew, quizzed on all occasions, not being an educated sailorman, but what we designated on shipboard a "landsman." "Connemara" was the nickname attached to him, suggested by the county in which he was born. King, who was of a hot, quick temper, had constantly resented the practical jokes of the men at his expense, causing the vexed first lieutenant to wonder if it was practical to keep Con-nemara out of the brig. He was for all this a generous, open-hearted Irishman, and his attachment was strong for officers and ship. He was mortally wounded; and just as his com-rades were about to lift him into the boat destined for the *Kearsarge*, he sent for Kell, and stretching out his feeble hand to him, remarked, "I have sent for you, Mr. Kell, to ask your forgiveness for all the trouble I've caused you since my en-listment on the ship. Please forgive poor Connemara now he is going to his long home." Kell, kneeling by his side, sup-porting and stroking his head, said, "My poor, dear boy, I have nothing to forgive; nothing against you, my brave lad; and I trust you will be in better trim soon."—"No," was the reply; "Connemara is going fast. Good-bye, Mr. Kell. God bless you, Mr. Kell!" He died on the *Kearsarge*.

Michael Mars was another son of Erin, a splendid type of the English man-of-war's man, and appropriately named. He was in many ways the most remarkable figure among our crew, and trustworthy to the uttermost. Still, strange to say, constantly in the brig for minor offenses, such as playing practical jokes on his messmates, and even at times including the younger officers if the field was clear for the exercise of his pranks. Nothing vicious or of serious moment happened among his offenses, making it therefore a worry to Kell to report and Semmes to punish him. An admirable part of his composition was his indifference to rum.

Mars distinguished himself in this memorable fight. He was compresser-man of the after pivot-gun, commanded by Lieutenant Joseph D. Wilson, manned by twenty-two men, ten on each side and two captains, first and second, in the rear. The gun, a very heavy one, eight-inch solid shot or shell weapon, had just been loaded and run out to fire, and Mars had stooped on his knees to compress (to retard recoil), when an eleven-inch shell from the enemy struck full in the middle of the first man on the port side of the gun, passing through the entire lot, killing or wounding them, and piling up on the deck a mass of human fragments. Such a ghastly sight the writer never saw before, and hopes never to see again. Mars at once rose to his feet uninjured, seized a shovel from the bulwarks, and soon had the mass of flesh overboard and the deck resanded. To have observed the man, you would have supposed him engaged in the ordinary morning-watch cleaning of decks. The pivot-gun had a picked crew, selected principally from the coal heavers and firemen, they being heavy, powerful men. At this stage the quarterdeck thirty-two-pounder of Wilson's division, and commanded in person by midshipman Anderson, was "secured," and the crew sent to man the more important gun, depleted of half its crew.

Later in the action, when the *Alabama* had settled with her spar-deck flush with the water and all hope was abandoned, the order was given, "All hands save yourselves!" through the boatswain and his mates. Semmes, who with Kell was stripping for the swim, seated on the quarterdeck, sent for Mars and Freemantle, and telling them that he (Semmes) was unable to save his diary and ship papers, his right arm being wounded by a fragment of shell, asked if they could take care of them. The seamen accepted the trust; and Bartelli, wading into the cabin, returned with them. Easing themselves down in the sea, Mars swam with one arm to the boat of the *Deerhound*, holding the documents above the water, and Freemantle to a French boat. Semmes and Kell followed suit; and the former had the gratification of knowing his notes were safe and once more in his possession. Mars would deliver the precious papers to none other on the yacht, though told Semmes was safe in the cabin. He wished to deliver them in person and succeeded. This latter fact was learned by the writer from Captain Jones of the *Deerhound*.

We were soon steaming in the yacht to Southampton, which port we reached without further adventure. Here Mars left us, sailorlike, for another cruise. As the years roll by the writer often thinks of Mars and wonders what is his fate; whether he who did such gallant deeds was at last swallowed by insatiable old ocean, or whether we shall meet again and tell each other of our later pilgrimage through life. If toiling here yet, may God, as in the past, keep watch and ward over the jovial, generous, and brave Irishman!

Captain Jones narrates a pleasing instance of noble self-sacrifice on the part of our captain of the forecastle. In coming up to a number of men struggling in the water, he observed an old gray-haired seaman swimming along contentedly, and while engaged pulling some others into his boat called out to the old fellow, "Come this way, and get on board." To which the old fellow replied, "Oh, I can keep up for a while longer! Save those other lads, they need your services more than I do. Your boat can't carry all of us."

SEEKING A HOME AFTER THE FIGHT

Upon landing at Southampton, a party of us started from the yacht on our own hook to look up a hotel. We were rigged out in a most outlandish manner, as may be supposed, most of us without pants, coats, or shoes, the yacht people being unable to supply forty-odd unfortunates with a complete outfit. We could hear the newsboys crying out the "extras," and of course supposed everybody knew of the sinking of the *Alabama*. Our first attempt was at the most fashionable hotel in the city. The bell of the private entrance was rung; and upon being answered by the bellboy, we asked to see the proprietor. The boy looked at us, taking stock all over, and hesitated to obey the request. However, he did so; and the landlord appeared and, hastily glancing over our persons, in a half-apologetic strain proceeded to explain that the hotel was full and directed us to another. He, of course, had heard the news of the fight and its result; and while professing to credit our identity and explanation, we were not swell enough for him or his hotel—at least, not in our present rig. This is the true translation of it. Foolish and shortsighted fellow! We were as independent as mine host, and withdrew, held a consultation (for it was late in the night, and no time to swap horses), and an idea striking us, off we started for the wharf front. Our idea was to seek out some hostelry, the rendezvous of coasting skippers and mates. We discovered and "hove-to" at one of them, and found the reading room of the hotel all agog at the news; and our reception was right royal. "Come in, lads!" was the answer to our request for lodgings. "God bless you! Come in, and make yourselves at home." And to attempt to convey the wealth of hospitality showered upon us would beggar language. The landlord was a retired coast skipper of the Bunsby order, and as jolly and great-hearted as Bunsby's friend, Captain Cuttle. A generous meal was after a while placed before us, our lads in the meantime telling the tale of the ill-starred *Alabama*. Little sleep for us this night. In the morning tradespeople were sent for, and each of us fitted out with all requirements and money handed us besides. Our strongbox had not as yet arrived. Our landlord of the swell hotel was quite well "rasped" by the press for his churlish reception of us. Blessings on him for it! As it turned out, by his selfish conduct we secured a real home.

CAPTAIN JONES'S STATEMENT

ON June 9, 1864, we were lying at St. Malo, where we landed Mr. Lancaster and family after a cruise among the Channel Islands. On their leaving, we immediately set sail for Cherbourg, calling on our way to Jersey for letters. We arrived at Cherbourg and came to anchor close to the *Alabama* and to an English sailing yacht, the *Hornet*. We had no communication with the *Alabama* during our stay in the harbor except to send alongside asking permission to visit, which they refused, saying that they were too busy. We could see from our vessel that they were practicing boarding drill, and surmised that they had it in view to board the *Kearsarge* in the engagement, which rumor in Cherbourg had it was to take place on the following Sunday.

On the day previous to the fight I met Mr. Lancaster and family at the station (as was my custom), and informed him that the *Alabama* was lying in the harbor. I reminded him that she was built at Messrs. Lairds' yard, at Birkenhead, during the time that the *Deerhound* was there being lengthened. I also told him that the *Kearsarge* had steamed in at the east end of the harbor and out at the west, evidently taking a survey of the enemy. No doubt this was a great advantage to Captain Winslow, who also got at the same time a full report of the *Alabama*'s condition from the American consul of the port—especially as to the condition of her boilers, which I believe were in a very bad state.

After the family came on board, they held a consultation as to whether they would go out on Sunday morning to see the fight. Mr. Lancaster put it to the vote, and Miss Lancaster (now Mrs. Part) gave the casting vote for going out. Early the next morning we noticed that the *Alabama* was getting up steam, and I ordered the same to be done on our little craft. Soon after breakfast we steamed quietly out of the harbor; and when about four miles out, we observed the *Kearsarge* well down on the eastern horizon and that the *Alabama* was steaming out of the harbor with a strong starboard list. She passed us close, heading directly for the enemy, and shortly afterward fired two or three shots with the starboard guns. The *Kearsarge* replied, also with her starboard battery. Both vessels were soon firing rapidly, steaming slowly on a circle about half a mile distant from each other. About thirteen minutes after the fight began, we noticed that there was a little confusion on the *Kearsarge*. I ascertained afterward that a shell had struck and entered the sternpost of the *Kearsarge*; but unluckily for the *Alabama* it did not explode. Had it done so, there can be no question but that the *Alabama*'s plan of boarding would have been successfully carried out. As it was, the greater speed of the *Kearsarge* frustrated her evident wish to come to close quarters, which we could make out plainly enough. In my opinion, had boarding been practicable, the *Alabama* would have made short work of her opponent; for her crew were daredevils from all nations and picked for splendid physical qualities. I was under the impression at the time that the American consul had warned Captain Winslow of the purpose of his enemy, as indicated by the incessant drills she was keeping up, and that the latter thought it as well not to accommodate. This was very much against the *Alabama*, as her ammunition was old and damp. I understand Semmes tried to get a fresh supply, but the French government prohibited it.[1] The *Kearsarge*, as it was, had her well in hand the whole time, her superior speed enabling her to choose position and distance. As to the chain armor, no doubt it saved her greatly; but the *Alabama*'s list to starboard was perhaps almost as great an advantage, presenting so much less surface to the enemy's shot. It was a fair, stand-up fight. The two vessels were constructed of the same materials, and the chances at first seemed to be even enough.

After the *Alabama* went down, we steamed round the starboard quarter of the *Kearsarge*, and Captain Winslow asked us to render all assistance possible to the drowning crew. We picked up forty-two, including Captain Semmes, who had a life belt on when rescued. William Roberts, our chief steward, recognized Semmes in the water from having seen him previously on the Confederate steamship *Sumter* at Gibraltar, where the *Deerhound* happened to be at the same time. Mr. Kell, the first officer of the *Alabama*, was rescued with Semmes; and Semmes probably owed his life to him, as he unquestionably did his liberty. It was Kell who suggested that Semmes should lie flat in the bottom of the boat to prevent his recognition by the party in the *Kearsarge*'s launch, which was close by us, and who donned himself one of our crew hats, with the word "DEERHOUND" on it, and took an oar so as to pass for one of our men. The question was asked from the launch whether Semmes had been saved or not. Kell promptly replied, "He is drowned"; and the assur-

---

1. I suppose Jones refers here to our ammunition. He is mistaken in stating the *Alabama* was refused fresh powder. No request was made in this connection. We had not discovered our ammunition damaged until the fight was opened. Neutrality laws would not have disallowed us a fresh powder supply.

ance was accepted, thus securing Semmes's escape. We were sorry we did not succeed in saving Mr. Llewellyn, the surgeon. Our boat was but a few yards off and pulling toward him when he went down.

When we had saved all we could, we prepared to sail for Southampton. I consulted Mr. Kell as to the international law in the case (he having a deal of experience in such matters), whether we were bound to deliver the persons we had rescued to the *Kearsarge*. He replied that as long as we kept the English flag flying, there could be no question that those who had found refuge under it were entitled to its protection. This decision was later fully confirmed from higher quarters. At the time the *Kearsarge* was about two miles from us, evidently taking breath and looking over her damages.

On our way to Southampton we passed the sailing yacht *Hornet*, Hewitt, master; and one of the saved men remarked that they had all their treasure, including about sixty chronometers, on board her. The same evening we arrived off Cowes, where Mr. Lancaster went on shore and reported himself at Cowes Castle as a member of the Royal Yacht squadron. We landed all the saved men at Southampton. The next day Mr. Lancaster gave the *Times* correspondent all the details. Afterward Mr. Mason (of the Mason and Slidell episode) came on board and thanked Mr. Lancaster and family for their kindness and humanity.

When Semmes came on board he was wounded and exhausted, and a most miserable object to look at. But after a little nursing he came on deck as bright as a dandy cock. Semmes seemed to be greatly reverenced by his crew, but I think Kell had their deepest regard. According to their idea, Kell was Semmes's mainstay and chief counselor, and the commander owed much of his success and reputation to his first officer's sagacity and promptness of resource.

The *Deerhound* was sold to Sir George Stuckley and was

at the opening of the Suez Canal in 1869, with Sir Stafford Northcote on board. She was the first British yacht to enter the canal. She was subsequently sold again and went to the coast of Zanzibar, where she was the means of rescuing many slaves. She eventually foundered in a storm. Thus ended the days of the historic little *Deerhound*.

EVAN P. JONES, *Captain*
Yacht *Deerhound*

Following is an incomplete facsimile list of the *Alabama*'s killed, wounded, and drowned (as hurriedly compiled and handed Captain Jones by one of the *Alabama*'s seamen).

LIST OF KILLED

JOHN ROBERTS	CHRISTIAN PUST	ANDRES PHEIFFER
JAMES KING II	CARL PJAVA	JOHN MAIR
JOHN WELLAN	CHRISTIAN OLSEN	PETER DUNCAN

Nine in all

WOUNDED

COMMANDER RAPHAEL SEMMES (Severely in right arm)
LIEUT. RICHARD F. ARMSTRONG
MIDSHIPMAN EDW. M. ANDERSON

JAMES BRODERICK	JOHN NEIL	SAMUEL. WILLIAMS
PETER HUGHES	THOMAS WINTER	JACOB BERBOT
WILLIAM MORGAN	ROBERT WRIGHT	DAVID WILLIAMS
THOMAS MCMILLAN	MARTIN KING	ROBERT B. HOBBS
WILLIAM MCGINLEY	JAMES MASON	CHARLES SEYMOUR

JOHN RUSSELL   JOHN ADAMS
Twenty in all

DROWNED

WILLIAM ROBINSON, Carpenter
JAMES HART
WILLIAM ROBERTSON, 3d. Asst. Engineer
DAVID HERBERT LLEWELLYN, Surgeon
GEORGE APPLEBEE, Yeoman
FREDERICK JOHNS
A. G. BARTELLI, Captain's Steward
HENRY FISHER
WALTER VAN ASS
THOMAS MURPHY
MARTIN WIDITCH
DAVID H. WHITE, Wardroom Boy
Twelve in all

Recapitulation: Total, forty-two

LIST OF PARTY AND CREW ON THE YACHT *DEERHOUND*

JOHN LANCASTER, Owner	JOHN LANCASTER JR., Son
MRS. LANCASTER, Wife	G. G. LANCASTER, Son
ROBERT LANCASTER, Son	CATHERINE LANCASTER, Daughter
MISS WILSON, Niece	MISS BROWN, Maid

EVAN P. JONES, Captain	———— ————, Seaman
ROBERT HUGHES, Mate	WILLIAM ROBERTS, Steward
HARRY ADAMS, Seaman	R. DURHAM, Cook
— PAGE, Seaman	WILLIAM BELL, Engineer
JOHN ROE, Seaman	WILLIAM JONES, Fireman
ROBERT BRODERICK, Seaman	— MARSHALL, Fireman

Twenty in all

[COPY]

CONFEDERATE STATES OF AMERICA,
EXECUTIVE DEPARTMENT,
RICHMOND, VA, *March 1st, 1865*

MR. JOHN LANCASTER,
Lancashire, England

Sir—It becomes my pleasing duty to transmit to you a certified copy of a Joint Resolution of thanks to Mr. John Lancaster, of England, for his friendly conduct towards the Commander, Officers, and Crew of the *Alabama*, passed by the Congress of the Confederate States of America and approved 14th February, 1865.

Permit me, as the Executive of the Confederate States, to join in returning to you the thanks of the people of the Confederacy, and to express my own appreciation of the gallant and humane conduct displayed by yourself and the Crew of your Yacht, the *Deerhound*, in the rescue of Captain Raphael Semmes, the Commander, and a portion of the Officers and Crew of the late Confederate States steamer, *Alabama*.

Be assured that my countrymen will never cease gratefully to remember your generous conduct, and I trust that our seamen under similar circumstances will ever be prompt to emulate your noble example.

Accept the tender of the esteem and regard with which I am,

Very respectfully,

Your friend,
JEFFERSON DAVIS

Joint resolution of thanks to MR. JOHN LANCASTER, *of England, for his friendly conduct towards the Commander, Officers, and Crew of the* Alabama.

RESOLVED by the Congress of the Confederate States of America, That the thanks of Congress and of the people of the Confederate States are due, and are hereby tendered to MR. JOHN LANCASTER, of Lancashire, England, for his friendly and humane conduct in receiving in his Yacht, the *Deerhound*, from the imminent peril of death by drowning, Captain RAPHAEL SEMMES, the Commander, and a portion of the Officers and Crew of the late Confederate States steamer *Alabama*, on the occasion of the combat between that vessel and the United States Steamer *Kearsarge* in the waters of the British Channel on the Nineteenth day of June, Eighteen Hundred and Sixty-four; and that his Excellency, the President of the Confederate States, be requested to inform Mr. Lancaster of the passage of this resolution, and to communicate to him a copy thereof.

(Signed)   TH. S. BOCOCK,
                      Speaker of The House of Representatives

                      R. M. T. HUNTER,
                      President of the Senate pro tempore

APPROVED 14TH FEB., '65.
            JEFFERSON DAVIS

CONFEDERATE STATES OF AMERICA,
                  DEPARTMENT OF JUSTICE

I do hereby certify that the foregoing is a true copy of a resolution of the congress of the Confederate States of

America, approved on the fourteenth day of February, One thousand Eight hundred and Sixty-five, and of which the original roll is on file in this office.

In faith whereof I have hereunto set my hand and affixed the seal of the said Department, this Seventeenth day of February, Anno Domini, One thousand eight hundred and sixty-five.

GEO. DAVIS,
Atty. Gen'l.

24 UPPER SEYMOUR STREET,
PORTMAN SQUARE, LONDON,
June 21, 1864

Dear Sir—I received from Captain Semmes, at Southampton, where I had the pleasure to see you, yesterday, a full report of the efficient services rendered under your orders by the officers and crew of your yacht, the *Deerhound*, in rescuing him, with thirteen of his officers and twenty-seven of his crew from their impending fate, after the loss of his ship. Captain Semmes reports that, finding the *Alabama* actually sinking, he had barely time to ship his wounded in his own boats to the enemy's ship, when the *Alabama* went down, and nothing was left to those who remained on board but to throw themselves into the sea. Their own boats absent, there seemed no prospect of relief, when your yacht arrived in their midst and your boats were launched; and he impressively told me that to this timely and generous succor he, with most of his officers, and a portion of his crew, was indebted for their safety. He further told me that on their arrival on board of the yacht, every care and kindness were extended to them which their exhausted condition required, even to supplying all with dry clothing. I am fully aware of the noble and disinterested spirit which prompted you to go to the rescue of the gallant crew of the *Alabama*, and that I can add nothing to the recompense already received by you and those acting under you, in the consciousness of having done as you would be done by; yet you will permit me to thank you, and through you, the captain, officers, and crew of the *Deerhound*, for this signal service, and to say that in doing so I but anticipate the grateful sentiment of my country, and of the Government of the Confederate States.

I have the honor to be, dear sir,

>Most respectfully and truly,

>>Your obedient servant,

(Signed)   J. M. MASON.

JOHN LANCASTER, ESQ.,

>>*Hindley Hall,*

>>>Wigan

Captain Evan Parry Jones
YACHT *DEERHOUND*
Photographed just after *Alabama-Kearsarge* engagement.

1. John Lancaster
2. Mrs. John Lancaster
3. John Lancaster Jr.

4. Albert Lancaster
5. G. G. Lancaster
6. Catherine Lancaster

John Lancaster, owner Yacht *Deerhound*, and Family
(Photographed just after the *Alabama-Kearsarge* engagement.)

EPILOGUE TO
ARTHUR SINCLAIR'S
NARRATIVE

When the *Alabama* sank beneath the waves of the English Channel, the bitterness it had engendered in the North did not sink with it. Nor did the issues of international law dissipate when the guns of war were silenced at Appomattox.

After his rescue and safe landing in Southampton, as described by Sinclair, Commander Raphael Semmes was warmly welcomed by friends whom he had met during his former stay in England following the abandonment of the *Sumter* in Gibraltar. Feted by the public, he received many letters from admirers and from young men wishing to serve under him as well as a specially inscribed sword from a group of British naval officers to replace the one he had lost in the Channel. His stay included a six-week tour of Europe and the Swiss Alps before he made plans to return and rejoin the Confederate cause.

Not wishing to risk running the blockade, he took ship via Havana and made land in Mexico at the mouth of the Rio

Grande, journeying on to Galveston where he was greeted as a hero. From there he had made a rugged journey across the plains of Texas and the swamps of Mississippi, reaching Mobile at the end of December 1864. He was promptly summoned to Richmond where he was honored by the Confederate Congress and appointed Rear Admiral with command of the James River squadron.

By this time the Confederate cause was all but lost, and shortly after taking command he was obliged to destroy his fleet to prevent its capture. Commandeering a train in Richmond, he joined the remaining Confederate forces at Danville, Virginia, and enlisted his crews as an artillery brigade in the final Confederate resistance. Then, with the end of hostilities following Lee's surrender at Appomattox, he, like other Confederate soldiers, was paroled and obliged to find his way back home to Mobile as best he could.

But Gideon Welles, the Union Secretary of the Navy, had not let go. On December 15, 1865, a lieutenant of marines arrived at Semmes's home with an order for his arrest on charges of treason and breach of parole when he escaped to England and reenlisted in the Confederate cause after the *Alabama* sank. Semmes was held in Washington for three months, but charges were dropped as Congress worked out terms to demobilize the Confederate army and reintegrate the Southern states.

Returning again to Mobile, he took up lecturing on the war and the *Alabama*'s exploits, publishing his memoirs in 1867. After holding various public positions—as probate judge for Mobile County, then as professor of Moral Philosophy and Literature at Louisiana State University, and finally as editor of the *Memphis Daily Bulletin*—from which he was effectively forced out by political pressure, he returned to his law practice. He died in 1877 in Mobile, where his statue now stands.

Much less is known about the author's later years. Following his stay in Southampton, Sinclair remained in Europe expecting to serve on another raider. Bulloch was still active and effective in commissioning other vessels for the Confederate navy—and in circumventing the restrictions of Britain's neutrality laws. It seems that Sinclair intended to enlist with the *Texas,* a raider built on the Clyde in Scotland, but the end of the war intervened before she could be put to sea. Finally returning to Norfolk, Virginia, he made a living as a merchant, though he always thought of himself as a naval officer. In 1895 he published this book, which was reprinted the following year. He outlived all his shipmates and died in 1925.

The Alabama Claims

When Lee surrendered at Appomattox, Charles Francis Adams was still the United States representative in London. The later years of the war had done nothing to improve his relationship with Lord Russell.

Although the British government had finally acted to seize the *Alabama*—albeit too late—it was generally believed on both sides of the Atlantic that private British money had in fact financed its construction. And by the time of the *Alabama*'s escape, Bullock had already commissioned the building of two ironclads at the Laird shipyard (to be known as the *Laird Rams*). Their state-of-the-art design and armament represented a real threat to the Union blockade. Soon uncovered by Dudley as intended for the Confederacy, Charles Adams found himself frustrated once again in his attempts to have the vessels seized—this time by a cunning ploy of Bulloch's to have the contract transacted through a French shipbuilder. Lord Russell flatly rejected taking any action until matters reached a crisis pitch, causing Adams to write to him: "It is superfluous for me to point out to your Lordship that this is war." Whether this letter or the recent Union victory at Gettysburg changed Russell's mind is hard to know, but he finally acted to detain the ironclads.

At the end of the war, Russell was further embarrassed when another famous raider sailed into Southampton, choosing to surrender to the British government rather than to the Union. Following the sinking of the *Alabama*, Bulloch had hurriedly purchased an East India merchantman, armed in Madeira and commissioned into the Confederate navy as the *Shenandoah*. She caused widespread devastation of Union whaling fleets, and with no certain knowledge of the Confederate surrender at Appomattox continued her depredations off the coast of Alaska for several months after the war had ended.

Mutual resentment and distrust ran deep. When Adams pressed his case for compensation, Russell bridled at the implied impropriety on his part, responding characteristically: "Her Majesty's Government are the sole guardians of their own honor."

There the matter rested until the USS *Miantonomoh*, on a courtesy visit, caught the public's attention. The ironclad, based on the *Monitor* design, outclassed anything that the British navy had afloat. As the *Times* reported: "There is not one (British warship) that the foreigner could not have sent to the bottom in five minutes. . . ."

The British government, now under new leadership, proceeded to make an offer to review Adams's petition for compensation; but it was so circumscribed by conditions that William Seward, Secretary of State and long standing Anglophobe, rejected it out of hand.

Seward's priority at that time was territorial expansion. Having just completed the purchase of Alaska from Russia, he wanted to exploit the claims issue to further his designs in the Northwest and had in mind to negotiate a settlement by the transfer of British Columbia to the United States. He sent his representative, Reverdy Johnson, to London to work out an agreement of all the outstanding territorial disputes together with the *Alabama* claims. However, the British Foreign Secretary, Lord Clarendon, outwitted the ill-qualified Johnson. The resulting draft bore no mention of national damages or of territorial compensation; it was essentially a protocol to recompense all individual parties who had suffered losses—including English blockade-runners.

By the time the document reached the Senate Committee, Ulysses S. Grant had been elected President and Seward was no longer the Secretary of State. The chairman of the Senate committee, Charles Sumner, was now to become the champion of the *Alabama* claims. Sumner was a passionate orator whose anti-slavery diatribes leading up to the Civil War had provoked one Southerner to physically assault him on the floor of the House. When he read the draft of the agreement he saw in it another grand cause.

On April 13, 1869, in ringing tones, Sumner denounced the craven language of the draft agreement. He reviewed Britain's role from the outset of the war: her immediate proclamation of neutrality which, he said, was a tacit recognition of the legitimacy of the Confederate government; Lord Russell's reluctance to act on the Union's repeated demands to seize the *Alabama*; and the welcome and assistance accorded the *Alabama* when she berthed in Jamaica, a British possession. Then he expounded in righteous fury on British perfidy in supporting the cause of slavery, in contradiction to British activism in abolishing the slave trade in the British Empire fifty years earlier.

But this was just the preamble. He then went on to enumerate not just the direct damages caused by the British-built raider but all the consequential damages—perhaps some $100 million. The climax of his speech came when he cast Britain as not simply a perfidious opportunist but the active abettor of the Confederate cause and thereby responsible for the prolongation of the war—in Sumner's estimate by some two years. Therefore the total damages that the United States was entitled to seek were not of the order of some tens of millions of dollars, but half the total cost of the war—some two billion dollars.

The speech had its intended shock value. Some in London even saw war as inevitable. However, Grant, the great warrior of the recent conflict, was not of that mind. He saw the issue as a needless distraction from the internal priorities and accelerating growth of the newly united republic.

But tensions remained high and there appeared to be no obvious way out of the impasse—until in 1872, when the landscape of world politics changed. In a few short weeks, the army of the new German Confederation under the leadership of Prussia had crossed the border into France and threatened the city of Paris. Britain realized that continuing hostility with the United States, who might one day be a needed ally, was not in its interest.

Very shortly thereafter, a British minister was in Washington negotiating terms to settle all outstanding disputes, chief among them the *Alabama* claims. It was agreed to settle them by the novel procedure of an international tribunal to be held in Geneva with one representative each from the United States and Britain and three from other countries to be appointed independently. Charles Adams served as representative from the United States, and it was understood that the tribunal would only address the matter of claims for direct damages. After a perfunctory opening session of the tribunal, each side was allowed several months to prepare its brief to be submitted to the other—and the court—prior to the hearing.

When British government officials finally read through

the voluminous document prepared in Washington, they were horrified. The aggrieved party was now claiming the full extent of damages brandished by Sumner—plus 7 percent interest! Britain immediately submitted a case for postponement, which Adams quickly recognized as no more than a ploy for indefinite deferment. He also knew that the United States' exaggerated claim was more for the benefit of the public and to gratify the patriotic fervor in Congress than as a realistic legal argument. If the United States were to receive any damages and the matter be resolved, his government would have to modify its position. As a result of his intervention, he persuaded the arbitrators to consider only the direct claims, allowing the hearing to proceed and the fire-eaters in the United States to claim that they had sought the maximum redress.

Ultimately the tribunal confined the case to damages related to three Confederate raiders: the *Alabama*, the *Florida*, and the *Shenandoah*. From widely diverging estimates of appropriate damages, the arbitrators agreed on a sum of $15,200,000, with the largest amount relating to the *Alabama*.

THE *ALABAMA* REEMERGES

The *Alabama* did not make headlines again until one hundred years later. In 1982, the sonar of the French minesweeper the *Circe* registered a large object some seven miles out from the French coast near Cherbourg. Divers soon confirmed its identity as the *Alabama*. Further dives revealed that the starboard hull, which was largely submerged, together with the propeller, lifting gear, cannon, and many artifacts had been preserved, but the exposed portside hull had been eaten away.

With the discovery, the *Alabama* had found herself the subject of yet another international controversy. Although American, the vessel lay within French territorial waters. Ambiguities as to ownership were resolved by an agreement that confirmed the United States ownership of the wreck but provided for shared management of recovery operations.

The strong currents in the channel have made recovery efforts difficult and treacherous, but they have proceeded steadily. In 2000, the History Channel produced an excellent documentary about the discovery and recovery. For the latest information regarding the *Alabama*, readers may contact the CSS Alabama Association.

—S. W.
November 2003

BIOGRAPHICAL NOTES

RAPHAEL SEMMES
Commander

The commander of the *Alabama* during her famous career entered the United States Navy as midshipman, April 1, 1826. He was appointed from Maryland, the state of his birth, and first saw service in September of the same year on the sloop-of-war *Lexington*, making the cruise on the vessel and pursuing at the same time his studies. After a short leave of absence in October 1828, was ordered to the sloop *Erie*, making a cruise on this vessel; and next, in January 1830, was ordered to the frigate *Brandywine*. In November 1831, ordered to the Norfolk Navy Yard and Naval School at this point. Passed examination January 1832, and received warrant as passed midshipman. The Naval School at Annapolis had not as yet been organized. In March 1833, ordered to service in the bureau of navigation. In July 1835, ordered to frigate *Constellation* as acting master. In March 1837, promoted to lieutenant and ordered to Norfolk Navy Yard. In May 1839, to the steamer *Poinsett*. In June 1839, to the receiving ship at Norfolk. In September 1840, to the *Consort*, on coast survey. In May 1841, to the Navy Yard, Pensacola. In July 1843, to sloop-of-war *Warren*; and in August 1843, to command of steamer *Poinsett*, on coast-survey duty. In September 1845, ordered to the brig *Porpoise*, home squadron. Made this cruise, and after leave of absence ordered in January 1848, to the command of the *Electra*, coast survey. Served in the Mexican War on the brig *Somers*. Commissioned commander October 1855, and served on lighthouse board in various capacities until February 1861, when he resigned his commission in United States Navy and at once tendered his services to the Confederate States government, at this time making Montgomery, Alabama, the capital of the Confederacy. He was in February 1861 placed on the Confederate naval list, with rank of commander.

Semmes's first duty in the new navy was a mission north for the purchase of war material and vessels suitable for cruisers. In the former he was eminently successful, purchasing immense quantities of war stores; but he failed to find a type of vessel, in the mercantile marine of the North, suitable for cruising. At the outset of the war, fully appreciating the immense interests at stake in the commerce of the enemy and the value of armed cruisers to prey on it, Semmes bent all his eloquence to impress upon the Secretary of the Navy the importance of fitting out, at as early a day as possible, a fleet of this class of vessels. As a pioneer of this arm of service, he suggested the purchase of the *Habana*, a packet steamer between New Orleans and Havana, the only vessel available at the time at all suited to the work. He was authorized to purchase and equip this steamer, pending the building abroad of a type of cruisers fully suited for the work. This vessel became the Confederate States steamer *Sumter*. The cruise in this vessel, after running the blockade at New Orleans, though short (from June 30, 1861, to January 18, 1862), was phenomenally successful, making eighteen captures and fully establishing the wisdom of the move. This steamer was succeeded by the *Alabama* and others of similar type, the result being that the foreign commerce of the United States was literally, in two years, swept from the high seas, leaving the carrying trade of the world mostly in English hands. On the completion of the *Alabama* cruise and subsequent sinking of the vessel, Semmes returned to the Confederate States via Mexico and Texas. In February 1865, he was promoted to rear admiral, Confederate States Navy, and ordered to command of James River ironclad fleet, assisting in defense of Richmond. Upon the evacuation of the capital, Semmes destroyed his fleet and, forming his command into a battalion, escaped to Danville per rail. He surrendered his command at Greensboro, North Carolina, May 1, 1865.

Semmes practiced law in Mobile, Alabama, the home of his adoption, from the close of hostilities to the end of his earthly career. A man of varied talents and perhaps without an equal for the work required, all things considered, in any navy of the world. As an expounder of international law he had few, if any, superiors. He had made the study of it not only a self-imposed duty but the pleasure of his life from early years, and lived to reap the benefit and satisfaction arising from having thoroughly mastered its intricacies. He was not once finally defeated in all his numerous tilts with the legal talent of foreign powers; and as a strategist on the ocean he was eminently successful in outwitting the plans of the commanders sent in pursuit of him. He rarely came in contact with them, and then gave them the slip with little trouble. He only came to blows with the enemy's cruisers by his own choosing. The career of

Semmes on the high seas will probably rank as the most re-markable for daring and success in the annals of naval history.

Semmes's verbal and written utterances manifest a bitterness of feeling toward his foes which are calculated to greatly mis-lead one respecting his real character. That he also pursued Northern commerce on the high seas with a vigor and relent-lessness that seemed absolutely malignant is not to be denied. In a sense, his heart was undoubtedly in his work. But he was uniformly just in his decisions. He respected private property and private feelings. And it was the rule, rather than the excep-tion, that he provided in the best possible way for his prisoners, military and civilian; and we have often seen that he gave them their boats and whatever their ships afforded of comfort and luxury to get away with. This was not the conduct of a malevo-lent partisan, but distinctly that of a generous and chivalric foe.[1] It is by his acts rather than by his utterances that a man like Semmes should be judged. He had a noble and generous soul.

JOHN McINTOSH KELL
First Lieutenant and Executive Officer

The subject of our sketch was born in Georgia and entered the United States Navy as acting midshipman, September 9, 1841. First saw service in this year on the sloop-of-war *Fal-mouth*, on the Gulf Station. His next service was in 1843, on board frigate *Savannah*, Pacific Station. He was present at the hoisting of the United States flag at Monterey when the United States forces took possession, and was in two engage-

---

1. Winslow himself paid a high compliment to Semmes; for upon learn-ing he proposed bringing the *Alabama* out for a fight, he (Winslow) did not for a moment doubt it, and evidenced it by ceasing to blockade the port at the marine league, keeping ten to twelve miles from the mole. Winslow honored the message and the man.

ments with the Californians, receiving flattering notice. Returned home in 1847 and was ordered to Naval Academy, passed examination, and was ordered to sloop-of-war *Albany*, Gulf of Mexico. On this cruise was tried by court-martial and dismissed the service for refusing to obey the order of the executive officer to light the candles for the wardroom officers. Young Kell refused to do this menial service as beneath the dignity of an officer and a gentleman. The finding of the court was reconsidered, and young Kell honorably acquitted and reinstated to former rank. In this trial Kell was defended by Raphael Semmes as counsel.

In 1852 ordered to United States steamer *Susquehanna*, flagship of East India squadron, under Commodore M. C. Perry, and was on the staff of Perry during the negotiation of the treaty of commerce with Japan, 1854; then transferred to United States steamer *Mississippi* of same squadron, returning home by the way of California and Cape Horn. Ordered to surveying schooner *Arago* on the Texas coast. Next ordered to receiving ship *Pennsylvania*, Norfolk. Next ordered to store ship *Supply*, Brazil Station. Next to Pensacola Navy Yard, where he remained until the breaking out of the Civil War and secession of Georgia, when he tendered his resignation from United States Navy, and offered his services to his native state.

In April 1861, commanded the state steamer *Savannah* for coast defense. May 26, 1861, received his commission as lieutenant, Confederate States Navy, and ordered to report at New Orleans to Captain Raphael Semmes, and assisted in fitting out the *Sumter* for service on the high seas. Here his services were invaluable. Ran the blockade on her through the Federal fleet at New Orleans and was chased by the United States steamer *Brooklyn* for forty miles off the coast, escaping in a rainstorm. Made the full cruise on this vessel. The *Sumter* being condemned by survey at Gibraltar,

Kell was ordered home, and proceeded with Semmes to Southampton en route to Confederacy via Nassau, West Indies. At latter point met orders to join Confederate States steamer *Alabama* fitting out at Liverpool. Proceeded to Liverpool. Found *Alabama* had escaped a few days before. He reembarked and joined her at Terceira, Western Islands, as executive officer. Here he at once entered upon the arduous task of converting an as yet merchant vessel into a full-fledged man-of-war—mounting battery, organizing crew, etc.

Upon his return from England to the Confederacy through the blockade after the sinking of the *Alabama*, Kell was ordered to the ironclad *Richmond* at Drury's Bluff, James River, under command of Captain Mitchell. During his service at this point, an unsuccessful attempt was made by the squadron to destroy the pontoon bridges of the enemy, constructed lower down the river. The attempt failed. Later on Kell was invalided, after having remained some time in the hospital. From this date he was totally unfitted for service up to the surrender of the Army of Northern Virginia. Since the war, Kell served on the staff of Governor John D. Gordon of Georgia, as adjutant-general of the state, and is, at this writing, occupying the same position on the staff of Governor W. J. Northen. His official residence is Atlanta. General Kell's private residence is at "Sunny Side," near Griffin, Georgia, where, residing upon his plantation, he has turned his sword into a plowshare and only "dreams of battles."

RICHARD F. ARMSTRONG
Second Lieutenant

Born in Eatonton, Georgia. Entered the United States Naval Academy as cadet from the state of Georgia, April 21,

1857. Made two practice-ship cruises on the United States sloops-of-war *Preble* and *Plymouth*, visiting Cherbourg, Cadiz, Madeira, Azores, and Canaries. Upon the secession of the state of Georgia, resigned warrant as acting midshipman, United States Navy, January 30, 1861. Appointed midshipman of the navy of the state of Georgia, and assigned to command of brig *Bonita*, used as a receiving ship, February 26, 1861. Detached from *Bonita*, and ordered to steamer *Savannah*, Commander John M. Kell, executive officer, March 1861. Detached from the *Savannah* and ordered to Georgia. Naval steamer *Huntress*, Commander C. Manigault Morris, flagship of Commodore Josiah Tatnall, March 1861.

April 17, 1861, appointed a midshipman in the Confederate States Navy and ordered to proceed to New Orleans and report to Commander R. Semmes in command of Confederate States steamer *Sumter*. June 30, *Sumter* ran the blockade, consisting of a strong fleet of steam vessels. Made the full cruise of six months on this ship, burning eighteen vessels of the enemy; and upon the arrival of the *Sumter* at Gibraltar, where she was condemned as unseaworthy, Armstrong with a crew was left by Semmes in charge of her, pending further orders from the Secretary of the Navy as to her disposition. July 1862, relieved of the command of the Sumter by master's-mate Andrews, he was ordered to report to Honorable James M. Mason, commissioner of the Confederate States at London.

Reported, and was ordered to await arrival of Captain Semmes, who was to command the *290* (*Alabama*). Reported for duty on this vessel August 10; and on August 13 embarked on steamer *Bahama* from Liverpool and joined the *Alabama* at Terceira, Western Islands, August 20, 1862. At anchor here was a barque transferring guns, stores, ammunition, etc., to the *Alabama*; and the subject of our sketch was soon in his element, assisting the executive officer in mounting guns, stowing the magazines, stationing the crew, etc. All was chaos and excitement; and order had to be brought out of it, and that quickly, as the enemy might at any time be down on us. Who better able to carry out our executive's orders? None. In the engagement with the *Kearsarge* off Cherbourg, June 19, 1864, Armstrong was wounded and was picked up out of the water by a French pilot-boat, nearly exhausted, and taken into Cherbourg. He was confined for some time to his bed at the Hotel de l'Europe. Upon his recovery he was ordered to the Confederacy. Embarked on the blockade-runner *Caroline* for Halifax, Nova Scotia, thence to Nassau; from Nassau to Southern Coast; and after many attempts to enter Wilmington was finally landed on the beach, crossed the Pedee River in a canoe to Georgetown, made his way to Richmond, and delivered his dispatches.

Next ordered to Wilmington. December 24, 1864, finds Armstrong a volunteer in Fort Fisher, placed in command of a division of three guns by Colonel Lamb commanding. Was present during the bombardment of Fort Fisher by Admiral Porter and received honorable mention for marked gallantry in the official dispatches.

Here is what Armstrong says of the fight in a letter to the writer: "When I arrived in Richmond, I found an application on file in the Bureau of Orders and Detail from Admiral Semmes for my assignment to him as flag-lieutenant, and had some difficulty in declining it. I did, however, get off, and was ordered to Wilmington to await orders. While there, the bombardment of Fort Fisher took place; and, like a fool, I had to be in it. It was the *merriest* Christmas Day I ever spent, old man; and if ever there was hell on earth, the inside of that fort was surely!"

Next ordered to Charleston as second lieutenant of the ironclad *Columbia*, which vessel was sunk, in coming out of dry dock, through treachery. Detached from her, was ordered to take *Columbia*'s crew to Richmond to reenforce Drury's Bluff. January 1865, ordered to Charleston to command a torpedo boat. Upon the evacuation of Charleston, the officers and crews of the fleet were formed into a brigade under Admiral Tucker and known as "Tucker Brigade"; and Armstrong was appointed captain of Company A. Marched to Fayetteville, thence to Durham, North Carolina, and was there detached and ordered to Richmond.

March 1865, ordered to school ship *Patrick Henry* as instructor in gunnery. April 2, Richmond was evacuated; and the midshipmen of the school were ordered out as escort to the President and cabinet, and guard to the specie of the Confederate States. Upon reaching Washington, Georgia, Armstrong was detached from the command and soon after left for his home under parole. Armstrong settled shortly after the war in Halifax, Nova Scotia, and is at this time general agent of the Grand Trunk Railway for the Maritime Provinces of Canada. Armstrong was not wanting in any of the essentials in the makeup of a naval officer, and though but twenty years of age at the time of joining the *Alabama* was as matured of judgment, as cool and unconcerned in danger, as an old and trained veteran. As an officer, with all the requisites for such a cruise as the *Alabama* was to make, Lieutenant Richard F. Armstrong had no superior. As a sailorman thoroughly up in his profession, and a typical graduate of the Naval Academy, Armstrong justly commanded the confidence of Semmes and amply answered to it. The division he commanded, embracing the one-hundred-pounder rifle gun, was under his guidance brought to a state of almost perfect efficiency. The steamer *Ariel* would most likely have escaped us but for Armstrong's splendid shot. His baffled effort to sink the *Kearsarge* with his rifle gun, reflects, in the state of our powder, no discredit on his judgment. The rapid destruction of the Hatteras was certainly due, I think, to his marksmanship.

JOSEPH D. WILSON
Third Lieutenant

For reckless daring and fierce fighting instincts, "Fighting Joe," as he was dubbed by his shipmates, stood almost alone among his comrades. He was sui generis, a man out and out framed for war, a veritable Othello. Appointed an acting midshipman in the United States Navy from his native state of Florida, he entered the Naval Academy September 21, 1857, and during his course of study made two cruises on the practice ships *Preble* and *Plymouth*, visiting Cherbourg, Cadiz, Madeira, Azores, and Canary Islands, fitting himself for the profession he was to take so distinguished a position in. Little could he at this time have imagined that circumstances would arise to force him from allegiance to the service and flag he was at the time so proud of and array him, heart, soul, and energies, against its principles and purposes. Upon the secession of his native state, Wilson resigned from the United States Navy and on April 7, 1861, was appointed midshipman in the Confederate States Navy and ordered to the Confederate States steamer *Sumter*, Commander R. Semmes, then being fitted out at New Orleans for a cruise against the enemy's commerce. Upon the laying up of the *Sumter* at Gibraltar, Wilson was ordered to London, with instructions to report for duty to Honorable J. M. Mason, commissioner of the Confederate States to Great Britain. On the 10th of August, 1862, he was ordered to Confederate States steamer *Alabama* and left Liverpool on steamer *Bahama* for Terceira where he joined us, and served until the sinking of the ship. Wounded and a prisoner, we next find

Wilson in a role not at all to his inclination or taste. But we will let his shipmate of both services, Second Lieutenant Armstrong, tell the story:

"On the *Alabama*, as you know, he commanded the second, or after-gun, division. Just before the ship sank he was sent off in charge of the wounded men, who were transferred to the *Kearsarge*, and thus became a prisoner of war. Subsequently the *Kearsarge* transferred Wilson to the sloop-of-war _____ (I cannot recall the name of this ship), which ship came into Dover, England.

"Wilson had been treated by the officers of both ships with consideration; and upon the suggestion of the captain of the _____, he came up to London on parole. He wired me from Dover, and I met him upon his arrival. Together we visited the Honorable John M. Mason, Confederate commissioner. Wilson had been entrusted with a letter from the captain to deliver to Honorable Charles Francis Adams, American minister, and which he was assured related solely to his release; but he resented the fact that the letter was sealed. You know how obstinate Wilson could be on occasions, and this was one of the times when he showed the greatest pigheadedness. Neither Mr. Mason nor myself could convince him that, owing to his mission, it was not infra dig for him to convey a sealed letter to Mr. Adams. He was extremely sensitive and feared a rebuff from the United States representative. The long and short of it was that 'old Joe' took the next train for Dover and Fort Warren. But it was not to be. I had an engagement to accompany Mrs. Greenough to an evening party; and, being full of regret for the unfortunate predicament of my shipmate, I called early upon her and stated Wilson's case. Mrs. Greenough was an extraordinary woman, very talented, quick in perception, ready in resource. She had elaborated a scheme to obtain Wilson's release in ten minutes. I hurried off to the telegraph station and sent several messages so as to catch Wilson before he had gone aboard ship; and in this I was fortunate enough to succeed and had the old boy safe in my rooms that night. Next day, accompanied by Mrs. Greenough (wax he was in her hands—and who was not?), he waited upon the American minister, was received with courtesy, and came forth the bearer of a letter to Captain _____ of the United States ship _____, which Mr. Adams assured him would meet his wishes. Wilson repaired to Dover, gave the usual parole, and was released a prisoner of war awaiting exchange. To one of Wilson's sensitive temperament his position was extremely galling; and although, like the rest of us, he was full of scurvy and needed recuperation, he never rested until he secured passage for the Confederate States, his whole thought night and day being to negotiate a speedy exchange and become once more a fighting man. And was not the old boy the devil incarnate in a fight? Did you see him on the 19th, just after the half of his pivot-gun's crew had been ground to powder? I did, and a cooler, braver daredevil of a fighter I never saw. Well, Mrs. Greenough, under Wilson's escort, embarked for the Confederate States in the same steamer. In attempting the blockade at Wilmington, the steamer was chased onshore under the guns of Fort Fisher, and poor Mrs. Greenough lost her life by the boat capsizing in the surf. Wilson speedily effected his exchange and was assigned to the James River squadron, in command of the gunboat *Hampton*. At the evacuation of Richmond, Wilson burned his ship and took the field in the brigade of Admiral Semmes, composed of the personnel of the James River squadron, and surrendered at Greensboro, North Carolina. This completes the official record of Lieutenant Joseph D. Wilson. He afterwards engaged in various capacities; indeed, a multitude of ventures.

Here are some of the things he attempted—cottonplanter,

druggist, photographer (success), telegraph operator (success), civil engineer (success), railroad contractor (success), auditor of railroad. Truly he was an all-round man— "General Dependence" for the Democratic Party in Florida during Reconstruction times. If the history of these times is ever written, Wilson's name will stand forth prominently. The people of middle Florida, in their postbellum troubles, looked up to, and depended on Joe for everything.

Wilson was killed in a railroad accident near Quincy, Florida, some years ago. He was a true friend, a generous, bighearted, gallant fellow. We will only add that Wilson's devotion to Mrs. Greenough was simply sublime. Her sad death must have been the severest blow of his life.

JOHN LOW
Fourth Lieutenant

Born at Liverpool, England, and educated in the merchant marine of his native country, the advent of the Civil War found Low an adopted son of Georgia and residing in Savannah. His excellent abilities attracted the attention of Captain James D. Bulloch; and he was appointed second officer of the *Fingal*, a steamer purchased by Captain Bulloch for the Confederate States government and loaded with war material. In company with Bulloch, he ran the blockade into Savannah. The *Fingal* being unable to get out of Savannah, owing to increased vigilance of the blockading squadron, Low, in company with Bulloch, proceeded to Wilmington and took passage for Liverpool on the *Annie Childs*. Prior to his departure for Liverpool, he was commissioned a lieutenant (dating from November 5, 1861), March 26, 1862. He took passage on the steamer *Florida* for Nassau as bearer of dispatches to Captain John N. Maffitt, who had been detailed to command this cruiser, arriving at Nassau, April 28. From this point he returned to Liverpool and joined the *Alabama* at Terceira. June 20, 1863, he was given command of the *Conrad* (*Tuscaloosa*). His orders were to cruise in the South Atlantic and Indian Oceans and in the neighborhood of Cape of Good Hope, and rejoin the *Alabama* at Cape Town at a date fixed. She was not destined to rival her parent ship in captures; for soon after parting, stress of weather forced her into Simon's Town, Cape of Good Hope, where she was seized by order of the British government, at the suggestion of the American consul, as having been unlawfully fitted out. Low, despairing of having his vessel released within a definite time, took steamer for England with his lieutenant and men. He did not succeed in rejoining the *Alabama* to participate in the fight with the *Kearsarge*.

ARTHUR SINCLAIR
Fifth Lieutenant

Lieutenant Sinclair comes from a naval family dating from Revolutionary times. His grandfather, Commodore Arthur Sinclair, commanded the United States sloop-of-war *General Pike* on Lake Ontario during the War of 1812–1815, rendered distinguished service, and received honorable mention and promotion. His father, Commander Arthur Sinclair, was from 1823 to 1861 in the United States Navy, when he resigned his commission as commander and cast his fortunes with his native state, Virginia, receiving his commission as commander in the Confederate States Navy, in which capacity he rendered signal service to the Confederacy.

Lieutenant Sinclair entered the naval service of the Confederacy May 1861, as master's-mate, and was assigned to duty on the gunboat *Winslow*, serving in the fleet of Commodore Lynch in the sounds of North Carolina, and took part in the defense of Fort Hatteras. Upon the surrender of this fort to the fleet of Commodore Stringham, he was detached and ordered to report at Norfolk; was ordered to the ironclad *Virginia (Merrimac)*, and served as aide to Captain Franklin Buchanan in the memorable engagement in Hampton Roads, March 8 and 9, 1862. After this engagement he was ordered to report to the Honorable Secretary of the Navy at Richmond, bearer of an official letter from Captain Buchanan recommending his promotion; received his commission as sailing-master and was ordered to report at New Orleans to the commanding officer of the station, Captain William C. Whittle, as sailing-master and acting lieutenant of the ironclad *Mississippi*, under the command of Arthur Sinclair, at the same time being entrusted with the conveyance of the battery destined for the above vessel. Was present at the surrender at New Orleans but did not participate in the action, the *Mississippi* being in an unfinished state at the time and moored to the dock at the navy yard. She was fired and destroyed by order of her commander. Escaped on river steamer *Platona*, landed at Vicksburg, and proceeded to Richmond. At the suggestion of Admiral Buchanan, ordered thence to Confederate States steamer *Alabama* and instructed to proceed to Charleston. Ran the blockade from this port on the steamer *Lucille* for Nassau. Arrived safe and reported to Captain Semmes for duty, at the same time delivering to him important dispatches from the Secretary of the Navy. Took passage, July 1862, on the steamer *Bahama* with Semmes and other officers detailed for the *Alabama*. Upon arrival at Liverpool, found the *Alabama* had slipped the authorities and put to sea. After gathering the remainder of the officers destined for the cruise, the head of the *Bahama* was turned south, steaming for the Western

Islands, at which point their future vessel was to be met. Was raised to rank of lieutenant by Commander Semmes.

After the sinking of the *Alabama*, Lieutenant Sinclair was granted leave of absence to recuperate his health; and just before the surrender was detailed as one of the lieutenants of the cruiser *Texas*, about completed on the Clyde, Scotland. Lee surrendered, and Othello's occupation was gone.

Lieutenant Sinclair's naval life dates from his 13th year. He had the advantage of serving four years under his father in the United States Navy; first on the United States ship *Supply* in the Mediterranean and on the Brazil Station, and also in the Japan expedition of Commodore Perry, 1852–1855. His father spared no pains to ground him thoroughly in his destined profession. Secretary Mallory distinguished him with marked favor, and he was practically a volunteer in every position he filled during the war.

IRVINE S. BULLOCH
Sailing-Master

Sailing-master Irvine S. Bulloch was appointed a midshipman in the Confederate States Navy, August 29, 1861, from the state of Georgia, and first saw service on the gunboat *Savannah*, Savannah River, under Captain John N. Maffitt (afterwards the commander of the Confederate States cruiser *Florida*). His next service was on board steamer *Nashville*, Captain R. B. Pegram. This vessel ran the blockade as a cruiser, making the run to Southampton, England, and returned, penetrating the blockade again at Beaufort, North Carolina. This vessel burned two prizes en route. In February 1862, ordered to steamship *Nansemond*, Norfolk, as aide to Commander Sydney S. Lee. Next ordered to Charleston, and thence through blockade to Nassau; thence to Liverpool, and per steamer *Bahama* to Terceira, Azores, and joined the *Alabama*. Bulloch joined the vessel as midshipman and was a most promising young officer, born and cut out for a sailor. With a few months' practice and experience he had so far mastered his profession as to earn from Semmes promotion to master, and ably navigated the vessel the remainder of the cruise, assuming also the duties of watch officer. He was an indefatigable student of his profession, pursuing its study at every spare moment, and at the end of the cruise had little to learn of the duties of a sailor.

In August 1864, Bulloch was ordered in steamship *Laurel* to Madeira and joined the Confederate States steamer *Shenandoah*, Captain J. I. Waddell, and made the memorable cruise in this vessel as sailing-master, visiting the North Pacific and Arctic Oceans, capturing many whalers, and completing the destruction of the United States merchant marine in the Pacific. When off San Francisco in the *Shenandoah*, August 1865, it was learned the war was over. The ship was brought to Liverpool, and on the 6th of November, 1865, turned over to the English government. Here Bulloch found his commission as lieutenant awaiting him, but no country to serve. At this writing, Bulloch is engaged in the peaceful pursuit of a cotton broker at Liverpool. For him also,

Grim-visag'd war hath smooth'd his wrinkled front.

BECKETT K. HOWELL
Lieutenant Marines

Howell entered the United States Marine Corps as first lieutenant of marines, his commission dating August 1, 1860. His appointment was from the state of Louisiana. Howell comes from a distinguished family of the South and was nurtured in chivalry and love of arms. He was a thorough soldier and drill officer, taking pride in his profession and, although without a marine guard on the *Alabama*, was indispensable in drilling the crew at the manual of arms. Howell first saw service at Washington Barracks, but upon the secession of his state resigned his commission and accepted service with the Confederate States, under commission of lieutenant of marines, dated March 29, 1861, and was ordered to the cruiser *Sumter* at New Orleans, organizing her marine guard and commanding it during the memorable cruise of that vessel. Proceeded from Gibraltar, upon laying up of the *Sumter*, to England, and was ordered to the *Alabama*, making the entire cruise on her. He was quite active after the fight in rescuing the wounded and assisting in transferring them to the *Kearsarge*. Howell took passage later for the Confederacy and served the remainder of the war on shore duty. He died some years since from fever contracted on the Mississippi River. He was a bighearted, generous fellow, ever ready to please a shipmate. Semmes's affection for him was marked, and he was distinctly the favorite with him among the ship's officers.

FRANCIS L. GALT
Surgeon and Acting Paymaster

F. L. Galt, a Virginian by birth, was appointed assistant surgeon in the United States Navy from the state of Georgia, September 28, 1855, and made his first cruise on the frigate *St. Lawrence*, flagship of Commodore French Forrest, to the Brazil Station, being absent four years. Upon his return was assigned to duty on the receiving ship *Pennsylvania* at Norfolk Navy Yard. Soon after transferred to the naval hospital, same station. From this duty was ordered to the gunboat *Pocahontas*, home station, cruising principally in the Gulf of Mexico. Returned in her to Norfolk, April 1861; and at that port, Virginia having seceded from the Union, resigned his commission as post assistant surgeon.

Entered Confederate States Navy, April 15, 1861, as surgeon, and ordered to report at New Orleans to Commander R. Semmes for duty on Confederate States steamer *Sumter*. Made the entire cruise in this vessel, and upon her being condemned, and laid up at Gibraltar, in company with Commander Semmes and executive officer Kell left for London, and thence with them for the Confederacy via Nassau. Finding at this latter port orders to join Confederate States steamer *Alabama*, embarked later for Liverpool per SS *Bahama*, thence per same steamer to Terceira. He entered upon his duties, making the entire cruise. After the destruction of the *Alabama*, Galt took passage on a blockade-runner, arriving at Wilmington, North Carolina; and was soon after, October 1864, ordered to the heavy batteries on the James River, between Drury's Bluff and Howlett's, and for some time acted as fleet surgeon to the James River ironclads, in absence of the fleet surgeon. Upon the retirement of the army from Richmond, he joined the naval battalion under the command of Commodore John R. Tucker, General Custis Lee's division, which was captured at Saylor's Creek fight. From this point the remnant of the division marched to Appomattox Courthouse. Here surrendered and was paroled April 9, 1865. Galt was next appointed surgeon on the "Hydrographic Commission of the Amazon," an expedition fitted out by the Peruvian government, under the command of Admiral Tucker of the Peruvian navy. The object of this expedition was to explore the headwaters of the Amazon River with a view to finding an outlet to the Atlantic. This was a most dangerous and adventurous undertaking, the route being through an almost unknown and primeval wilderness. The expedition finished its work and was disbanded in 1875. Galt returned to his native state, Virginia, and is at this time practicing his profession at Welbourne, Loudoun County, "far from the madding crowd's ignoble strife." The highest endorsement as to ability in his profession is to be expected from us. Surgeon Galt during the entire cruise of the *Alabama* in all climates, the officers and crew undergoing hardship of every sort, did not lose by disease one soul out of the two hundred and thirteen men serving from first to last on the vessel. A gratifying and remarkable record. Galt also performed the duties of paymaster, in absence of a regular officer of this grade, and was as apt at figures as with his instruments and pills. Indeed, it is the opinion of the writer that, upon a pinch, Galt could have performed the duties of a line officer, having looked on for so many years with intelligent appreciation the exigencies and resources of sailor craft.

DAVID HERBERT LLEWELLYN
Assistant Surgeon

Assistant surgeon Llewellyn was born in Wiltshire, England, a grandson of Lord Herbert and son of a divine of the Church of England. He graduated in 1860 and was appointed surgeon of the steamer *Bahama*, chartered to convey the officers destined for the *Alabama* to Terceira. Upon completion of the arming of the cruiser, Llewellyn, who had made application, was commissioned by Semmes assistant surgeon and made the entire cruise in the ship.

After the engagement with the United States steamer *Hatteras* off Galveston, he rendered valuable assistance to the surgeons of latter vessel in attention to their wounded.

Llewellyn was made surgeon at Kingston, Jamaica, when Galt was installed as paymaster; and later on was conspicuous for his devotion to the wounded of our own vessel in the engagement off Cherbourg with the *Kearsarge*. Not until the water was knee-deep in the sick bay, and the ship rapidly sinking, did he hearken to the order, "All hands save yourselves!" After seeing his wounded safe under the care of the *Kearsarge* surgeons, he took to the water and lost his life. A monument to his memory, we learn, stands in Charing Cross Hospital courtyard, erected by his fellow students. Llewellyn joined the Southern cause from sympathy for a people struggling, as he believed, for liberty and firesides; hence especially sad was his end. We look surely for decided action from those to the manor born; they have done but their duty. But a foreigner, simply guided by a generous impulse to aid people whose cause appeals to his sense of justice and right, and because the odds are against them, becomes the champion of principle, pure and simple, and merits a deeper reverence and admiration. Llewellyn's motives admit of no question by those who knew him, and they place him in the same class with the honored Marquise de Lafayette.

MILES J. FREEMAN
Chief Engineer

Miles J. Freeman, chief engineer of the Confederate States steamer *Alabama*, was born in Wales, and after a technical education in Scotland, removed to New Orleans, Louisiana, and served as chief engineer of the merchant steamer *Habana*, of the Havana line. When this steamer was purchased by the Confederate government, Freeman was, by the recommendation of Semmes, appointed chief engineer in the Confederate States Navy from the state of Louisiana, ranking from February 15, 1861. He had charge of the altering and refitting of the *Habana,* changed to the Confederate States steamer *Sumter.* Freeman was a man of fine ability in his profession; and no little credit is due him for the manner in which, under many disadvantages, he succeeded in putting on the ocean a fairly serviceable cruiser. Upon the completion of the *Sumter* he was ordered to her as chief engineer and made the entire cruise in her; and upon her being laid up at Gibraltar, after a cruise of between six and seven months, was detached and ordered to England. He was again chosen by Semmes as chief engineer of the Confederate States steamer *Alabama* and joined this vessel with the detail of officers taking passage from Liverpool in the English steamer *Bahama.* He made the entire cruise on this vessel and was, after the fight off Cherbourg, taken prisoner by the *Kearsarge,* transferred to Fort Warren, Boston Harbor, and served his time out there until the close of the war. After the close of the war Freeman again entered the merchant service as chief engineer and was up to the time of his death, some years since, in the employ of a steamship line out of New York. Freeman was of a phlegmatic disposition and exceedingly reticent. He did not avail himself of his opportunities of parole. Had he sought an audience with the United States minister at London through the commander of the *Kearsarge* after his capture, he doubtless would have been paroled, as Lieutenant Wilson was, and need not have pined the remainder of the war in prison. Freeman was an able officer and true friend. His wheel has ceased to turn. May he rest in peace!

WILLIAM P. BROOKS
First Assistant Engineer

Engineer Brooks was born in Charleston, South Carolina, and after serving his apprenticeship was appointed first assistant engineer of the merchant steamer *Habana*, of which Miles J. Freeman was chief. He was likewise selected by Commander Semmes as an engineer of the *Sumter*, receiving his commission in the Confederate States Navy from the state of Louisiana as first assistant engineer, May 11, 1861, and assisted fitting the *Sumter* for sea. He made the entire cruise on that vessel and was also ordered with the rest of the *Sumter*'s officers to London. Brooks and his party of officers came near losing their lives by the foundering of the steamer in which they had taken passage to London. He awaited orders for some time in London; and upon the return of Commander Semmes from Nassau to Liverpool, Brooks, at his request, was detailed for the *Alabama*, reaching her by steamer *Bahama* to Terceira. He made the entire cruise on the vessel participating in the fight off Cherbourg, and was among the rescued by the yacht *Deerhound*. After a short furlough he was ordered to the Confederate iron-clad *Stonewall*, completed the latter part of the war, and made the short and uneventful though exciting cruise in this ship as chief engineer. At the close of the war Brooks entered the Spanish navy as chief engineer; but the service not proving congenial to his taste, he resigned his commission and took service with the Ocean Steamship Company as chief engineer of the *Tallahassee*. Brooks died some years since, in the service of the above company.

MATHEW O'BRIEN
Second Assistant Engineer

Of the officers of the Confederate States Navy serving on cruisers, O'Brien ranks among the most fortunate in the nature of his service, being attached for the entire period of the war to the three most-noted Confederate cruisers afloat. Starting upon the lowest rung of the ladder, his abilities and faithfulness raised him in this short period to the very topmost. He was born in County Limerick, Ireland, in 1837. His parents immigrated to this country and settled at Tuscaloosa, Alabama, when he was six years old. Five years later they moved to New Orleans. In 1852 O'Brien was entered an apprentice at Leed's foundry, serving his time in the machine shop until the breaking out of hostilities. On May 20, 1861, he was commissioned third assistant engineer, Confederate States Navy, from the state of Louisana, and assigned to duty on the *Sumter*. When the *Sumter* was laid up at Gibraltar he was ordered to Liverpool, and taking passage on the British Steamer *Euphrosyne*, with other of his brother officers was wrecked in Vigo Bay, Spain, and narrowly escaped with his life. Eventually arriving at Liverpool, he was assigned to the *Alabama*, and upon the arrival of Semmes took passage on the *Bahama* for Terceira. After the destruction of the *Alabama* he was placed on waiting orders; and in October 1864, he was ordered to the *Shenandoah* and made the full cruise in this vessel as chief engineer. On the surrender of the *Shenandoah* at Liverpool, seven months after the close of hostilities, he returned home and soon entered the employ of the Morgan Steamship Line, where he remained until he was appointed to his present position. O'Brien is now United States supervising inspector of steam vessels for the tenth Louisiana district, with headquarters at New Orleans.

O'Brien's skill and resource were very unusual, even in the

line to which officers of his grade are most carefully trained. The *Alabama* cruised for two years without opportunity to avail herself of machine shops and dockyards, and at the end of that time her machinery was in excellent condition and her boilers still available. Candor requires the statement that this circumstance was due principally to O'Brien's mechanical skill and long practical training as a machinist.

But O'Brien possessed another trait of almost equal value, when the monotony and hardships of our cruise are considered with reference to their effect upon our temper and spirits. He was without exception the jolliest fellow I ever met, and possessed a wonderful power of imparting cheerfulness and good nature to every person with whom he came in contact. He had a marvelous faculty for discovering the ludicrous side of misfortune and could point out the silver lining of hope on the darkest clouds of our discontent. Who shall say whether the mechanical or moral value of such a comrade is to be deemed the greater?

WILLIAM ROBERTSON
Fourth Assistant Engineer

There is little data at my disposal respecting Robertson. He was appointed assistant engineer by Commander Semmes to fill the vacancy caused by the death of Cummings. He was an Englishman. He had left an English steamer at Cape Town and was looking out for a position in the line of his profession. Semmes appointed him on the strength of his letters of recommendation. He proved an efficient engineer and stood gallantly at his post in the fight off Cherbourg like a true Briton. He is believed to have lost his life in the engine room, owing to the rapid sinking of the ship after receiving her death wound. At any rate, he perished in the fight, which is a sufficient testimony of his devotion to the cause he had espoused, and should entitle him to the grateful remembrance of those to whom it was dear.

BARON MAXIMILIAN VON MEULNIER
Master's-Mate

This gentleman was an officer in the Prussian navy and was on leave of absence at the time of joining the *Alabama*. While making a tour of the world he was shipwrecked near Table Bay, and on the arrival of the *Alabama* applied to Semmes for a position on board. Semmes questioned him carefully, and finding him a thoroughly able and educated officer gave him an appointment as acting master's-mate. He was especially valuable to us because besides his abilities as an officer, he was familiar with the language of most places it might be necessary for us to visit. He was permitted to remain with us during the entire cruise, securing the confidence and friendship of his brother officers and from the first the respect of the crew. Upon the *Alabama*'s arrival at Cherbourg, and before it was known that a fight would take place, he was paid off and released from duty. He proceeded to Paris, but there learning of the impending fight, managed to return to the ship and to render the bravest and most important service during the engagement. We parted with him at Southampton, from which port he returned to his native place, Berlin. Of his subsequent career the writer has been able to obtain no information. May his lines fall in pleasant places was and is the prayer of his sometime shipmates. With him, as with Llewellyn, the motive to service was not merely adventurous. He possessed a strong sympathy for the Southern cause and seemed as deeply pained as any of us at its ill success.

JULIUS SCHROEDER
Master's-Mate

Julius Schroeder was likewise of noble birth and an officer of the Prussian navy. He was traveling with Von Meulnier and was also his companion in the shipwreck, and with him applied to Semmes for a place on the *Alabama*. He likewise served on the entire cruise, and after being discharged at Cherbourg returned with his friend to participate in the fight with the *Kearsarge*. Schroeder had a peculiar, genial temperament and was a great favorite with his shipmates. He was rather a phlegmatic, undemonstrative fellow, cool as a cucumber in danger and when all about him was excitement, thoroughly unselfish, always ready to take a fellow's watch or otherwise relieve a tired soul from trying duty. After his return to Prussia, his scientific and literary tastes apparently supplanted the military ardor of his youth. I am informed that he is at present a professor of mathematics in one of the great German universities.

JAMES EVANS
Master's-Mate

At the breaking-out of the war, Evans was a pilot at Charleston, South Carolina, and owner of the pilot-boat *Rover*. His first feat was to take into this port an English sailing-vessel, the *"A and A,"* through the blockade maintained by the United States steam frigate *Niagara* and other war vessels. He next ventured out of port as prize-master of the privateer *Savannah*, capturing the merchant brig *Joseph*. Evans took his prize into Georgetown. Southern coast-pilots being wanted for the blockade-runners leaving Europe, Evans took passage on the Confederate States steamer *Nashville* for England, arriving about the time of the *Alabama*'s escape from Liverpool. His services being needed, orders were duly issued assigning him to the *Alabama*, with the rank of master's-mate. Evans was a thorough sailor, a clearheaded, sagacious officer, and possessed a gift or acquirement of the greatest value to us. Upon a report of a sail from the masthead, Evans would be ordered aloft with his spyglass to report upon her probable nationality. As to whether the sail was a Yankee or otherwise, his report could be absolutely relied on. Not once during the entire cruise did he make a mistake in this respect. After testing him for some time, Semmes would simply decline to chase when a sail was pronounced by Evans to be neutral.

After the war Evans returned to Charleston and resumed his profession as a harbor pilot. As the writer has had occasion in the body of his narrative to speak of Evans at some length, and his naval experience was confined to the cruise of the *Alabama*, no further information respecting his history belongs properly to the public.

GEORGE T. FULHAM
Master's-Mate

George T. Fulham was an Englishman by birth and received his earlier nautical education in the English merchant service. His sphere of usefulness to us began in conjunction with our various agents abroad, engaged in blockade-running, cruiser building, and fitting-out. Fulham attracted the attention of Captain James D. Bulloch; and when the latter officer took passage on the *Bahama* for Terceira to superintend the arming of the *Alabama*, Fulham was in the party accompanying him and was warranted a master's-mate by Semmes. He made the entire cruise and was as capable and trustworthy an officer as we had in the line of his duty. Fulham was called upon to board more vessels than any officer of our ship, relieving the lieutenants and watch-officers of much of this arduous and dangerous duty. From his previous experience and education he understood the character of merchant officers and service thoroughly, and could expedite the business in the minimum time. He was foremost in all sports improvised for our mutual pleasure and health; the greater part of the fun evolved in the steerage was the product of his fertile and original brain. Fulham served with marked gallantry in the fight and was conspicuous with Howell in looking out for the wounded after the surrender. Since the close of the war Fulham has been engaged as mate in the English merchant service.

THOMAS C. CUDDY
Gunner

This officer received his early education at the Ordnance Department, Washington Navy Yard. On the secession of South Carolina he resigned and returned to his native city, Charleston, April 1, 1861. He was appointed gunner, Confederate States Navy, with orders to report to New Orleans for service on the Confederate States steamship *Sumter*. Cuddy made the entire cruise in this ship, and when she was laid up at Gibraltar left with other officers for England. Upon Semmes's arrival at Liverpool he was assigned to the *Alabama*. Cuddy belonged to an old Irish family, the McGillicuddys, and possessed the best traits of a thoroughbred Irishman. He was a most efficient and energetic officer in his line of duty. After the destruction of the *Alabama* he was for some months on leave of absence. He took passage for home on the blockade-runner *Lelia*, and was drowned off the mouth of the Mersey River, January 19, 1865.

W. BREEDLOVE SMITH
Captain's Clerk

This gentleman shares with O'Brien the exceptional record of service on the *Sumter*, the *Alabama*, and the *Shenandoah*, and of serving the entire cruise on each of them. His social, not less than his business, qualities are abundantly manifest in the bare fact, for a captain's clerk, like a private secretary, must necessarily share the confidence of his superior and be able to assist his counsels, and must also be happy and tactful in personal association. Smith had a peculiar man to deal with in Semmes, and probably few could so have understood and pleased him. Smith received his credentials immediately on the commissioning of the *Sumter*. After her condemnation he returned to Liverpool and was promptly tendered his former office by Semmes on the *Alabama*. After his return to England he attracted the attention of Waddell and soon received promotion to the rank of paymaster, in which capacity he was assigned to the *Shenandoah*. He is at present a successful merchant of St. Louis and New Orleans, and domiciled at the latter city. It is perhaps unnecessary to state that such a man must have been popular with his shipmates, and that the qualities which so eminently fitted him for success as a "cruiser" (a thing which can hardly be said of some of the rest of us) would be pretty sure to ensure a similar result in commercial and social life.

SIMEON W. CUMMINGS
Third Assistant Engineer

Simeon W. Cummings was born in New London, Connecticut, and was, at the commencement of hostilities, a citizen of New Orleans and in the employ of a coastline steamship company. The attention of Commander Semmes was called to him while serving as engineer as above; and he was, at Semmes's suggestion, appointed a third assistant engineer in the Confederate States Navy, his commission dating from May 20, 1861. He reported for duty immediately and assisted in the fitting-out of the *Sumter*, rendering valuable service in this connection and making the entire cruise on her. The *Sumter* being condemned at Gibraltar, Cummings took passage on the Spanish steamship *Euphrosyne* for London, and suffered with his brother officers of the *Sumter* the perils and hardships of shipwreck. Leaving Vigo, Spain, the scene of the disaster, he took passage for England, was on leave of absence some months, and upon the completion of the *Alabama* was ordered to and joined her at the Western Islands. Cummings made the cruise on the *Alabama* up to the arrival of the ship at Saldanha Bay, South Africa, where he accidentally lost his life. Elsewhere the particulars of his sudden death have been related. Cummings, though of Northern birth, was an enthusiastic and faithful follower of the cause he had espoused, and deserves the more credit in that his determination was taken and carried out in spite of the protests of his immediate family, resulting in his having their sympathy and love withdrawn. Cummings was a most capable engineer officer, cool and collected in hours of danger, a true friend, generous and broad in his views and, as stated before, at most times sad and reflective, yet most satisfactory company. He served the flag of his adoption with all the ardor of his great soul, and our cause and ship suffered a great loss in his sudden taking off.

JOHN PUNDT
Third Assistant Engineer

John Pundt was born at Charleston, South Carolina, and after completing his mechanical education removed to New Orleans. He was appointed third assistant engineer of the Confederate States steamer *Sumter* from the state of Louisiana, his appointment dating May 20, 1861. Pundt assisted also in the fitting out of the ship, being a first-class practical mechanic. He made the entire cruise of the *Sumter*, leaving her at Gibraltar for London under special orders, and was wrecked with the other detail of the Sumter's officers on the *Euphrosyne* in Vigo Bay, Spain. Proceeding from here to London, he was detailed for the *Alabama* and was of the party taking passage from Liverpool on the British steamer *Bahama* for Terceira. Pundt made the entire cruise of the *Alabama* participating in the engagement with the United States steamer *Hatteras* off Galveston, Texas, and with the United States steamer *Kearsarge* off Cherbourg, France, and rendered valuable service in both engagements. Pundt was made prisoner by the *Kearsarge* after the fight, being picked up out of the water by one of her boats, but was eventually released on parole and avoided the horrors of prison life. Pundt was an unusually cool officer under fire. He returned to the merchant service after the close of the war and engaged in the coast trade in the line of his profession, dying a few years since at his post. South Carolina had a gallant and efficient officer in Pundt, and may be proud to keep his memory green.

WILLIAM H. SINCLAIR
Midshipman

This young gentleman was an offspring of the old navy, being a grandson of Commodore Arthur Sinclair and a son of Commander George T. Sinclair. The latter had the superintendence of the building of the Confederate States cruiser *Texas*, on the Clyde, Scotland, which vessel was sold to the Spanish government and, under the name of the *Pampero*, captured the blockade-runner *Virginius* during the Cuban rebellion. It will be remembered that Captain Joseph Fry, commander of the *Virginius*, and his officers and crew were shot without trial. Midshipman Sinclair entered the Confederate States Navy August 18, 1861, making his first cruise in the *Nashville* to Southampton and return, running the blockade into Beaufort, South Carolina. In June 1862, he was ordered to the *Alabama* and again ran the blockade from Charleston to Nassau, arriving at Liverpool with other officers on the *Bahama*. Midshipman Sinclair was called by Semmes his "handsome middy." He was selected as assistant to the lieutenant who boarded the mail steamer *Ariel* off the east end of Cuba. In the absence of Captain Jones, detained on board the *Alabama* as a prisoner, Mr. Sinclair assumed the honors of the dinner table with remarkable success and entirely won the confidence, if not the hearts, of the lady passengers. His return to the *Alabama* minus his coat buttons has been elsewhere noted and is the one instance on record where the absence of coat buttons seems to have been made to testify to an officer's success and good conduct. When the barque *Conrad* was made a prize and fitted out as the Confederate cruiser *Tuscaloosa*, Sinclair was detached to her as acting lieutenant. Her cruise and subsequent fate have already been chronicled. His disappointment was keen at his inability to join us in the fight off Cherbourg. He remained in Europe some time, pending the construction of cruisers at English ports, and on the cessation of hostilities he returned to his native state. Subsequently he removed to Halifax, Nova Scotia, where he died. That he was a young officer of great promise will be understood from his selection by Semmes as executive officer of the *Tuscaloosa*. He had all the instincts and aptitudes which might be expected from his lineage. He was an excellent sailor and a brave fighter.

E. M. ANDERSON
Midshipman

Entering the Confederate States Navy, November 18, 1861, as midshipman, appointed from his native state, Georgia, Anderson's first service was on board the gunboat *Savannah*, of the squadron under Commodore Tatnall, stationed in the Savannah River. In February 1862, ordered abroad, running the blockade from Wilmington. On reaching Liverpool, he was detailed for the *Alabama*, then being constructed at Birkenhead. In August 1862, took passage for the Azores in the Confederate States steamer *Bahama*, joining the *Alabama* and assisting in the work of completing her as a man-of-war. Made the entire cruise in this vessel, was wounded in the fight with the *Kearsarge* but managed to keep afloat some considerable time in the water. Was rescued by a boat from the *Deerhound* and, with the rest of the officers saved by this vessel, was taken to Southampton. Was on waiting orders from July to October 1864, when he was ordered to the Confederacy. En route at Bermuda, he met the government blockade-runner *Owl*, commanded by Captain John N. Maffitt, formerly commander of the Confederate States steamer *Florida*, and was by him retained as navigating officer with the rank of acting master, and remained on her until the close of the war. We may here add that Anderson was promoted to the grade of lieutenant just before the closing of the war. Anderson commanded the thirty-two-pounder gun of Lieutenant Wilson's division and did most effective work with it during the first part of the *Kearsarge* fight. Later on, when the after pivot-gun was depleted of nearly every man on its port side, Anderson was ordered to secure his gun and take his crew to the pivot, where he did service for the remainder of the action under the personal supervision of his lieutenant.

Anderson descends from one of the oldest and most distinguished families of Georgia. His father was at one time mayor of Savannah and a gentleman of sterling worth. The fact of this young gentleman's promotion from acting midshipman through all intermediate grades to that of lieutenant, in the short period of two years, attests his high qualifications. He was a most efficient officer, rapidly mastering his profession in all its branches and having the full confidence of his commander and respect and admiration of his brother officers. Since the close of hostilities he has resided at Savannah. The writer had the pleasure of meeting him some years since and reviewing the memories of our adventures of 1862–1864.

E. A. MAFFITT
Midshipman

Appointed an acting midshipman in the Confederate States Navy from the state of Georgia, November 15, 1861. Was ordered to the gunboat *Savannah*, of the fleet of Commodore Taltnall, stationed on the coast of Georgia, serving with distinction in this fleet until ordered abroad. In August 1862, ran the blockade from Wilmington, North Carolina, on the steamer *Annie Childs*, under orders to report for duty on the

Alabama; and with Semmes and other officers reached the Western Islands via *Liverpool*, assisting in the fitting-out of the cruiser, and made the entire cruise on her. Was one of the lucky ones rescued by the *Deerhound* after the Channel fight; taken to Southampton, England, and was in waiting orders for some months. October 1864, was ordered home. On reaching Bermuda, found the *Owl*, government blockade-runner, in port, and was ordered by Commander Maffitt (his father) back to Liverpool for duty on one of the cruisers under construction in England. Maffitt was, while with us, midshipman of the first division, under command of Lieutenant Armstrong, consisting of a hundred-pounder rifle-gun and two thirty-twos. He had charge of the latter guns in the engagement between the *Alabama* and *Kearsarge*, earning well-merited promotion for his steady gallantry. Unlike his father in disposition, young Maffitt was of the unruffled order, calm as a summer day, of few words, but at all times thoroughly efficient. The commander was noted for dash and almost reckless impetuosity. Witness his plunge into Mobile through a heavy fleet of the enemy blockading the port; his vessel, the *Florida*, having at the time but a handful of men on duty, the rest either dead or disabled by yellow fever, and Maffitt himself piloting his vessel through the fleet lying upon a mattress on the topgallant forecastle ill with fever! Of such stock was our young middy. At the close of hostilities Maffitt made Wilmington, North Carolina, his home. He died some few years since, surrounded by wife and little ones. If no other comfort remains to his loving helpmate, she can gather her little ones around her and tell them they inherit the blood of heroes.

HENRY ALCOTT
Sailmaker

Henry Alcott is another of our adopted shipmates, an Englishman by birth and a protégé of Bulloch, joining the *Alabama* at Terceira, receiving a warrant from Semmes as sailmaker, and making the entire cruise in our ship. Alcott was of the sturdy type of our sympathetic English coworkers. He was like Pat's parrot, slow of speech but profound of thought, and hard to convince that canvas was not the most important part of the *Alabama*. Alcott did good service in the shot-and-shell division in the action, and was among the rescued by the *Deerhound*. His next service was as sailmaker of the *Shenandoah*, making the entire cruise in her and losing his warrant as sailmaker in the Confederate States Navy only by the result of the war.

GEORGE ADDISON
Carpenter's-Mate

George Addison, carpenter's-mate, should be honorably mentioned. He was cool and collected; and though helpless to stop the huge rents made in our sides by the formidable eleven-inch guns of the *Kearsarge*, he was on hand to assist and obey his superior, carpenter Robinson. Addison had the honor of being the only man wounded on our ship in the *Hatteras* fight, a small fragment of shell passing through his cheek. In the first fight Addison did most efficient service, the smaller shot holes of the light battery of the *Hatteras* being easily plugged.

JAMES BROSMAN
Boatswain's-Mate

James Brosman, boatswain's-mate, was one of the original crew of the *Alabama*, making the entire cruise, and was captain of the after pivot-gun, under command of Lieutenant Wilson. He was a splendid specimen of an English man-of-war's man. A thorough sailor, and could pipe as sweet a "call" as a sailor would care to move by. He served in both engagements and was paid off and honorably discharged at Southampton after the fight. He afterwards served on the *Shenandoah* with a boatswain's warrant.

WILLIAM ROBINSON
Carpenter

Carpenter Robinson was born at Boston, Massachusetts, removed to New Orleans, making it his home, and at the breaking out of the Civil War was engaged in a private shipyard in the line of his trade. His ability was brought to the notice of Commander Semmes, who engaged his services to help fit his vessel for sea. The *Habana* had to be altered, indeed, half reconstructed, being a simple passenger and freight boat plying between New Orleans and Havana; and before she could be metamorphosed into man-of-war *Sumter*, much intelligent skill and labor were required. The subject of this sketch was fully equal to the task. Upon the completion of the alterations, and the Sumter being ready for her armament and stores, Robinson was, at the suggestion of Commander Semmes, warranted as a carpenter in the Confederate States Navy from the state of Louisiana, his warrant dating May 20, 1861. He made the entire cruise of the *Sumter*, and under orders was one of the party taking passage from Gibraltar for London in the ill-fated steamer *Euphrosyne*. Awaiting orders for some time in England, upon the arrival of Commander Semmes he was detailed for the *Alabama* and joined her per steamer *Bahama* from Liverpool at the Western Islands. Assisted again at this point in fitting the *Alabama*'s battery, etc., his ability coming into play. Robinson made the entire cruise on this vessel, was most distinguished in both fights, and lost his life by drowning after the sinking of the *Alabama*. The writer, standing in the starboard pivot-gun port, saw the last of poor Robinson. He left the sinking ship among the last. His duties calling him to the point where shot holes were to be plugged, made his task exceedingly arduous and active; and the presumption is he lost his life more from prior exhaustion than want of skill in the water. He was an active swimmer, a man of strong nerve and fertility of resource.

The last seen of the carpenter, William Robinson, by the writer was while standing near the port gangway with Evans. It was soon after the order issued: "All hands save yourselves!" Robinson was at this time on the port rail, nearly stripped, and apparently about to leave our ship from that side. The rest had gone from the starboard side nearest the two vessels. He must have left the ship before O'Brien and self. He was a good swimmer and should have been saved. There was no observance of sharks about the vessel at the time or afterwards. How Robinson lost his life is wrapped in doubt. No one saw him in the water after the fight; all we realized was he never answered to the last muster roll. He was popular with his messmates, jolly, and full of fun. "Rest thee!"

BENJAMIN P. MECASKEY
Boatswain

The subject of our sketch was born in Philadelphia, Pennsylvania, and during his earlier days served in the navy of the United States, as boatswain's-mate. The advent of the war found Mecaskey at New Orleans, where he attracted the attention of Commander Semmes and assisted in the rigging-out of the *Sumter* after her conversion into a man-of-war. He made the cruise of this vessel, and was also of the party making the voyage from Gibraltar to Liverpool, and was among the rest a temporary castaway at Vigo Bay, Spain. Mecaskey, I should have stated above, was warranted a boatswain in the Confederate States Navy from the state of Louisiana, his warrant dating from May 20, 1861. Being on waiting orders at the time of the return of Semmes from Nassau to Liverpool, Mecaskey was ordered to the Confederate States steamship *Alabama*, and with his brother officers joined her at Terceira. He was as useful an officer as we had on board, fitting the gun-tackle, etc., and otherwise making the ship a man-of-war. He made the entire cruise, and after the fight was captured by the *Kearsarge* and served the remainder of the war a prisoner, first on the enemy's ship and later at Fort Warren. Mecaskey, as was the case with Freeman, did not seem to know how to go about it for his parole. Simply stood on his dignity and took the consequences accordingly. He was a typical sailor; looked it all over. They have passed away, this type, but thirty years or more ago you could have picked out on board any American man-of-war his counterpart. Born, as the navy saying goes, "with web feet and barnacles on his back." Possessed of a strong and musical voice, his "call" could be heard from deck to main-royal truck; and his word of command passed to the crew was electrifying. A man of fearless makeup; and in all times of peril a picture of steadiness, standing like old Palinurus, stern as fate.

The writer has lost sight of the old boatswain. Whether he has tripped his anchor for the unknown country this deserved tribute to his worth may discover.

GEORGE FREEMANTLE
Seaman

Another conspicuous seaman of our ship, and one first brought to the attention of our appreciative commander by Captain James D. Bulloch, the gentleman already referred to frequently in these pages. Freemantle had made the passage in the blockade-runner *Fingal* with Bulloch and Lieutenant Low, the latter afterwards one of our lieutenants and subsequently commander of the *Tuscaloosa*, our tender. Both these officers had a high appreciation of Freemantle. We have frequently referred to him before; and after recording that he filled the important trust of coxswain of the captain's gig and captain of the maintop, you need not be told that he was a thorough sailorman as well as a trusty subordinate. I am not sure, but think he must have gotten into the "breakers" through no fault of his own, judging from his past stable characteristics. It is the only defense I shall offer, viz., "past good character"; and let him now tell the story and explain, then judge for yourself, even you, lady readers. We now find our hero after the sinking of the *Alabama*, rescued by a French fishing smack and carried to Cherbourg. From this time, for some months, the writer lost sight of him; when one day, being at my hotel in London, a servant announced a sailor below anxious to see me. Imagine my surprise and joy to have Freemantle stand before me in "shore togs" and looking so well. A hearty grasp of the hand, and then to the primary object of the visit. It seems he was now on his way to Liverpool to ship for the East Indies, and wanted from me some funds to reach his destination. After supplying the needful, I remarked: "Now, Freemantle, tell me all about yourself since we jumped overboard from the *Alabama* in the English Channel." "Well, you see, Mr. Sinclair, I was paid off with a lot of dollars, married a little craft at Cherbourg, and rented a cottage; furnished it cozily, and tried to settle down; but bless your soul, sir, matters got tame. She couldn't *parle vous* English, and I couldn't *parle vous Français;* so I 'sheered off,' leaving her the traps; and I'm off to sea." So like a sailor! I have never seen the fine fellow since and am not likely to after all these years, nor do I imagine he has mastered French and returned to his "little craft." Freemantle was one of the men in charge of the captain's papers, and upon his being landed at Cherbourg by a fishing smack, sought out Commander George T. Sinclair of the Confederate States Navy and handed him the papers for transmission to Semmes. It need scarcely be added they were safely delivered.

ROBERT WRIGHT
Seaman

A reliable and valuable seaman was Robert Wright, who joined our ship at Terceira, making the entire cruise, escaping the snares and blandishments of his tempters while on liberty. Wright was a cool man in all emergencies, an accomplished sailor, and remarkably courteous to superiors. It was the pleasure of the writer to have him as captain of one of the guns of his division. He was badly wounded in the latter part of the fight but escaped capture by sheer good fortune, managing to keep afloat on a fragment of our wreck, and was picked up by a fishing smack and carried to Cherbourg. After leaving the French hospital, he was paid off and honorably discharged. Wright was the only man seriously hurt at either of the writer's guns.

SCENE OFF BRAZIL COAST, MAKING
SHIP SNUG FOR A NIGHT HUNT

The evening is on us; the cruiser to be stripped for her night hunt—placed under low canvas, single-reefed topsails. The "first luff" takes the deck. "All hands reef topsails," echoes along the spar-deck to the pipe of boatswain and mates. "Stand by the topsail halyards"; "round in the weather topsail-braces"; "settle away the topsail halyards"; "haul out the reef-tackles"; "haul up the buntlines"; "stand by to lay aloft." In a flash the lower rigging is a mass of topmen, bunched just above the rail, and, with a grasp of the lower rigging, eyes and faculties intent, they anxiously await the next order, not a motion among them. The order rings out from the trumpet, "Aloft, topmen"; and springing up the lofty lower rigging like a troop of squirrels, two ratlines a jump, and over the futtock-shrouds they pause at the "slings" of the topsail-yards. "Man the boom tricing-lines"; "trice up"; "lay out"; "take one snug reef." Out they scramble on the foot ropes, each striving for the weather-earing, the post of honor, next the captain of the top. As the latter throws his leg over the yardarm, as the trooper over his saddle, "Light over to windward," comes the cry from him; and in a twinkle he has caught a turn or two of the weather-earing. "Haul out to leeward," again from the captain of the top; the reef-points are secured, the maneuver accomplished. The finished work aloft has been noted by the deck officers. From the trumpet comes, "Lay in"; "down booms"; "lay down from aloft"; and helter-skelter. Some by the backstays, others by the lower rigging, the deck is reached in a jiffy. Again the trumpet order, "Man the topsail halyards"; "tend the weather topsail-braces"; "overhaul the reef-tackles and buntlines"; "hoist away the topsails." The weather braces are hauled taut, and the boat snug. "All hands splice the main brace," to the musical pipe of Mecaskey and mates. Now observe the bright, laughing eye and jaunty step of our gallants as they file around the grog-tub. The "first luff" hands the trumpet to the deck-officer; the captain gives his order to the latter, "Keep her 'full and by,' sir," and returns to his cabin. The officer of the deck conveys the course to the quartermaster at the "con," mounts the horse-block, glasses and trumpet in hand. The watch coil up under the weather bulwarks to dream of home or Molly, the lookouts to speculate on sails and prize-money. And now

All the air a solemn stillness holds,

save the slight splash of the sea in the propeller-well. The trap is set for the game.

A SOUVENIR OF THE *ALABAMA*

THE following communication from the author to his mother is a facsimile of one of the few letters reaching its destination through the blockade. Its itinerary was to England per British mail, thence to the Confederacy, "through the kindness of any blockade-runner"—an uncertain and irresponsible mail system. But two letters from the author reached destination during the cruise. No postage could be prepaid on it beyond England. From this time forward it was a tramp.

SIMON'S BAY, *August 16th, 1863*
(Near Cape Town)

MY DARLING MOTHER,

We arrived here a few days since from the coast of Brazil via Saldanha Bay and Cape Town. At the former place I was called upon to witness the first and only accident that has happened to any of us. I was in charge of one of our boats with Mr. Bulloch, our master, and Mr. Cummings, one of our engineers. We were hunting wild fowl, and under sail at the time. Mr. C.'s gun went off, and the entire charge of duck-shot entered his breast. He sprang up in the boat, and his only exclamation was, "Oh, me!" and expired immediately. You can imagine our horror and grief at seeing a companion endeared to us all by mutual cares and privations, thus taken from us in a moment, without even time to send a message of love to the dear one at home. His funeral was the saddest sight I ever witnessed. Here in this lonely and desolate spot we were forced to leave all that was earthly of one of the noblest fellows that ever lived. He was the entire cruise of the "Sumter" with Captain Semmes, and it seemed so hard that he should not return home with us to share our honors (if it is God's will that we shall). We have fitted out a vessel (one of our captures) under the command of Acting

Master Low, and Willie is her First Lieutenant. She carries two guns (also captured), and since we fitted her, which is about two months since, has captured a Yankee valued at $150,000. She has just come in and joined us again. I was delighted to see once more her First Luff. Think of Willie's luck; $1,200 per annum, and executive officer of a "Pirate." I have been promoted to Lieutenant, and bear my position with becoming dignity. Bye-the-bye, I must mention her name, the sloop-of-war "Tuscaloosa." We have just captured (coming from Cape Town here) another vessel with two guns, and shall transfer them to Low's vessel. The interest expressed by the world in the "Alabama" is beyond anything. We have sometimes thought we could get an idea of it from the newspapers, but they give but a faint one. When we were telegraphed as approaching Cape Town, men, women, and children left business and pleasure, and rushed to the beach to get a view of the far-famed "Pirate." They not only saw her, but saw her at her work; for as we neared the land, a vessel also standing in showed Yankee colors, and in a moment we were on her, as a hawk on a chicken. The capture in sight of the city added to the excitement, and the most unlikely reports found circulation as—that the "Alabama" was engaged with one of the enemy's cruisers," the " 'A' was sinking a merchant vessel at the time because she would not show her colors," etc., etc. We had scarcely anchored before the decks were crowded with both sexes, and all conditions from boatmen to lords; and question after question was put faster than we could answer them. A few moments after our arrival the mail-steamer from England arrived, and passing under our stern, manned the rigging, and gave three cheers for the "gallant 'Alabama,' " which we returned. Her captain came on board, and invited us to a breakfast the next morning, to which all who could be spared from duty went. This steamer brought us news to the 6th of June. We shall have another in from England in a few days with news to the 6th of August from America. When is this war to end? I sometimes think never. What a loss we have met with in the death of Jackson! but we have given them glorious whippings at Fredericksburg and Vicksburg, and have a great deal to be thankful to God for. Unless England or France interferes (and there are no indications that they will at present) this war must last a great many years, I think. Perhaps you wish to know something of Willie and myself. I can only say we are enjoying magnificent health, the ocean agreeing with us both.

The captain of one of the vessels just captured by us was taken on his last trip (a few months since) by the "Florida," and he tells me that Terry was well and hearty. We sighted the "Florida" on the coast of Brazil, but did not run down to her, as at the time we were uncertain it was she, and our policy is to avoid (if honorable) a fight. She went into Pernambuco and we into Bahia; and we got from the "B" papers a long account of her, and she of us. We have quite a fleet of Confederates down here at present. The "Florida" was spoken a few days since, the "Georgia," the "Lapwing," fitted out by Maffitt (Terry is not in her but still on the "F"), the "Tuscaloosa" now with us, making five in all here, and in the North Atlantic several, including an "iron-clad" of 21 guns, under Captain B. You cannot imagine how we appreciate the kindness of all abroad to us (exiles as we are), particularly the French and English. Their affection for the South is about equal to their contempt and hate of the Yankees. If a Yankee man-of-war comes in they drive her off in 24 hours; and if they complain that they are in want of repairs, they order a board of their own (English) officers, and they always decide that the repairs are not necessary; but in our case they only say, "We are glad to see you, old fellows, make yourselves at home, and anything you want let us know." The English and French admirals come on board and make official calls in full uniform. And the admiral here has gone so far as to say that had we saluted him he would have returned it, which you know would have amounted to a recognition of the C. S. I enclose a view of the "Alabama" taken on board by an artist. It is not a good picture, but truthful. In it you will notice your humble servant in the act of furling sails, and the prominent gun in sight is one of the guns of my division, and the one I fought in the engagement with the "Hatteras." You can form some idea of her great length from the picture. We are soon to have an addition to our armament, and shall then be a very formidable vessel, able to cope with anything we shall meet.

Another Confederate cruiser, a brig-rigged steamer, is telegraphed today as standing into Table Bay. I think after a while "John Bull" will give us a large navy. Yesterday one of our boats with a crew in her got adrift from our stern, and, owing to a strong gale blowing at the time, was unable to reach us again, and went on shore to leeward. The admiral, who lives on shore, sent for them, and had breakfast prepared in his dining-room for them, and entertained them the whole morning. They drank his health so often that they were in a fine state by the time they reached us again, which was late in the afternoon. They were put in irons for it. I could not help quoting the old Latin proverb, "Tempora mutantur et nos mutamur in illis," first breakfasting with an admiral, and then in double irons in the "brig."

You will receive by the same mail a full account of our adventures since leaving England. It is taken from the private journal of our officers, and put together by an editor of this place. If you receive it be sure and preserve it, as I shall not be here when it comes out, but have left an order for a copy to be mailed to your address.

The "Tuscaloosa" sailed this morning on a cruise. Willie is well, but now has to work hard as First Luff.

LIST OF OFFICERS

OF THE

CONFEDERATE STATES STEAMER *ALABAMA*
AS THEY SIGNED THEMSELVES

RAPHAEL SEMMES
Commander

JOHN MCINTOSH KELL
First Lieutenant and
Executive Officer

RICHARD F. ARMSTRONG
Second Lieutenant

JOSEPH D. WILSON
Third Lieutenant

JOHN LOW
Fourth Lieutenant

ARTHUR SINCLAIR
Fifth Lieutenant

FRANCIS L. GALT
Surgeon and Acting Paymaster

MILES J. FREEMAN
Chief-Engineer

WM. P. BROOKS
Assistant-Engineer

MATHEW O'BRIEN
Assistant-Engineer

SIMEON W. CUMMINGS
Assistant-Engineer

JOHN M. PUNDT
Assistant-Engineer

WM. ROBERTSON
Assistant-Engineer

BECKET K. HOWELL
Lieutenant Marines

IRVINE S. BULLOCH
Sailing-Master

D. HERBERT LLEWELLYN
Assistant-Surgeon

WM. H. SINCLAIR
Midshipman

E. ANDERSON MAFFITT
Midshipman

E. MAFFITT ANDERSON
Midshipman

BENJAMIN P. MECASKEY
Boatswain

HENRY ALCOTT
Sailmaker

THOMAS C. CUDDY
Gunner

WM. ROBINSON
Carpenter

JAS. EVANS
Master's-Mate

GEO. T. FULHAM
Master's-Mate

JULIUS SCHROEDER
Master's-Mate

BARON MAX. VON MEULNIER
Master's-Mate

W. BREEDLOVE SMITH
Captain's Secretary

A GENERAL MUSTER ROLL

OF THE

OFFICERS, PETTY OFFICERS, SEAMEN, AND FIREMEN OF THE CONFEDERATE STATES STEAMER *ALABAMA*,

From the day she was commissioned, August 24, 1862, to the day she was sunk, June 19, 1864.

The list contains the name of every person who served on the *Alabama*, with the exception of three, and was copied from the Official Roll.

Those marked with an* composed the original crew, and those whose names are followed by a † were in the fight off Cherbourg.

IN COMMAND

NAME	RANK	STATE	SERVICE	SERVICE	REMARKS
* Raphael Semmes †	Captain	Alabama	U.S.	Sumter	Promoted Rear Admiral.

WARDROOM OFFICERS

NAME	RANK	STATE	SERVICE	SERVICE	REMARKS
* Jno. Mcintosh Kell †	1st Lieut.	Georgia	U.S.	Sumter	Promoted Commander.
* R. F. Armstrong †	2d Lieut.	Georgia	U.S.	Sumter	
* Jos. D. Wilson †	3d Lieut.	Florida	U.S.	Sumter	Captured by enemy, June 19.
* Jno. Low	4th Lieut.	Georgia			Afterwards in command *Tuscaloosa*.
* Arthur Sinclair, Jr. †	Sailing-master	Virginia			Promoted Lieut. and Watch Officer.
* Irvine S. Bulloch †	Midshipman	Georgia			Master *Shenandoah*. Prom. Master and
* Francis L. Gait †	Surgeon	Virginia	U.S.	Sumter	Watch Officer.
* D. Herbert Llewellyn †	Asst. Surgeon	England			Acting Paymaster.
* Miles I. Freeman †	Chief Eng.	Louisiana		Sumter	Drowned, June 19.
* B. K. Howell †	Lieut. Marines	Louisiana	U.S.	Sumter	Captured by enemy, June 19.

STEERAGE OFFICERS

NAME	RANK	STATE	SERVICE	SERVICE	REMARKS
* Wm. H. Sinclair	Midshipman	Virginia			1st. officer *Tuscaloosa*.
* E. A. Maffitt †	Midshipman	No. Carolina			
* E. M. Anderson †	Midshipman	Georgia			Prom. Paymaster C.S. Afterwards steamer
* W. B. Smith †	Secretary	Louisiana		Sumter	*Shenandoah*.
* Geo. T. Fulham †	Master's-Mate	England			
* James Evans †	Master's-Mate	So. Carolina			
Max Von Meulnier †	Master's-Mate	Prussia			Joined at Cape Town.
Julius Schroeder †	Master's-Mate	Hanover			Joined at Cape Town.
* Wm. P. Brooks †	2d Asst. Eng.	Georgia		Sumter	

STEERAGE OFFICERS (Cont'd)

NAME	RANK	STATE	SERVICE	REMARKS
* Matthew O'Brien †	3d Asst. Eng.	Louisiana	Sumter	Afterwards Chief Engineer, *Shenandoah*.
* Simeon W. Cummings	3d Asst. Eng.	Louisiana	Sumter	Accidentally shot, Saldanha Bay.
* John M. Pundt †	3d Asst. Eng.	So. Carolina		Captured by enemy, June 19.
* Wm. Robertson †	3d Asst. Eng.	England		Drowned, June 19.

WARRANT OFFICERS

NAME	RANK	STATE	SERVICE	REMARKS
* Benj. P. Mecaskey †	Boatswain	Louisiana	Sumter	Captured by enemy, June 19.
* Thos. C. Cuddy †	Gunner	South Carolina	Sumter	Drowned on blockade-runner *Lelia*, Jan. 19, 1865.
* Wm. Robinson †	Carpenter	Louisiana	Sumter	Drowned, June 19.
* Henry Alcott †	Sailmaker	England		Afterwards Sailmaker, *Shenandoah*.

Officers present when ship went into commission   25
Officers who joined ship afterwards   3
   28

Officers detached, 2; Casualties, 1   3
Officers present and participating in action June 19   25

PETTY OFFICERS.

NAME	RANK	ENLISTMENT	REMARKS
* H. Marmalstein	Quartermaster	Aug. 24, 1862	2d Officer *Tuscaloosa*.
* I. G. Dent †	Quartermaster	Aug. 24, 1862	Paid off and honorably discharged at Southampton.
R. B. Hobbs †	Quartermaster	Aug. 16, 1862	Paid off and honorably discharged at Southampton.
* W. F. Forrestall†	Quartermaster	Aug. 24, 1862	Paid off and honorably discharged at Cherbourg.
* Jas. King, I †	Quartermaster	Aug. 24, 1862	Paid off and honorably discharged at Southampton.
* George Harwood†	Boatswain's Mate	Aug. 24, 1862	Paid off and honorably discharged, Feb. 27, 1863. Afterwards, Boatswain *Shenandoah*.
* Brent Johnson	Boatswain's Mate	Aug. 24, 1862	Deserted. Left on shore (ship having to sail) on liberty.
* James Brosman †	Boatswain's Mate	Aug. 24, 1862	Paid off and honorably discharged at Southampton.
* Thos. Weir	Gunner's Mate	Aug. 24, 1862	Deserted.
* Wm. Crawford †	Quarter-gunner	Aug. 24, 1862	Paid off and honorably discharged at Southampton.
* Ralph Masters †	Quarter-gunner	Aug. 24, 1862	Paid off and honorably discharged at Southampton.
* Geo. Appelbee †	Yeoman	Aug. 24, 1862	Drowned, June 19.
* Geo. Addison †	Carpenter's Mate	Aug. 24, 1862	Paid off and honorably discharged at Southampton.
* Fred'k-Johns †	Paymaster's Steward	Aug. 24, 1862	Drowned, June 19.
* Wm. Purdy t	Sailing-master's Mate	Aug. 24, 1862	Paid off and honorably discharged at Southampton.
* Geo. Freemantle †	Captain's Coxswain	Aug. 24, 1862	Paid off and honorably discharged at Cherbourg.
* Edw'd. Rawse †	Ship's Corporal	Aug. 24, 1862	Paid off and honorably discharged at Cherbourg.
* James Smith	Captain of Forecastle	Aug. 24, 1862	Deserted, Dec. 24, 1863.
* Peter Hughes †	Captain of Foretop	Aug. 24, 1862	Wounded. Paid off and honorably discharged at Cherbourg.
* Wm. Morgan †	Captain of Maintop	Aug. 24, 1862	Wounded. Paid off and honorably discharged at Cherbourg.
* Thos. McMillan †	Coxswain	Aug. 24, 1862	Wounded. Paid off and honorably discharged at Southampton.

PETTY OFFICERS (Cont'd)

NAME	RANK	ENLISTMENT	REMARKS
* James Higgs †	Captain of Hold	Aug. 24, 1862	Paid off and honorably discharged at Cherbourg.
* A. G. Bartelli †	Captain's Steward	Aug. 24, 1862	Drowned, June 19.
* R. Parkinson †	Wardroom Steward	Aug. 24, 1862	Paid off and honorably discharged at Cherbourg.
* Henry Fisher †	Coxswain	Aug. 24, 1862	Drowned, June 19.
* Robert Wright †	Captain of Maintop	Aug. 24, 1862	Wounded in action, 19th. Paid off and honorably discharged at Cherbourg.
* H. Ustaker †	Captain of Head	Aug. 24, 1862	Drowned, June 19.
* Owen Daffy †	First-class Fireman	Aug. 24, 1862	Paid off and honorably discharged at Cherbourg.
* Jas. McFadgen	First-class Fireman	Aug. 24, 1862	Paid off and honorably discharged, Feb. 27, 1863.
* Frank Cunant	First-class Fireman	Aug. 24, 1862	Paid off and honorably discharged at Cherbourg. 3d Assistant Engineer, *Shenandoah*.
* Geo. Egerton †	First-class Fireman	Aug. 24, 1862	Paid off and honorably discharged at Cherbourg.
* Chas. Godwin †	Captain of After Guard	Aug. 24, 1862	Paid off and honorably discharged at Cherbourg.
* Mich'l. Mars †	Coxswain	Aug. 24, 1862	Paid off and honorably discharged at Cherbourg.

FIREMEN, SEAMEN, ORDINARY SEAMEN, LANDSMEN, AND BOYS

NAME	RANK	ENLISTMENT	REMARKS
* Chas. Seymour †	Captain of After Guard	Aug. 24, 1862	Paid off and honorably discharged at Southampton.
* Henry Tucker †	Wardroom Cook	Aug. 24, 1862	Paid off and honorably discharged at Cherbourg.
* Edgar Fripp †		Aug. 24, 1862	Paid off and honorably discharged at Cherbourg.
* John Emery †		Aug. 24, 1862	Paid off and honorably discharged at Cherbourg.

* H. Legris		Aug. 24, 1862	Transferred to *Tuscaloosa*, June 21, 1863.
* Jno. Doyle		Aug. 24, 1862	Deserted, Dec. 24, 1863.
* Jno. Duggan		Aug. 24, 1862	Transferred to *Tuscaloosa*, June 21, 1863.
* P. Henney		Aug. 24, 1862	Deserted, May 17, 1863.
* W. McGinley †		Aug. 24, 1862	Wounded in action, June 19.
* Jno. Carern†		Aug. 24, 1862	
* F. Townsend †		Aug. 24, 1862	
* Jno. Roberts †		Aug. 24, 1862	Killed in action, June 19, 1864.
* Samuel Henry †		Aug. 24, 1862	
* Jos. Connor †		Aug. 24, 1862	
* Edwin Jones		Aug. 24, 1862	Transferred to *Tuscaloosa*, June 21, 1863.
* Wm. Rinton		Aug. 24, 1862	Transferred to *Tuscaloosa*, June 21, 1863.
* Wm. Hearn †		Aug. 24, 1862	
* Jno. Neil †		Aug. 24, 1862	Wounded in action, June 19.
* Robt. P. Williams		Aug. 24, 1862	Transferred to *Tuscaloosa*, June 21, 1863.
* Thos. Williams		Aug. 24, 1862	Transferred to *Tuscaloosa*, June 21, 1863.
* Jos. Pearson †		Aug. 24, 1862	
* H. Yates †		Aug. 24, 1862	
* H. Cosgrove	Boy	Aug. 24, 1862	Deserted, Dec. 24, 1863.
* Jas. Wilson †	Boy	Aug. 24, 1862	
* Robert Egan	Boy	Aug. 24, 1862	Deserted, Sept. 21, 1863.
* Thos. L. Parker †	Boy	Aug. 24, 1862	
* Jno. Grady	Boy	Aug. 24, 1862	Deserted, Dec. 24, 1863.
* Jno. McAllee		Aug. 24, 1862	Deserted, Jan. 21, 1863.
* Jno. Lartram	Fireman	Aug. 24, 1862	Deserted, Jan. 21, 1863.
* David Roche	Fireman	Aug. 24, 1862	Deserted, Jan. 21, 1863.
* Andw. Shilland †	Fireman	Aug. 24, 1862	

FIREMEN, SEAMEN, ORDINARY SEAMEN, LANDSMEN, AND BOYS (Cont'd)

NAME	RANK	ENLISTMENT	REMARKS
* James Mair †	Fireman	Aug. 24, 1862	
* John Jack	Fireman	Aug. 24, 1862	Deserted, Sept. 18, 1863.
* Peter Laverty †	Fireman	Aug. 24, 1862	
* Jno. Harrigan †	Fireman	Aug. 24, 1862	
* Pat'k. Bradley †	Fireman	Aug. 24, 1862	
* Sam'l. Williams †	Fireman	Aug. 24, 1862	
* Thos. Potter †	Fireman	Aug. 24, 1862	
* Jno. Reilly †	Fireman	Aug. 24, 1862	
* Thos. Murphy †	Fireman	Aug. 24, 1862	Drowned on a blockade-runner.
* Jas. Foxton †	Fireman	Aug. 24, 1862	
* Martin King †	Fireman	Aug. 24, 1862	
* Wm. Levins †	Fireman	Aug. 24, 1862	
* Jas. Mason †	Fireman	Aug. 24, 1862	
* Thos. Winter †	Fireman	Aug. 24, 1862	Wounded in action, June 19.
* Peter Duncan †	Fireman	Aug. 24, 1862	
* M. McFarland †	Fireman	Aug. 24, 1862	
* Christian Pust †	Fireman	Aug. 24, 1862	Killed in action, June 19.
* Edw'd. Fitzmaurice	Ordinary Seaman	Aug. 24, 1862	Paid off at Blanquilla. Invalided.
* M. Gnischhas	Ordinary Seaman	Aug. 24, 1862	Paid off at Blanquilla. Invalided.
* Wm. Price	Ordinary Seaman	Aug. 24, 1862	Paid off at Blanquilla. Invalided.
* Thos. Walsh	Ordinary Seaman	Aug. 24, 1862	Paid off at Blanquilla. Invalided.

This complete list of original crew. . . . . 52 before the mast
Of the petty officers, Hobbs was not of the original crew . . . . 31 petty officers
The two unmentionables. . . . . 2 petty officers

Makes original complement of 25 officers and 85 men.

Name	Rating	Date	Notes
Abram Nordhock †	A. B.	Sept. 15, 1862	
Martin Molk	Ordinary Seaman	Nov. 25, 1862	Transferred to Tuscaloosa, Jan. 21, 1863.
Wm. Robinson †		Nov. 25, 1862	
James Williams		Nov. 8, 1862	Deserted, Dec. 24, 1863.
Wm. Burns †		Nov. 8, 1862	
Mich'l Shields †		Nov. 8, 1862	
Charles Stetson †		Nov. 8, 1862	
Jos. Martin		Nov. 8, 1862	Invalided, Aug. 12, 1863.
Sam'l. Brewer		Nov. 8, 1862	Transferred to *Tuscaloosa*, Jan. 21, 1863.
Jas. Raleigh		Nov. 8, 1862	Deserted, Sept. 19, 1863.
Jas. Clemments †		Oct. 12, 1862	
Jon. Allan		Oct. 3, 1862	Deserted, Dec. 24, 1863.
Wm. Clark †		Oct. 3, 1862	
David Thurston †		Oct. 3, 1862	
David Williams †		Oct. 3, 1862	
David Laget †		Oct. 8, 1862	
Thos. James		Nov. 17, 1862	Deserted, Aug. 12, 1863.
George Ross		Dec. 1, 1862	Deserted, Sept. 17, 1863.
Albert Gillman		Jan. 25, 1863	Deserted, July 31, 1863.
James Adams		Jan. 25, 1863	Discharged by Court-martial, Aug. 30, 1863.
Wm. Miller †		Jan. 25, 1863	
Walter Van Ass †		Oct. 27, 1862	Drowned, June 19, 1864.

FIREMEN, SEAMEN, ORDINARY SEAMEN, LANDSMEN, AND BOYS (Cont'd)

NAME	RANK	ENLISTMENT	REMARKS
Martin Miditch †	Drummer	Oct. 27, 1862	Drowned, June 19, 1864.
Alfred Morris		Oct. 28, 1862	Deserted, Aug. 12, 1863.
H. Godson †		Nov. 8, 1862	
Ivan Ochoa †		Nov. 10, 1862	
Louis Dupois †		Nov. 9, 1862	
Geo. Yeoman †		Nov. 25, 1862	
David H. White †	A slave from Delaware	Oct. 9, 1862	Wardroom boy. Drowned, June 19, 1864.
Wm. Halford		Oct. 9, 1862	Deserted, Jan. 21, 1863.
Jos. Neal		Nov. 8, 1862	Deserted, Jan. 21, 1863.
Valentine Mesner		Oct. 27, 1862	Deserted, Jan. 21, 1863.
Gustave Schwalbe		Sept. 20, 1862	Deserted, Jan. 21, 1863.
Jas. McGuire †		Jan. 25, 1863	
Jacob Verbot †		Feb. 21, 1863	
Jean Veal		Feb. 21, 1863	Deserted, Sept. 17, 1863.
Jos. F. Minor		March 25, 1863	3d officer *Tuscaloosa*.
Jno. Hughes		March 25, 1863	Deserted, Sept. 18, 1863.
Ch. Olson †		March 25, 1863	
Albert Hyer		March 26, 1863	Deserted, Dec. 24, 1863.
Wm. McClennan †		March 26, 1863	
Peter Jackson		March 26, 1863	Deserted, Sept. 19, 1863.
Wm. Nordstrom		March 27, 1863	Deserted, Aug. 1, 1863.
Fred Myers †		March 27, 1863	
John Benson †		March 27, 1863	

Name		Date	Notes
Chas. Coles		April 1, 1863	Deserted, Sept. 19, 1863.
Geo. Getsinger		April 18, 1863	Invalided, Aug. 1, 1863.
Robert Owens		April 18, 1863	Transferred to Tuscaloosa, Jan. 21, 1863.
Jas. Wallace		April 18, 1863	Deserted, Aug. 1, 1863.
Maurice Britt †		April 18, 1863	
Thos. J. Allman		June 21, 1863	Transferred to Tuscaloosa, Jan. 21, 1863.
Wm. Jones †		Jan. 4, 1863	From the Agrippina.
Wm. Wilson †		June 21, 1863	
Geo. Percy †		June 21, 1863	
Geo. Thomas		June 21, 1863	Deserted, Sept. 19, 1863.
John Williams, I †		June 21, 1863	
John Miller		June 21, 1863	Deserted, Sept. 21, 1863.
Jas. Wilson	Ordinary Seaman	June 21, 1863	Deserted, Sept. 21 1863.
Jas. Broderick †		July 7, 1863	
Fred Columbia †		July 7, 1863	A Frenchman who was from Cherbourg.
Wm. Bradford †		July 7, 1863	
H. Saunders		July 7, 1863	Deserted, Sept. zr, 1863.
Jno. Williams II		July 7, 1863	Deserted, Sept. 21, 1863.
James Welsh †		Aug. 15, 1863	Paid off and honorably discharged at Cherbourg. I owe my life to this man's assistance.— R. F. A.
P. Warton †		Aug. 15, 1863	
F. Mahoney		Aug. 15, 1863	Deserted, Dec. 23, 1863.
Rich'd. Ray		Aug. 15, 1863	Deserted, Sept. 21, 1863.
Nich. Maling		Aug. 15, 1863	Deserted, Sept. 21, 1863.
John Russell †		Aug. 15, 1863	
John Adams †		Aug. 15, 1863	
Sam'l. Volans		Aug. 15, 1863	Deserted, Sept. 21, 1863.

FIREMEN, SEAMEN, ORDINARY SEAMEN, LANDSMEN, AND BOYS

NAME	RANK	ENLISTMENT	REMARKS
John Smith †		Sept. 25, 1863	
Henry Angell †		Sept. 25, 1863	
John Mehan †		Sept. 25, 1863	
R. Evans †		Sept. 25, 1863	
John Welham †		Sept. 25, 1863	
Andres Pheiffer †		Sept. 25, 1863	
Thos. Kehoe †		Sept. 25, 1863	
Rich'd. Hambly		Sept. 25, 1863	Deserted, Dec. 23, 1863.
Thos. Brandon †		Sept. 25, 1863	
Geo. Conroy †		Sept. 25, 1863	
Geo. White †		Sept. 25, 1863	
James Hart †		Sept. 25, 1863	
Jno. Wilson †		Sept. 25, 1863	
Carl Pjava †		Nov, 11, 1863	
Thos. Watson †		Dec. 24, 1863	
Robert Devine †		Dec. 24, 1863	
James KingII †		Dec. 24, 1863	Wounded, and died of lockjaw, June 19.
H. Higgins †		Dec. 24, 1863	
Chas. Colson †		Jan. 16, 1864	
John Jonson †		Jan. 16, 1864	
John Buckley †		March 25, 1864	
Fred Lennen		March 25, 1864	
H. Micoy †		March 25, 1864	

Name		Date	Notes
Nich's. Adams †		March 25, 1864	Shipped from the prize *Rockingham*.
Robt. Longshaw †		April 30, 1864	Shipped from the prize *Tycoon*. The last man shipped on the *Alabama*.
Edwd. Burrell †		May 9, 1864	Deserted from the Sumter in ____. Captured on the brig *Dunkirk*,
George Forrest	Seaman		Oct. 8, 1862; tried by court-martial, and finally landed in irons, and dismissed the service at Blanquilla, Nov. 26, 1862.

RECAPITULATION	OFFICERS	MEN
Joined the ship at Terceira	26	85
Not enumerated in this list	1	2
Enlisted during the cruise	3	99
Totals	30	186
Death	1	
Desertions	1	42
Paid off during cruise		2
Invalided during cruise and sent to England		6
Transferred to *Tuscaloosa*	2	12
Dismissed the service by court-martial		2
Leaves present for duty, June 19, 1864	26	122

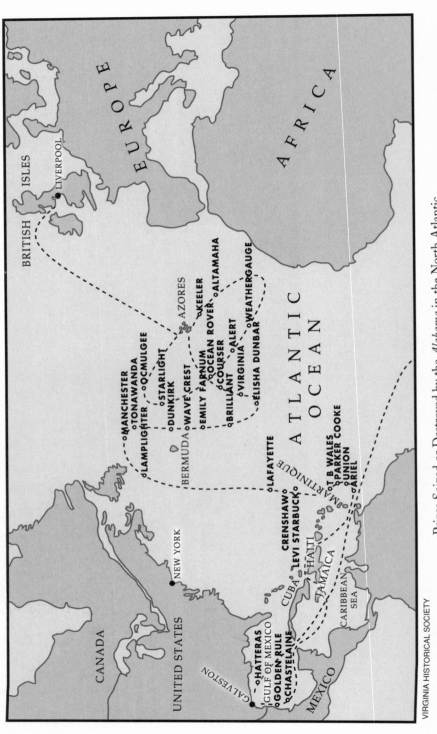

Prizes Seized or Destroyed by the *Alabama* in the North Atlantic